BROKERS AND BOUNDARIES
COLONIAL EXPLORATION
IN INDIGENOUS TERRITORY

Aboriginal History Incorporated

Aboriginal History Inc. is a part of the Australian Centre for Indigenous History, Research School of Social Sciences, The Australian National University, and gratefully acknowledges the support of the School of History and the National Centre for Indigenous Studies, The Australian National University. Aboriginal History Inc. is administered by an Editorial Board which is responsible for all unsigned material. Views and opinions expressed by the author are not necessarily shared by Board members.

Contacting Aboriginal History

All correspondence should be addressed to the Editors, Aboriginal History Inc., ACIH, School of History, RSSS, 9 Fellows Road (Coombs Building), Acton, ANU, 2601, or aboriginal.history@anu.edu.au.

WARNING: Readers are notified that this publication may contain names or images of deceased persons.

BROKERS AND BOUNDARIES
COLONIAL EXPLORATION
IN INDIGENOUS TERRITORY

Edited by Tiffany Shellam, Maria Nugent,
Shino Konishi and Allison Cadzow

Published by ANU Press and Aboriginal History Inc.
The Australian National University
Acton ACT 2601, Australia
Email: anupress@anu.edu.au
This title is also available online at press.anu.edu.au

National Library of Australia Cataloguing-in-Publication entry

Title: Brokers and boundaries : colonial exploration in indigenous territory / editors: Tiffany Shellam, Maria Nugent, Shino Konishi and Allison Cadzow.

ISBN: 9781760460112 (paperback) 9781760460129 (ebook)

Series: Aboriginal history monograph.

Subjects: First contact of aboriginal peoples with Westerners--Australia.
Aboriginal Australians--Biography
Aboriginal Australians--Social conditions.
Discoveries in geography--19th century.
Australia--Discovery and exploration.

Other Creators/Contributors:
Shellam, Tiffany Sophie Bryden, 1979- editor.
Nugent, Maria, editor.
Konishi, Shino, editor.
Cadzow, Allison, editor.

Dewey Number: 994.02

All rights reserved. No part of this publication may be reproduced, stored in a retrieval system or transmitted in any form or by any means, electronic, mechanical, photocopying or otherwise, without the prior permission of the publisher.

Cover design and layout by ANU Press. Cover images: Detail from 'Forrest expedition exploring party, 1874', 004541D. Sourced from the Collections of the State Library of Western Australia, and reproduced with the permission of the Library Board of Western Australia. Sir Thomas Mitchell, 'The south eastern portion of Australia showing the routes of the three expeditions and the surveyed territory', B.R. Davies (sculpt.), 1838, Map NK 1476, Rex Nan Kivell Collection, National Library of Australia, published with permission.

This edition © 2016 ANU Press and Aboriginal History Inc.

Contents

List of illustrations vii
List of contributors ix
Preface xiii

1. Brokering in colonial exploration: Biographies, geographies and histories 1
   Tiffany Shellam, Maria Nugent, Shino Konishi and Allison Cadzow

2. Bennelong and Gogy: Strategic brokers in colonial New South Wales 15
   Shino Konishi

3. 'Race', intimacy and go-betweens in French–West Papuan encounters 39
   Nicole Starbuck

4. Aboriginal guides in the Hunter Valley, New South Wales 61
   Mark Dunn

5. Guided by her: Aboriginal women's participation in Australian expeditions 85
   Allison Cadzow

6. Bobby Roberts: Intermediary and outlaw of Western Australia's south coast 119
   Clint Bracknell

7. Mediating the imaginary and the space of encounter in the Papuan Gulf 141
   Dario Di Rosa

8. Local agency and William MacGregor's exploration of the Trobriand Islands 161
   Andrew Connelly

9. Explorers & co. in interior New Guinea, 1872–1928 185
   Chris Ballard

List of illustrations

Figure 5.1: George Augustus Robinson, Aboriginal women and men taking Robinson across the river, 10 June 1830 98

Figure 5.2: Detail from map by Thomas Mitchell 102

Figure 5.3: Portraits of Turandurey (the female guide), and her child Ballandella, with the scenery on the Lachlan (10 May 1836) 103

Figure 5.4: 'Female and child of Australia Felix' 109

Figure 7.1: Detail of 'General Chart of Terra Australis or Australia: Showing Parts Explored Between 1798 and 1803 by M. Flinders Commr. of H.M.S. Investigator', 1822 [1814] 142

Figure 7.2: Detail of 'Chart of the northern part of the Great Barrier Reef including Torres Strait, & y.ᵉ adjacent Coast of New Guinea', 1847 144

Figure 7.3: H. S. Melville, 'Hut, and Natives of Darnley Id. [Island]', n.d. 150

Figure 7.4: Map of languages in Gulf of Papua area, 1981 153

Figure 8.1: William MacGregor, 1888 162

Figure 8.2: Map of Milne Bay Province, south-eastern Papua New Guinea, showing the Trobriands and surrounding islands in the Solomon Sea 164

Figure 8.3: First map of the Trobriands, 1807 165

Figure 8.4: William MacGregor, 'Sketch Map of the Kiriwina Group', 1893 168

Figure 8.5: Trobriand yam houses, 1897. Photograph
    by George Brown 170

Figure 8.6: Paramount Chief Numakala and son (possibly
    Puluaiwa), 1897. Photograph by George Brown 175

Figure 9.1: Interior New Guinea, showing explorers' routes 189

Figure 9.2: Patrol Officer Ivan Champion meets
    the 'Chief' of Bolivip Village. Untitled illustration
    by Pamela Lindsay 201

Figure 9.3: Charles Karius and company at Brumtigin rock,
    1927. Photograph by Ivan Champion 204

Figure 9.4: Ivan Champion and Tamsimal at Brumtigin rock,
    1927. Photograph by Charles Karius 205

Figure 9.5: Philip Pousai and Ray Kisol at Brumtigin rock,
    1997. Photograph by Chris Ballard 206

List of contributors

Chris Ballard is Associate Professor in the Department of Pacific and Asian History, College of Asia and the Pacific, The Australian National University. He has conducted long-term field research as an archaeologist, historian and anthropologist in Papua New Guinea, Vanuatu and eastern Indonesia. His present work focuses on resource ownership and land rights, colonial encounters and concepts of race, and Indigenous historicity and cultural landscapes. He was co-author and co-organiser of Vanuatu's successful nomination of Chief Roi Mata's Domain to UNESCO's World Heritage List (2008). His most recent ARC-funded project, in collaboration with Elena Govor, looks at the role of drawing in the early anthropological field research of Russian naturalist Nikolai Miklouho-Maclay.

Clint Bracknell is a Nyungar from the south coast of Western Australia and Senior Lecturer for the Sydney Conservatorium of Music and Division of Architecture and Creative Arts at the University of Sydney. His research explores the links between Aboriginal Australian song and languages, emerging technologies, and Indigenous creative futures. A musician and composer, he was nominated for 'Best Original Score' in the 2012 Helpmann Awards. His Nyungar cultural elders use the term 'Wirlomin' to refer to their clan.

Allison Cadzow is a Research Associate on 'Serving Our Country: A History of Aboriginal and Torres Strait Islander people in the Defence of Australia', an ARC-funded Linkage project based at The Australian National University. Allison is co-author of *Rivers and Resilience*: *Aboriginal people on Sydney's Georges River* (UNSW Press, 2009) with Professor Heather Goodall (shortlisted for the 2010 NSW Premier's History Awards). She co-edited *Nelson Aboriginal Studies* (Nelson Cengage, 2012) with Professor John Maynard. Her PhD, completed at the University of Technology, Sydney (2002), examined non-Aboriginal Australian women's involvement in expeditions of the 1840s to 1940s.

Andrew Connelly holds an MA from Sacramento State University and a PhD from The Australian National University, with broad research interests in Melanesian history and anthropology. More specifically, he is interested in Trobriand Island history and ethnography, colonial encounters and representation, ethnographic film and oral histories of the Pacific War.

Dario Di Rosa was awarded a BA and a MA in Anthropology in Italy, and is currently a PhD candidate in Pacific and Asian History at The Australian National University. Combining archival research and ethnographic fieldwork (conducted among Kerewo people of Papua New Guinea), he is investigating the relations between local narratives of the colonial past and the perceived marginality to the 'modernity project' encoded in specific understanding of 'the State' and 'development'. His main research interests are colonial history, ethnography of historical consciousness, epistemology of history, and history of social sciences.

Mark Dunn completed his PhD in 2015 at the University of NSW researching the colonial settlement, clashes and conflicts between 1820 and 1840 in the Hunter Valley, north of Sydney. He has a particular interest in the way the environment and the availability of resources shaped the way people interacted with each other. He has worked as a consultant historian and occasional archaeologist and is the 2016 C.H.Currey Fellow at the State Library of New South Wales.

Shino Konishi is a senior lecturer jointly appointed in the School of Humanities and the School of Indigenous Studies at the University of Western Australia. She is currently working on an ARC-funded project on Aboriginal histories of Australian exploration with Maria Nugent and Tiffany Shellam. She is the author of *The Aboriginal Male in the Enlightenment World* (Pickering and Chatto, 2012), and co-edited *Indigenous Intermediaries: New Perspectives on Exploration Archives* (ANU Press, 2015) with Maria Nugent and Tiffany Shellam. She is Aboriginal and descends from the Yawuru people of Broome, Western Australia.

Maria Nugent is a Fellow in the Australian Centre for Indigenous History, School of History at The Australian National University. She is the author of *Botany Bay: Where Histories Meet* (Allen & Unwin, 2005) and *Captain Cook was Here* (Cambridge University Press, 2009), and co-edited *Indigenous Intermediaries: New Perspectives on Exploration Archives* (ANU Press, 2015) with Shino Konishi and Tiffany Shellam. She publishes in the fields of memory studies and Indigenous history. In 2015–16, she is Visiting Professor of Australian Studies at the University of Tokyo.

Tiffany Shellam is Senior Lecturer in History at Deakin University. She publishes on the history of encounters between Aboriginal people and Europeans in the contexts of exploration, early settlement and mission stations in the nineteenth century. Her book *Shaking Hands on the Fringe: Negotiating the Aboriginal world at King George's Sound* was published by UWA Publishing in 2009. She also co-edited *Indigenous Intermediaries: New Perspectives on Exploration Archives* (ANU Press, 2015) with Maria Nugent and Shino Konishi.

Nicole Starbuck is a lecturer in History at the University of Adelaide. She is also a Senior Research Associate on the ARC Discovery Project, 'Revolutionary Voyaging: Science, Politics and Discovery During the French Revolution (1789–1804)'. Nicole studies the contact history of French scientific explorers in Oceania, with particular attention to the culture, politics and thinking about human nature, 'civilisation' and empire in Revolutionary and post-Revolutionary France. She is the author of *Baudin, Napoleon and the Exploration of Australia* (Pickering and Chatto, 2013).

Preface

In July 2013 we held a conference called 'Local Intermediaries in International Exploration' at The Australian National University in Canberra. This conference sparked a range of stimulating conversations about the diverse experiences and histories of people who acted as intermediaries, brokers and go-betweens in exchanges between European explorers, travellers and colonial administrators, and the Indigenous and local people whose lands they entered. One conversation about the challenges of recovering such hidden histories through European archives led to a collection of essays edited by Shino Konishi, Maria Nugent and Tiffany Shellam, *Indigenous Intermediaries: New Perspectives on Exploration Archives* (Aboriginal History Inc. and ANU Press, 2015).

This collection stems from two other common themes that many of the conference participants explored. Firstly, it highlights the importance of individual biographies in understanding the diverse and complex histories of Indigenous intermediaries. While earlier studies have identified and defined different types of Indigenous guides and intermediaries who assisted European explorers and travellers in Australia and Africa, such generalised typologies do not necessarily accommodate all of the particular experiences of individual brokers. Further, many of these more generalised discussions explore the reasons why local guides were recruited by explorers, but pay less attention to the myriad factors that motivated Indigenous intermediaries to join such expeditions. Consequently, the chapters in this collection reveal that the particular stories of individual brokers still need to be reconstructed in order to deepen our understanding of the histories of Indigenous intermediaries, and especially to recover the individual agency of such figures. Another common theme which arose at the conference was the important reminder that exploration was essentially a colonial enterprise, and that the explorers' reliance on Indigenous guides highlights their often unspoken awareness that they were in Indigenous territory, not unexplored wilderness.

We would like to thank all of the participants who generously contributed rich insights to the conference conversation, and especially thank the authors who contributed to this volume. We also thank the Australian Centre for Indigenous History who hosted the conference, the ANU College of Arts and Social Sciences, which provided financial support, as well as the Australian Research Council, for funding the two projects from which the conference stemmed (DI100100145 and DP110100931). For this collection in particular we thank Rani Kerin the Aboriginal History Inc. monographs editor, copyeditor Geoff Hunt and Emily Tinker from ANU Press who all provided incredible assistance and support in bringing this project to fruition. We also acknowledge the many institutions that allowed us to reproduce their images in this collection. Finally, we pay our respects to the Indigenous brokers whose stories are told in this book.

1

Brokering in colonial exploration: Biographies, geographies and histories

Tiffany Shellam, Maria Nugent,
Shino Konishi and Allison Cadzow

The history of exploration has often been thought of as a heroic drama in which the explorer is the principal, sometimes exclusive, protagonist and narrator. This edited volume – along with a companion volume *Indigenous Intermediaries: New Perspectives on Exploration Archives* – treats exploration as a collective effort and experience involving a variety of people from across social strata and cultures coming together, sometimes for a sustained time, at others only briefly, in various kinds of relationships and interactions. It engages with the recent resurgence of interest in the history of exploration by focusing primarily on the intermediaries – the guides, translators, hosts, labourers and myriad other 'locals' – who became involved in expeditions and assisted and facilitated European explorers who ventured out into the world from the eighteenth through to the twentieth centuries.[1]

---

1   See, for instance, Driver and Jones 2009; Kennedy 2013; Metcalf 2005; Schaffer et al. 2009; Thomas 2015. Earlier works include Reynolds 1990; Baker 1993; Baker 1998.

While the myth of the solitary intrepid explorer has long been questioned, the notion of exploration still suggests the discovery of a wilderness. This collection unsettles this persistent mythology by examining the extent to which the territories and regions that attracted explorers and travellers, who were often themselves impelled by the romance of 'first discovery' or the idea of untouched wilderness, were in fact peopled landscapes, long inhabited by Indigenous people as well as by the vanguards of empire – fortune-hunters such as beachcombers, sealers, labour-recruiters and miners, as well as missionaries and patrol officers, among others. In some Pacific contexts, local peoples were used to the arrival of strangers and traders, and extended their hospitality to itinerant Europeans, or incorporated them into their *taio* (friendship) ceremonies.[2] This was also true of many northern Aboriginal coastal groups who had established transactional relationships with Macassan trepang fishermen prior to exploration encounters with Europeans.[3]

In recent years, there has been renewed interest in the ways in which European explorers, travellers and other sojourners depended fundamentally for support, food, shelter, protection, information, guidance, emotional solace and other resources on local Indigenous people – both those who joined exploration parties and those who were encountered in the course of expeditions.[4]

The scholarship of Henry Reynolds and other scholars in Australia and overseas such as Don Baker, Tim Flannery, Felix Driver and Lowri Jones, and D. Graham Burnett, to name just a few, has been an important step in recognising and recuperating the contributions that Indigenous guides made to the history of exploration, and exploring the agency that they had in terms of the expedition's goals. In *With the White People* (1990) Henry Reynolds dedicates a chapter to 'those valiant heroes', the Indigenous advisers who assisted European explorers in 'conquering the [Australian] interior', pointing out that 'their role has rarely been fully appreciated in the innumerable works which have celebrated the achievements of the explorers'.[5] In response to this lack of recognition, Reynolds charted the contributions made by numerous Aboriginal guides to the colonial enterprise of exploration: providing

---

2 See Smith 2010; Salmond 2003; Matsuda 2012; and Connelly's chapter in this book.
3 See Macknight 2011; Mitchell 1995; Konishi and Nugent 2013: 51–54.
4 See, for example, Burnett 2002; Driver and Jones 2009; Roller 2010; Kennedy 2013.
5 Reynolds 1990.

local knowledge and bushcraft as they travelled through country, acting as ambassadors and envoys to the Indigenous inhabitants of new territories entered, and serving as 'private assistants' not only to explorers, but also to colonists and travellers 'venturing into the bush'. Like Reynolds' earlier works, this was an important historiographic intervention, drawing attention to the Indigenous side of the history of Australian exploration. Yet in many respects Reynolds' recasting of Aboriginal guides as 'black pioneers', did little to unsettle the colonial underpinnings of exploration.

However, an understanding of Indigenous perspectives and motives for participating in expeditions is harder to elucidate. Interest in the social subtleties, labour relations and economies of expeditions has contributed to fresh analysis which is alert to the shifting and contingent power relations that emerged *within* exploration parties. This adds to a more sustained interest over the last two or three decades in the nature of cross-cultural relations that emerged during interactions between explorers and Indigenous people.[6] Indeed, as a number of historians have noted, the challenge for leaders of expeditions, whether on sea or over land, was not only to navigate new terrain but also to manage the interpersonal interactions that were part of the grind – and pleasure – of exploration and travel. While more attention has been given to this aspect of the social history of exploration, it has not generally included the ways in which Indigenous participants in imperial exploration also manoeuvred within the social and interpersonal contexts of exploration.

Dane Kennedy argues in *The Last Blank Spaces: Exploring Africa and Australia* that the power dynamics inherent in exploration were complex and uneven, and many Indigenous guides had little choice in joining expeditions. He describes such brokers as 'marginal men' who had been 'ripped from their own communities and forced by the circumstances of their estrangement to forge a new niche for themselves at the intersection of cultures'.[7] Kennedy also highlights the 'remarkable ability' of Aboriginal brokers Charley Fisher and Harry Brown 'to retain a real measure of autonomy, dignity, and even authority in their dealings with [Ludwig] Leichhardt' during his

---

6   Greenblatt 1991; Pratt 1992; Thomas 2004; Salmond 2003; Jolly et al. 2009; Shellam 2009; Nugent 2009; Smith 2010; Konishi 2012; West-Sooby 2013; Douglas 2014.
7   Kennedy 2013: 166.

expedition.⁸ While this is an important reminder of the dynamics at play in some expeditions, not all Indigenous intermediaries involved in exploration were able to assert their influence or have their authority recognised, as many of the chapters in this collection reveal.

Recent international scholarship on go-betweens in colonial contexts highlights the 'complex and shifting loyalties' at play. In *Go-Betweens and the Colonization of Brazil: 1500–1600*, Alida Metcalf explores the lasting effect brokers had, from translating during first encounters to becoming prominent figures during possession and colonial settlement. She argues that 'go-betweens clearly took centre stage, for they were the means of communication in the middle grounds of encounters'.⁹ Drawing on the now iconic Nahua go-between Malintzin, or Doña Marina, who mediated for Hernán Cortés, Metcalf highlights the capacity for brokers to open up spaces for the colonisers and themselves, stressing the triangular dynamic that their presence created.¹⁰ In this triangular relationship, Metcalf argues, brokers 'occupied an intermediate space between worlds where a boundary could become a borderland'.¹¹ Australian scholar David Turnbull has similarly illuminated the ways in which brokers opened up boundaries and created borderlands, suggesting it was the cultural dexterity or mobility of these go-betweens that created new knowledge spaces and gave them the ability to draw new boundaries. Turnbull reflects on the power and changing loyalties of brokers who can 'both dissolve and create boundaries in the process of linking people, practices and places in networks'.¹² Metcalf also stresses the mobility of brokers, suggesting that they were not neutral figures, but people whose fluid alliances could influence the power dynamics at play in the relations between Indigenous and European worlds. Focusing on the third space that a broker's presence enabled, she argues that they created a further dimension of power and could 'exploit their positions for their own benefit because he or she is indifferent to the outcome'.¹³

---

8   Kennedy 2013: 162.
9   Metcalf 2005: 8. See also Yannakakis 2008.
10   Metcalf 2005: 8. See also Godayol 2012.
11   Metcalf 2005: 8.
12   Turnbull 2009: 396.
13   Metcalf 2005: 3.

The authors in this collection tease out the ways in which Indigenous people or individuals, whether attached to expeditions or encountering them on their own estates, made their own 'strategic' and adroit uses of expedition parties or of particular members of them. Some authors glean and speculate about what it might have meant for some Indigenous people – men and women, young and old, single and attached – to build relationships with expedition leaders and expedition members. Both Clint Bracknell and Shino Konishi, for instance, highlight the way in which expeditions provided opportunities for Indigenous individuals to increase their own political sway within their polities. Allison Cadzow analyses the complexities that arose when the intermediaries were Aboriginal women: they were assumed to pose less of a threat to Aboriginal groups wary of strangers, but at the same time viewed with suspicion by the explorers as duplicitous Eves, who might collude with 'the natives'. These Indigenous travellers, who were experiencing and embracing new forms of social as well as geographical mobility,[14] had to be – or to become – adept at handling fraught and unpredictable social situations that were riven with competing interests, difficult personalities, contradictory desires, impossible expectations and unfamiliar values, all of which could be intensified and magnified by the cheek-by-jowl living arrangements that exploring inevitably involved. Relationships between explorers and Indigenous guides were never merely contractual or transactional in a purely economic sense. Typically they functioned according to unstated expectations on all sides around patronage and favour, honour and trust, faithfulness and obedience, obligation and incentive.[15] Teasing out what might have been the stakes involved for Indigenous intermediaries in exploration parties in terms of forming alliances, earning debts and obligations, leveraging resources and status, currying favour and gaining advantage not only with Europeans but also their own kin, allies and enemies, reflects and generates a particular emphasis on Indigenous people and perspectives within histories of exploration that provides a necessary and long called for correction to the broader historiography of exploration.

---

14 Carey and Lydon 2014.
15 Russell 2010.

Australia and its neighbour New Guinea provide the geographical scope of the collection. In addition to the long history of Indigenous cultural exchange between Indigenous Australians and Papuans conducted via the Torres Strait, Australia and New Guinea have overlapping histories of exploration, stemming from the Dutch VOC whose explorers in the seventeenth century charted the coastlines of both, and continuing into the nineteenth century when explorers such as Louis Freycinet landed at sites in both countries (see Nicole Starbuck's chapter). They also have entwined histories of colonisation, with key colonial figures having established their careers in both colonies.[16] For instance, William MacGregor, the subject of Andrew Connelly's chapter, was a colonial administrator in British New Guinea before becoming the Governor of Queensland. Such entangled histories of exploration and colonisation illustrate how cross-cultural interactions and (mis)understandings were not only shaped by the immediate actions of European and Indigenous individuals involved. They were also the legacy of earlier interactions with other Indigenous peoples from different parts of the empire.[17]

The chapters on Australian exploration in the collection include Bracknell's study of Bobby Roberts, a Noongar intermediary from south-western Western Australia, and Cadzow's account of Aboriginal women's role in expeditions in Tasmania, Victoria and New South Wales. Konishi and Mark Dunn both examine exploration in New South Wales. Konishi offers a study of two intermediaries: Bennelong, who was an infamous cultural broker in the early years of the Port Jackson colony, and the lesser known and seemingly mercurial guide Gogy, who was involved in Barrallier's thwarted attempt to cross the Blue Mountains. Dunn's is a survey of the diverse roles of Aboriginal guides in a number of excursions in the Hunter region, which included tracking runaway convicts, carrying messages, and guiding expeditions. The chapters on New Guinea include Chris Ballard's evocation of five actual and fictional expeditions into the interior; Starbuck's reading of the influence of interactions with Papuan intermediaries at Waigeo and Dorey Bay in 1819 and 1827 on French 'racial' thought; and Dario Di Rosa's examination of Francis Blackwood's 1845 exploration of the Gulf of Papua. Connolly's chapter

---

16 For a broader study of such imperial mobility and networks, see Lambert and Lester 2006.
17 For more on imperial mobility, see Lester 2005; Lambert and Lester 2006; Ballantyne and Burton 2009; Carey and Lydon 2014.

is a study of colonial administrator William MacGregor's 'discovery' of the Trobriand Islands (now part of the Milne Bay Province in Papua New Guinea), and the islanders he was ostensibly to superintend.

Common to many of the chapters is attention to the specificities of locality. This has some advantages, not least of which is that they can provide a level of local-based knowledge that provides the bedrock on which to build nuanced insights into and speculations about the often opaque meanings of interactions, episodes and shifting emotions and moods. Some of that knowledge has been gained through intensive fieldwork, revealing, as it does in di Rosa's chapter, the depth in knowing a historical archive, a landscape and local community intimately. Other authors are able to draw upon knowledge that comes with personal and familial connections, such as Bracknell's to the Wirloman Noongar community, and in which one's own relatives are a source and guide within the analysis.

It is not only local knowledge that is brought to the analysis. Some authors also productively ask questions of what the 'local' means, or what it means to be 'local'. These lead also to consideration of ideas of space – and to questions about incommensurate or conflicting ideas about the meanings and significance of space, place or 'country', as well as the meanings and histories of particular locations, sites or 'routes'. For example, Dunn prioritises the political space of Aboriginal country in his chapter on Aboriginal guides in the Hunter region, showing how Aboriginal social spaces frequently dictated explorers' routes through country. By both exploring cross-cultural interactions in particular locations, as well as conceptualising how particular places or conceptualisations of space influenced the nature of such interactions, the collection extends in empirically rich ways some of the earlier 'inroads' into exploration history and writing made by scholars such as Paul Carter, Ross Gibson, Mary-Louise Pratt and Simon Ryan a decade or two ago.[18] Other contributors to this volume bring frameworks of 'race' and 'gender' to bear on the narratives of exploration. Cadzow's chapter discusses the absence of women in the historiography of exploration arguing that Aboriginal women were actually present and active agents in exploration in particular, political ways. Starbuck's chapter on French–West Papuan

---

18 Carter 1987; Ryan 1996; Pratt 1992; Gibson 2012.

encounters reads French expedition texts to reveal how discourses on 'race' within these encounters also suggest the presence of strong Indigenous agency.

A focus on the local in this volume is matched by an emphasis on the biographical. Biographical-influenced approaches, where analysis is focused closely on an individual life or a group of lives, is a methodology and narrative strategy used by several of the authors in this collection, to powerful effect. This reflects a growing appreciation that 'the detailed analysis of individual or collective lives offers one of the best ways to explore' diverse experiences as well as wider histories of race, gender, and class.[19] More recently, Jane Carey and Jane Lydon have also recognised the important value of biographical approaches, asserting that they allow us 'to vividly demonstrate the experience and impact of individuals within global trajectories of movement and exchange'. They add that '[l]ife stories link the transnational and the personal by incorporating both the specificities and intimacies of individual lives with macro circulations of trade, knowledge and state power'.[20]

Still, some historians take a disdainful view of biography, seeing it as a 'faintly suspect' historical method.[21] Certainly, there are reasons to be wary. Biography can be too individualising at the expense of understanding broader processes, contexts and group associations. Felix Driver has argued there is the risk of substituting, merely replacing a heroic myth of an individual (the explorer) with another (the broker or intermediary).[22] Similarly, David Philip Miller has warned against too great a focus on intermediaries, for it could lead 'us to neglect the larger forces within which they operated'. He states that it is 'easy in our fascination' with these colourful, puzzling characters to overstate their agency.[23] Miller is right to urge us to find a balance between the mythic explorer-hero narrative from which intermediaries were excluded, and the 'add guides and stir' approach.

---

19 Caine 2010: 3.
20 Carey and Lydon 2014: 10–11.
21 Evans and Reynolds 2012: 1.
22 Driver 2013: 8.
23 Miller 2011: 613.

However, these concerns can be mitigated by situating individual studies carefully, in a manner akin to microhistory and ethnohistory, where the examination of a broker's life can serve to tease out a broader picture, while respecting its particularities, as in Bracknell's reflective discussion of the life of Bobby Roberts. This is an approach that other authors in the volume also take. In addition to discussing the work brokers do within an expedition, the authors also study brokers by tracking their lives beyond the expedition and speculating about their possible motivations for participating in exploration. A focus on their larger lives provides a powerful counterpoint to historical representations that cast them as anonymous assistants: the 'native boy' or the 'blackfellow'. The analysis needs to take account of Indigenous brokers' views, agendas and actions too. Comparisons can be drawn between key figures to ascertain common tactics, rather than presenting an account of an artificially isolated individual. This is evident in Konishi's chapter where Bennelong and Gogy are compared, which enables new ways of reading Gogy's actions. What results is a more subtly rendered picture of the dynamic nature of expedition relationships. These various approaches reinforce just how productive a contextualised biographical approach can be. It creates a space for a deeper investigation of brokers' lives and actions, which explorer accounts too often discuss fleetingly, gloss over, or give the impression that the broker lived and breathed for the moment of the expedition and nothing more.

The chapters in this collection remind us of the pivotal and enduring role that exploration played in European imperialism and colonisation, as the European newcomers grappled with understanding and negotiating the diverse environments and landscapes of Australia and New Guinea in order to claim it as their own. Despite their obfuscating representational practices and the myth that these new lands were a *tabula rasa* – a blank slate to be inscribed by European territorial claims – European explorers were keenly aware that they traversed Indigenous lands, made up of distinct territories, occupied by different peoples and clans. This was one of the many reasons why the Europeans sought out Indigenous brokers who could mediate their encounters with different groups, and negotiate their needs and desires, be it basic wants such as water, food, and peaceful passage, or to facilitate their colonial ambitions and cement imperial reputations through acquiring esteemed geographic knowledge, or to attempt to secure administrative control over the 'natives', or just to establish nascent communication networks over vast areas. This volume adds to exploration scholarship more broadly by uncovering new stories of Indigenous brokers as well as offering new readings of their experiences. But it is not only to histories of exploration that this volume contributes. The work of brokering was necessitated by and embedded in colonial structures, relations and histories. And so by studying the ways in which these men and women tested, pushed and remade boundaries, shared or withheld their knowledge, forged and managed relations with explorers and their own countrymen and women, new insights and perspectives are also offered on colonial processes. We hope this book follows their lead, brokering further discussions, debates, and understandings of the complexities, cross cultural impacts and historical significance of brokering and boundary crossing.

References

Baker, Don 1993, 'John Piper: Conqueror of the Interior', *Aboriginal History* 17(1): 17–37.

―― 1998, 'Exploring with Aborigines: Thomas Mitchell and his Aboriginal guides', *Aboriginal History* 22: 36–50.

Ballantyne, Tony and Antoinette M. Burton (eds) 2009, *Moving Subjects: Gender, Mobility, and Intimacy in an Age of Global Empire*, University of Illinois Press, Urbana.

Burnett, D. Graham 2002, '"It is impossible to make a step without the Indians": Nineteenth-century geographical exploration and the Amerindians of British Guiana', *Ethnohistory* 49(1): 3–40.

Caine, Barbara 2010, *Biography and History*, Palgrave Macmillan, Houndmills, Basingstoke.

Carey, Jane and Jane Lydon (eds) 2014, *Indigenous Networks: Mobility, Connections and Exchange*, Routledge, London.

Carter, Paul 1987, *The Road to Botany Bay: An Essay in Spatial History*, Faber and Faber, London.

Douglas, Bronwen 2014, *Science, Voyages, and Encounters in Oceania, 1511–1850*, Palgrave Macmillan, Houndmills, Basingstoke.

Driver, Felix 2013, 'Hidden Histories made visible? Reflections on a geographical exhibition', *Transactions of the Institute of British Geographers* 38: 420–435.

Driver, Felix and Lowri Jones 2009, *Hidden Histories of Exploration: Researching Geographical Collections*, Royal Holloway, University of London, and Royal Geographical Society (with IBG), London.

Evans, Tanya and Robert Reynolds 2012, 'Introduction to this special issue on biography and life-writing', *Australian Historical Studies* 43(1): 1–8.

Gibson, Ross 2012, *26 Views of the Starburst World: William Dawes at Sydney Cove 1788–91*, UWA Publishing, Crawley.

Godayol, Pilar 2012, 'Malintzin/La Malinche/Doña Marina: re-reading the myth of the treacherous translator', *Journal of Iberian and Latin American Studies* 18(1): 61–76.

Greenblatt, Stephen 1991, *Marvellous Possessions: The Wonder of the New World*, Oxford University Press, Oxford.

Jolly, Margaret, Serge Tcherkézoff and Darrel Tryon (eds) 2009, *Oceanic Encounters: Exchange, Desire, Violence*, ANU E Press, Canberra.

Kennedy, Dane 2013, *The Last Blank Spaces: Exploring Africa and Australia*, Harvard University Press, Cambridge, MA.

Konishi, Shino 2012, *The Aboriginal Male in the Enlightenment World*, Pickering & Chatto, London.

Konishi, Shino and Maria Nugent 2013, 'Newcomers, c. 1600–1800', in *The Cambridge History of Australia: Volume 1: Indigenous and Colonial Australia*, Alison Bashford and Stuart Macintyre (eds), Cambridge University Press, Melbourne, 43–67.

Lambert, David and Alan Lester (eds) 2006, *Colonial Lives Across the British Empire: Imperial Careering in the Long Nineteenth Century*, Cambridge University Press, Cambridge.

Lester, Alan 2005, *Imperial Networks: Creating Identities in Nineteenth-Century South Africa and Britain*, Routledge, New York.

Macknight, Campbell 2011, 'The view from Marege': Australian knowledge of Makassar and the impact of the trepan industry across two centuries', *Aboriginal History* 35: 121–144.

Matsuda, Matt K. 2012, *Pacific Worlds: A History of Seas, Peoples, and Cultures,* Cambridge University Press, Cambridge.

Metcalf, Alida C. 2005, *Go-Betweens and the Colonization of Brazil: 1500–1600,* University of Texas Press, Austin.

Miller, David Philip 2011, 'History from between', *Technology and Culture* 52(3): 610–613.

Mitchell, Scott 1995, 'Foreign Contact and Indigenous Exchange Networks on the Cobourg Peninsula, North-Western Arnhem Land', *Australian Aboriginal Studies* 2: 44–48.

Moore, Clive 2003, *New Guinea: Crossing Boundaries and History*, University of Hawai'i Press, Honolulu.

Nugent, Maria 2009, *Captain Cook Was Here*, Cambridge University Press, Melbourne.

Pratt, Mary Louise 1992, *Imperial Eyes: Travel Writing and Transculturation,* Routledge, London.

Reynolds, Henry 1990, *With the White People: The Crucial Role of Aborigines in the Exploration and Development of Australia*, Penguin, Ringwood, Vic.

Roller, Heather F. 2010, 'Colonial collecting expeditions and the pursuit of opportunities in the Amazonian *Seratao* c. 1750–1800', *The Americas* 66(4) (April): 435–467.

Russell, Lynette 2001, *Colonial Frontiers: Indigenous-European Encounters in Settler Societies.* Manchester University Press, Manchester.

Russell, Penelope 2010, *Savage or Civilised?: Manners in Colonial Australia*, UNSW Press, Sydney.

Ryan, Simon 1996, *The Cartographic Eye: How Explorers Saw Australia*, Cambridge University Press, Cambridge.

Salmond, Anne 2003, *The Trial of The Cannibal Dog: Captain Cook in the South Seas*, Allen Lane, London.

Schaffer, Simon, Lissa Roberts, Kapil Raj and James Delbourgo (eds) 2009, *The Brokered World: Go-Betweens and Global Intelligence, 1770–1820*, Science History Publications, Sagamore Beach, MA.

Shellam, Tiffany 2009, *Shaking Hands on the Fringe: Negotiating the Aboriginal World at King George's Sound*, UWA Publishing, Perth.

Smith, Vanessa 2010, *Intimate Strangers: Friendship, Exchange and Pacific Encounters*, Cambridge University Press, Cambridge.

Thomas, Martin 2004, *The Artificial Horizon: Imagining the Blue Mountains*, Melbourne University Press, Melbourne.

—— (ed.) 2015, *Expedition into Empire: Exploratory Journeys and the Making of the Modern World*, Routledge, New York.

Turnbull, David 2009, 'Boundary-crossings, cultural encounters and knowledge spaces in early Australia', in *The Brokered World: Go-Betweens and Global Intelligence 1770–1820*, Simon Schaffer, Lissa Roberts, Kapil Raj and James Delbourgo (eds), Science History Publications, Sagamore Beach, MA, 387–428.

West-Sooby, John (ed.) 2013, *Discovery and Empire: the French in the South Seas*, University of Adelaide Press, Adelaide.

Yannakakis, Yanna 2008, *The Art of Being In-between: Native Intermediaries, Indian Identity and Local Rule in colonial Oaxaca*, Duke University Press, Durham.

2
Bennelong and Gogy: Strategic brokers in colonial New South Wales

Shino Konishi

Introduction: Intersecting and parallel lives

On the road between Parramatta and Prospect a meeting took place on Monday last for the purpose of inflicting punishment on a native well known at the above settlements by the name of Goguey … His crime was defensible upon custom immemorial, but so likewise was his extraordinary mode of arraignment an event consequent upon the former. Perceiving an unusual degree of rancour in the menaces of his judges, he endeavoured for a short time to avoid them by retiring; but being closely pursued he formed his resolution, and made a stand, with two adherents near him. The spears of his adversaries were barbed and rough-glazed, and three at once advancing upon him until within ten or twelve feet, he caught the first thrown on his target, but the second, discharged by Bennelong, entered above the hip, and passed through the side, so as to be afterwards extracted; but the third thrown by Nanbery as he wheeled to defend himself from the former, entered the back below the loins; when perceiving that his seconds had left him, he in a transport of rage and anguish turned his resentment upon those from whom he expected assistance but had deceived him, and then exhausted, fell.

Sydney Gazette and New South Wales Advertiser, 17 March 1805

Many historians have outlined the rationale behind European colonists' use of Indigenous guides. It has long been acknowledged that the guides' knowledge of the local environments informed and safeguarded the Europeans, as they played a crucial role in ensuring the expeditions had sufficient water and food. Increasingly, historians have recognised that such individuals were not mere guides, but rather acted as intermediaries, for their knowledge of local Indigenous languages and protocols allowed them to communicate the aims and interests of the explorers to any wary Indigenous people encountered. Historians have begun to map out the different reasons why Aboriginal people would become intermediaries for imperial and colonial expeditions, especially those who became known as professional guides, leading multiple excursions and traversing vast distances. Some of the broader synthetic studies such as Henry Reynolds's *With the White People* and, more recently, Dane Kennedy's *The Last Blank Spaces* have posited a range of factors, such as the temptation of material rewards, the desire for adventure, and, as Kennedy argues, the sad fact that some were 'deracinated', removed from their own kin networks, and had few alternative options.[1] Such typological studies are useful for sketching out the history of Aboriginal guides, but in order to gain deeper insights into the more complex motivations of Indigenous people to join expeditions, we need more detailed biographical portraits of the individual intermediaries and brokers, considering the Indigenous worlds that framed an individual intermediary's outlook, interests and intentions.

This chapter will investigate the experiences of two early Indigenous intermediaries: the infamous Wangal man Bennelong, the first intermediary between the local Eora clans and the British First Fleet (which, under the command of Governor Arthur Phillip, established the New South Wales colony); and his contemporary, the lesser known Dharawal man Gogy, who acted as a guide for NSW Corps Lieutenant Francis Barrallier on his colonial expedition into the Blue Mountains. Bennelong has long been subject to historical and biographical study, and long-standing representations of him as a tragic figure destroyed by alcohol have in recent years been replaced by the view that he was a highly mercurial yet strategic individual who was aware of

---

1   Reynolds 1990: 5–40; Kennedy 2013: 159–194.

his important role as a cultural broker.² Gogy, on the other hand, has been dismissed by the few historians who have discussed him as 'obnoxious' and seen as a failed intermediary who 'undermined' the expedition.³ My aim is to tease out the parallels in their actions and the relationships that Bennelong and Gogy deliberately cultivated with Phillip and Barrallier, in order to suggest that they were both driven by their standing in their own Indigenous polities and saw their roles as intermediaries as a means of elevating their status. Our knowledge of these two individuals derives from Western accounts. Yet most archival records about Aboriginal people are fragmentary, and written sources are often mediated through colonial prejudices, interests and assumptions. Consequently, informed speculation and 'reading against the grain' is often necessary in fleshing out the lives of past Aboriginal individuals. As Lynette Russell observes in her reflections on writing the biography of her Aboriginal grandmother, 'imagination plays an important role in constructing her narrative'.⁴ In this chapter, I argue that it is crucial to view intermediaries such as Bennelong and Gogy not only in terms of how they contributed to or were ruined by colonial society, but also in terms of their Indigenous life worlds.

Bennelong the cultural broker

Bennelong was a key cultural broker in the early Port Jackson colony.⁵ He was a member of the Wangal, one of the Eora clans whose territory spanned the southern side of Port Jackson between Darling Harbour and Rose Hill. He first became known to Governor Arthur Philip, who established the British colony in Sydney in January 1788, in November 1789 when he was 'about 26 years old, of good stature and stoutly made'. The British were initially struck by his appearance, as he had 'a bold intrepid countenance which bespoke defiance and revenge'.⁶

---

2   See Clendinnen 2003; Dortins 2009; Smith 2009; Turnbull 2009.
3   Lhuedé 2003: 13; Thomas 2003: 87.
4   Russell 2001: 148.
5   Bennelong advised the British colonists that he had five names 'Wol-lar-re-barre, Wog-ul-trowe, Ban-nel-lon, Boinba, [and] Bunde-bunda', according to Governor Phillip. Tench reported that his preferred name was Woollarawarre, however, he was most often referred to as Bennelong. See Smith 2009: 9.
6   Tench 1979: 159.

Phillip had long been eager to establish cordial relations with the local Eora Aboriginal people, not only because he had been instructed by the Admiralty to 'conciliate their affections', but also because he believed he could bring them 'into a voluntary subjection' through 'humane' and 'honourable' conduct, and prove that, in contrast to the Spanish conquest, 'a sanguinary temper was no longer to disgrace the European settlers in countries newly discovered'.[7] This ambition had been frustrated by the Eora's refusal to come into the colony, and their seemingly opportunistic attacks on lone or unarmed convicts. So in December 1788, Phillip decided to induce a definitive response from the Eora by 'capturing some of them by force'. He believed that this kidnapping would possibly bring tensions to a head and trigger a more decisive confrontation, but hoped that it would instead 'induce an intercourse' once the Aborigines realised that the captives had been treated with 'mildness and indulgence'.[8] Unfortunately for the British the first potential intermediary they captured, Arabanoo (also known as Manly), died whilst in their custody, so could not advocate the colonists' benevolence to the Eora people.[9]

The following November saw Phillip decide to try the same strategy, with the added hope that the new captives would inform the governor 'whether or not the country possessed any resources by which life might be prolonged'.[10] So Lieutenant William Bradley was dispatched and managed to carry off 'without opposition, two fine young men', Bennelong and Coleby. Despite the governor's instructions to 'treat them indulgently, and guard them strictly', Coleby escaped within the first week. Once alone it seemed to the British that Bennelong 'pretended, nay, at particular moments, perhaps [even] felt satisfaction in his new state'.[11]

Bennelong developed a close relationship with Governor Phillip, who took an active role teaching him English as well as the arts of British decorum and etiquette. Bennelong impressed the British with his

---

7   Phillip 1968: 44–45, 68.
8   Tench 1979: 138.
9   Arabanoo was captured on 31 December 1788 and died in May 1789 from smallpox. During this time two Aboriginal children, Nanbaree and Bòo-ron (known by the British as Abaroo), came to live in the colony. Both had been discovered by the British with a family member suffering from smallpox who had subsequently passed away. Tench 1979: 139–149.
10 Tench 1979: 158–159.
11 Tench 1979: 159.

quick grasp of the foreign language, leading Watkin Tench, a First Fleet lieutenant, to praise '[h]is powers of mind [which] were certainly far above mediocrity'. Tench observed that '[h]e acquired knowledge, both of our manners and language, faster than his predecessor [Arabanoo] had done. He willingly communicated information, sang, danced and capered, told us all the customs of his country and all the details of his family economy'.[12] During his period of incarceration, Bennelong shared Phillip's table and, unlike Arabanoo and Coleby, developed a taste for alcohol, often enthusiastically toasting the health of his acquaintances. He also entertained the governor by mimicking the 'actions and gestures of every person in [his] family'.[13] The two men shared regular walks around the governor's grounds, the younger dressed in his favourite red kersey jacket and 'a pair of trowsers' adorned with Phillip's small sword, 'a mark of [the governor's] confidence' in his prospective intermediary.[14]

Throughout his period of incarceration, Bennelong appeared to be a promising future go-between, one who could eventually return to the Eora people and testify to the good intentions of the British colonists, and lead to their 'coming in' to the colony. For instance, unlike Arabanoo, who would not tolerate any injury against his pride, Bennelong appeared to be 'very good-natured, being seldom angry at any jokes that may be passed upon him'. Bennelong's readiness to sing and dance at the officers' behest, the conscientiousness he displayed in learning British manners, and his adoption of Western dress seemed to demonstrate his acceptance of the British and desire to assimilate to their ways.[15] Governor Phillip also ensured that Bennelong was kept 'in ignorance' of the dire circumstances faced in the early colony, lest he give 'his countrymen such a description of our diminished numbers and diminished strength as would have emboldened them to become more troublesome'. To this end his rations were supplemented with extra fish and ground corn. While he was held captive, the British deemed Bennelong as 'pliant', and 'hardly anyone judged that he would attempt to quit us were the means of escape put within his reach'.[16] Yet when the opportunity finally arose, after five months

---

12 Tench 1979: 160.
13 King 1968: 267.
14 King 1968: 269.
15 King 1968: 269.
16 Tench 1979: 161.

in British custody, he absconded from the colony. After feigning an illness in the middle of the night, Bennelong was allowed outside, and once he 'found himself in a backyard ... he nimbly leaped over a slight paling and bade us adieu'.[17]

However, despite his escape from the colony, Bennelong did eventually become an intermediary, and has been recognised as the most significant cultural broker between the British and the Eora people. Contrary to British expectations, he did not simply become a 'pliant' advocate of their interests. Instead, he attempted to use the British to serve his own personal ambitions.[18] In *Dancing with Strangers* Inga Clendinnen reminds us that before Bennelong's capture the Eora clans had been ravaged by a smallpox epidemic that claimed untold lives, and in the wake of this tragedy, 'a radical redrawing of old political arrangements' would have been necessary.[19] Such a 'redrawing' perhaps provided opportunities for younger individuals, who otherwise would have deferred to the authority of elders, to try and elevate their position. Alternatively, the British presence may have been construed as a potential means of improving one's status; as Clendinnen speculates, Bennelong may have 'decided on trying for an alliance with the strangers shortly after his capture', or even 'toyed with the idea' earlier. She argues that this underlying motive better explains some of his 'actions and reactions', such as his 'tireless boasting of his sexual and fighting prowess', his 'swift adoption of British manners', and his 'use of clothing'.[20] David Turnbull similarly recognises that Bennelong's actions were deliberate and calculated, arguing that 'Bennelong was not a passive subject, he took an active, strategic, part in the spatial politics of positioning the cultural boundary in his role as negotiator and translator'.[21] Through a series of events, and negotiations, Bennelong 'skillfully [wove] the British into a series of reciprocal relations' which significantly advantaged his clan over others and, as Turnbull points out, allowed the Eora to dominate the trade with the British relative to other language groups in the area.[22] Thus recognising Bennelong's actions as strategic, rather

---

17   Tench 1979: 167.
18   Inga Clendinnen enthusiastically adopts this notion, suggesting that almost immediately after his capture he decided to try and forge an alliance with the British. Clendinnen 2003: 107.
19   Clendinnen 2003: 106.
20   Clendinnen 2003: 106–107.
21   Turnbull 2009: 394.
22   Turnbull 2009: 399.

than guileless as the British had, certainly recasts British reports of his actions and behaviours, including his exchange of names with Governor Phillip.

As previously mentioned, Bennelong had forged a close relationship with Phillip which endured after his escape. He even referred to the governor as '"*Beanga*" or Father; and the governor call[ed] him "*Dooroow*" or Son'.[23] Bennelong also exchanged names with the governor, a significant custom within Aboriginal society, and not just a 'mark of friendship' as asserted by Tench. Thus he called Phillip by his own preferred name 'Wolarawaree', and in turn adopted 'to himself the name of governor'.[24] This trading of Aboriginal and English names arguably endowed Bennelong with the authority to act as an intermediary between both societies, and garner prestige and power. Considering this exchange of names as strategic, rather than just as a symbol of friendship, explains some of Bennelong's inexplicable actions. For instance, the first time the British encountered Bennelong again after his escape was at a whale feast at Manly Cove.

Before the 200-odd Aboriginal people gathered on shore, Bennelong ostentatiously presented the sailors with a piece of whale meat as a present for the governor.[25] His gift of whale meat was effective, and Phillip rushed to Manly Cove where Bennelong reminded him of their friendship by performing their traditions and toasting to 'the king'. However, shortly after they were reunited the governor was speared by a visibly agitated man, Wil-le-me-ring.[26] Phillip perceived this attack as a 'momentary impulse of fear', but was more perplexed by Bennelong, noting that his behaviour in front of the Aboriginal crowd was 'not so easily ... accounted for. He never attempted to interfere when the man took the spear up, or said a single word to prevent him from throwing it.' Yet later, when Bennelong and Coleby were questioned by the British, they '*pretended* highly to disapprove the conduct of the man who had thrown the spear, vowing to execute

---

23 King 1968: 269. See also Hunter 1968: 141; Collins 1975: 452; Tench 1979: 160.
24 Tench 1979: 160. While Clendinnen sees Bennelong as politically minded and astute, she views this exchange of names simply as a mark of affection, and not strategic. Clendinnen 2003: 103–104.
25 Phillip 1968: 305.
26 Phillip 1968: 308–311. Clendinnen contests the accepted view that Phillip's spearing was a result of panic, and proposes that Bennelong had staged either a ritualistic spearing contest or Phillip's punishment for British transgressions. This is an interesting opinion, but the prevailing view of the First Fleet diarists was that it was a nervous reaction. Clendinnen 2003: 123–124.

vengeance upon him'. Phillip did not understand why his esteemed friend had not leapt to his defence, and was shocked when days later Bennelong bluntly 'enquired if the governor was dead'. Yet, crucially, Bennelong also claimed that he had beaten Wil-le-me-ring after the spearing.²⁷ Bennelong's seemingly duplicitous behaviour appears as strategically motivated, and as a determined effort not to turn either the British or the Eora against him. In front of the Aboriginal gathering he behaved as they did, by not reacting to Wil-le-me-ring's attack, yet to the British, he claimed solidarity with Phillip.

Bennelong's reason for adopting 'to himself the name of governor' was to muster British support against his rivals by presenting them as enemies. Phillip observed that 'from the first day he was able to make himself understood he was desirous to have all the [neighbouring] tribe of the Cammeragal killed'.²⁸ But this demand baffled the British, since he was frequently seen keeping amiable company with the Cameragal²⁹ and other clans that he had portrayed as enemies, including those from Botany Bay whom he accused of 'always kill[ing] the white men'.³⁰ Perhaps Bennelong's animosity towards the Cameragal was because they played an instrumental role in the *yoo-lahng erah-ba-diahng* ceremony which marked Aboriginal boys' transition to manhood.³¹ This ceremony was a prestigious event, in which large numbers of Aboriginal people from around the Sydney region would congregate at the '*yoo-lahng*', or ceremonial space, and dance through the night, awaiting the arrival of the Cameragal.³² The key part of the ceremony, the removal of the front tooth, was performed by the *carrahdis*, and the British understood that this role was an esteemed 'office' in Eora society. Significantly, Bennelong had boasted to Phillip that he had performed this operation himself: 'Bannelong had a throwing stick which he took pains to shew had been cut for the purpose of knocking

---

27 Phillip 1968: 308, 310–311. Tench claims that shortly after the spearing Bennelong and Colbee had both been interviewed by some of the boat's crew, and '[l]ike the others, they had *pretended* highly to disapprove the conduct of the man who had thrown the spear, vowing to execute vengeance upon him' (my emphasis). Tench 1979: 181.
28 Phillip 1968: 323–327.
29 While there are different historical spellings for this clan, the most widely accepted spelling is now 'Cameragal'. See, for example, Aboriginal Heritage Office 2015: 6, 8; Dictionary of Sydney n.d.
30 Phillip 1968: 323–327.
31 The ritual significance of the tooth removal ceremony was indicated by this name, whereas the loss of any other tooth was referred to by the term 'bool-bag-ga'. Collins 1975: 485.
32 Collins 1975: 467.

out the front tooth, and there was some reason to think he had performed that office'.[33] Bennelong's attempt to forge an alliance with the British was motivated by his desire to elevate his own position of power in the Eora polity, and eventually 'Governor Phillip began to suspect, though very unwillingly, that there was a great deal of art and cunning in Bennelong'.[34]

Throughout his interactions with the British, Bennelong always appeared to have one eye on his fellow Eora, ensuring that they were witness to the esteem with which the British treated him due to their desire to harness him as an envoy. After his escape, the British did not see him for four months. When they eventually did he was unrecognisable and had grown a long beard.[35] Before meeting with Phillip he requested a razor so he could shave, but was instead given scissors with which he trimmed his beard. Yet one week later when he again met some officers, his behaviour was markedly different. This time, in front of his family and friends, some of whom were 'timorous and unwilling to approach', Bennelong made a show of his familiarity with the British. After receiving a 'hatchet and a fish' he 'called loudly for' some 'bread and beef', which he offered to the others but only two were willing to taste it. Bennelong then 'made a motion to be shaved', and to the 'great admiration of his countrymen' was promptly shaved by the British barber. Bennelong clearly showed off in front of his countrymen, for they 'laughed and exclaimed' when he was shaved. Yet his performance was also a way of proving his own unique position as go-between, for after watching the British shave Bennelong, none of the others would 'consent to undergo it' themselves.[36]

Yet Bennelong's ostentatious displays were not just intended for his Aboriginal audience, his performances were also directed at the British, Phillip in particular, and were intended to assert and remind the colonists of his own political power. His determined efforts to have his authority recognised by the British came to a head during a protracted dispute over a young woman. Bennelong had kidnapped Boorong and announced that he would kill her in revenge for an

---

33   Phillip 1968: 332.
34   Phillip 1968: 323–327.
35   Tench 1979: 176.
36   Tench 1979: 183.

injury inflicted on him by her father.[37] After Bennelong was seen attacking Boorong several times, the colony's judge advocate David Collins attempted to 'reason' with him, telling 'him that if he killed the girl the governor would kill him'. Bennelong responded by 'mark[ing] with his finger those parts of the head, breast and arms where he said he would wound her, before he cut her head off'. When the governor offered her sanctuary, Boorong indicated that she would instead prefer to go to Bennelong's hut, where other Eora, including a young man thought to be her husband, were staying. After Phillip attempted to make the girl understand that 'if she went away she would be beat' by Bennelong, Bennelong suddenly promised the governor that he would not hurt her. While the other officers were suspicious of Bennelong's abrupt about-face, the governor believed him and let the woman go with Bennelong. The other officers were astounded by Phillip's decision, and their 'general opinion was that the girl would be sacrificed'. However, 'Governor Phillip himself was fully persuaded that Bannelong [sic] would keep his word' and, to everyone else's surprise, he did and Boorong remained unharmed.[38] Clendinnen sees this episode as a cultural misunderstanding, arguing that it was Bennelong's attempt to prove to Phillip that he too has a position of authority within the Eora polity, especially when resident within his own house.[39] Perhaps Bennelong's aim was even to remind the British of the continued jurisdiction of Aboriginal law within the boundaries of the colony, by asserting his right to punish Boorong. Certainly, Bennelong's performance was directed towards Phillip, testing Phillip's determination to publicly affirm their mutual respect and show his faith in Bennelong, and again confirming Bennelong's privileged position in the colony as a key cultural broker.

---

37   Phillip 1968: 321. Clendinnen sees this episode as a cultural misunderstanding. She argues that this was Bennelong's attempt to prove to Phillip that he too has a position of authority within his own polity, and had a level of autonomy within the colony, especially when resident within his own house.
38   Phillip 1968: 321–323.
39   Clendinnen 2003: 149–151.

Gogy the obnoxious guide

In 1802, Gogy was still a young man, as he only had one wife and a young son, but he had already led a turbulent life.[40] He belonged to the Dharawal whose territory spanned from Botany Bay southwards to the Shoalhaven River, and inland to Camden, where it bordered the lands of the Gandangara people who lived in the Blue Mountains. At that time it was not known as Dharawal country by the British colonists. They instead named these lands the County of Cumberland, but it was more frequently referred to as 'the Cowpastures', named after the cattle brought from England by the First Fleet to help feed and nourish their new settlement which had instead escaped south-west, running wild in the grasslands created by the local clans over many generations.[41] By then Gogy had already been exiled from his Dharawal country; instead of facing his punishment for a killing he had been involved in he fled west into Gandangara territory. There he was succoured by Goondel, forming a close relationship with the man who 'provid[ed] for all of his wants with the greatest friendship'. After a 'long time' Gogy returned to the Dharawal, and after 'submitt[ing] himself to the usual punishment' was 'well received'. 'Unfortunately … [Gogy then] made an incursion with a friend of his' back into Gandangara territory, and the friend, who was also Goondel's enemy, pursued, caught and killed a local woman, and both men then allegedly 'grilled and ate' some of her flesh.[42] Thus Gogy again fled, this time fearing Goondel's wrath and retribution, heading east, towards the British outpost at Prospect Hill.

It was here in October 1802 that Gogy met the 29-year-old French surveyor Francis Luis Barrallier, telling him this story of his troubled past. At the time, Barrallier was on a brief reconnaissance excursion to the foothills of the Blue Mountains scouting potential depot sites in preparation for his imminent expedition to find a route through the range. Since 1788, when the British had first arrived, the Blue Mountains had served as an impenetrable western boundary of the expanding Port Jackson settlement, and had already defeated numerous British attempts to discover what lay beyond. Barrallier, a Frenchman

---

40 By 1810 he would have two wives and more than one child. Liston 1988: 58.
41 Liston 1988: 50.
42 Barrallier 1975: 48n. See also Liston 1988: 57; Lhuedé 2003: 13.

whose Royalist family had escaped 'the wrath of the early French Revolutionaries' and fled to Britain in 1793, had sailed to Port Jackson in 1801 with the ambition of becoming the colony's Deputy Surveyor General.[43] On the journey out he met King, who was travelling with his French-speaking family to New South Wales to take up the colony's governorship after John Hunter. Having already established a close connection to King, Barrallier enlisted with the NSW Corps upon arriving in the colony, and soon undertook surveying missions in Bass Strait and the Hunter region. In 1802 he became Governor King's aide de camp. The governor had been particularly keen to discover what lay beyond the Blue Mountains primarily to quell the rumour, as 'wicked as it false', of an inland settlement which had tempted many convict to abscond and seek refuge there.[44] Barrallier was confident that he could succeed in crossing the mountains even though others had failed because he planned to establish a network of depots. He envisaged that this would allow his expedition to remain in communication with the colony, and more importantly receive regular provisions, as earlier attempts had failed when the explorers ran out of food.[45]

Upon encountering Gogy on this initial reconnaissance to find the site for the first depot, Barrallier believed that the 'native' had 'taken a fancy' to him. Meeting Gogy inspired Barrallier to employ a native guide, as he assumed that the Dharawal man would be 'useful to [him] when [he] advanced further inland'.[46] However, given Gogy's turbulent history with both the Dharawal and the Gandangara, it is likely that Gogy in turn saw an advantage in 'attaching' himself to the French surveyor. After having agreed that Gogy would serve as a guide on the eventual expedition, they arranged to rendezvous at Prospect Hill the following month.

The history of this failed expedition is well charted by historians, especially in local histories of the Blue Mountains. Barrallier set out with four soldiers, some convicts, and an ox-drawn cart, as well as Gogy and his wife and son. After establishing a depot, Barrallier and some of his men would generally set out on different excursions trying to make their way over the mountains by following the waterways.

---

43 Lhuedé 2003: 6–7.
44 Cunningham 1996: 98.
45 Barrallier 1975: 1.
46 Barrallier 1975: 1n.

Over the course of the expedition other Gandangara men and some of their wives and families joined the expedition. Some of the men would guide Barrallier on his excursions, and their families would camp at the depots, exchanging goods and food. Yet Barrallier never found a passage across the mountains: on 17 December 1802, six weeks after setting out, and thoroughly frustrated by his futile excursions, Barrallier realised that the chain of mountains 'could only be ascended by making almost superhuman efforts'.[47] The next day he made his way back to the depot, and a few days later embarked on the three-day walk back to Sydney.

In his report to King, Barrallier frequently disparaged Gogy as 'useless'. This assessment has been echoed by both local historian Andy Macqueen and French studies scholar Valerie Lhuedé. They perceived Gogy's disturbingly violent treatment of his wife, and his seemingly erratic behaviour in general as 'obnoxious' and troublesome.[48] Martin Thomas also suggested that the Gandangara's hostility towards Gogy 'undermined' Barrallier's expedition.[49] Such interpretations are somewhat short-sighted, taking Barrallier at his word. Instead, it is most likely that in his journal, Barrallier, like many other European explorers, effaced the significant contribution Gogy made to the expedition.

Kathrin Fritsch observes that many European explorers tended to obscure the contribution of Indigenous intermediaries in their accounts by reducing them to the status of 'mere servants', and refusing to admit the 'native' knowledge that formed the basis of the geographic knowledge they produced.[50] Her argument is borne out in Barrallier's account, even though his account has a relatively unusual level of detail about the Aboriginal people he met, including their names, and many of the people he describes appear as individuals with distinct personalities and manners. Yet, even though Gogy was not rendered invisible like the intermediaries in Fritsch's case studies, Barrallier nonetheless *reduced* Gogy's role, describing him as a follower and not a guide, and treating him as a retainer. Further, in his detailed description of Aboriginal place names, local resources,

---

47 Barrallier 1975: 50.
48 Macqueen 1993: 94; Lhuedé 2003: 13.
49 Thomas 2003: 87.
50 Fritsch 2009.

and cultural practices, he did not acknowledge Gogy as the source of information. For instance, on 6 November 1802, the first day of the expedition proper, Barrallier noted that the ford where they crossed the Nepean River was 'called Binhény by the natives', and that a swamp they arrived at later that day was known as 'Baraggel'. The next day they passed two more swamps called 'Manhangle' and 'Carabeely'.[51] The French surveyor also reported that he had learned that these swamps teemed with 'enormous eels, fishes, and various species of shells', which were 'sometimes used by the natives as food', along with the 'opossums and squirrels, which are abundant in this country'.[52] Barrallier also described in detail the local method for hunting kangaroos: a large group would form a circle one or two miles across, and slowly moving inwards, corral the animals with fire and noise so that they could be more easily speared.[53] Yet by reading Barrallier's account against the grain, it becomes evident that his detailed local and cultural knowledge must have been explained to him by Gogy. The only other Aboriginal people in the party at that stage of the expedition was Gogy's wife and son, whom Barrallier rarely mentions. Barrallier's account, then, not only effaced Gogy's contribution to the local knowledge accumulated on the expedition, but also significantly masked the close relationship that the two men must have developed. The level of detail in his account suggests that the pair must have spent considerable time together conversing about their immediate environs, planning possible routes, and Aboriginal food sources and hunting practices.

Unlike Bennelong, Gogy has not been perceived as strategic by historians. Perhaps this is because Barrallier, Gogy's only significant chronicler, was himself oblivious to Gogy's motives. Phillip had eventually become partially aware of Bennelong's strategic endeavours throughout the course of their four-year affiliation.[54] Barrallier on the other hand knew Gogy for less than two months, thus the motives behind Gogy's confusing actions remained opaque.

---

51   Barrallier 1975: 2.
52   Barrallier 1975: 2n.
53   Barrallier 1975: 2–3n.
54   Konishi 2007; Fullagar 2009.

As we have seen, Gogy had quickly attached himself to Barrallier, and he arguably found this to be a privileged position that he alone wanted to hold, so jealously guarded it. As Alida Metcalf has observed in her study of Brazilian go-betweens, intermediaries 'inhabit an "in-between" space which gives them mobility, information and power', and as a consequence they 'may exploit their positions for their own benefit'.[55] Arguably, Gogy tried to create and inhabit the space between Barrallier and the other Aboriginal people, and use this 'in-between' space to his own advantage. This became apparent when the expedition encountered Bungin and Wooglemai, two Gandangara, or 'mountaineer', men as Barrallier called them. Bungin, who had never seen a white man before, quickly impressed Barrallier by demonstrating his expertise in discerning the identity of individuals by their footprints. He also showed gratitude to the Frenchman's generous trade of a new axe for Bungin's old one by building a hut for the Frenchman. This, Barrallier learned, was a local custom extended to 'strangers they wish to receive as friends', since ordinarily 'the natives do not allow any stranger to inhabit the territories they have appropriated to themselves'.[56] Consequently, Barrallier decided to 'attach' himself to Bungin, believing he would be 'very useful in the country … he was in', and attempted to curry his favour by ensuring food was given to him.[57] As these exchanges and conversations would have been negotiated by Gogy, the expedition's sole translator at that point, it is most likely that he was conscious of his imminent displacement as the expedition's primary guide.

In response, Gogy tried to insinuate himself back into Barrallier's favour. His first opportunity soon arose when the expedition encountered new people: Bulgin and his wives and children. They had just been hunting and had in their possession two feet of an animal they called 'colo'.[58] Knowing that Barrallier was interested in collecting natural history specimens, Gogy obtained these in exchange for two spears and a tomahawk, presumably his own since the only trade items Barrallier mentioned bringing on the expedition were metal axes. Barrallier was delighted with these specimens (most likely they were koala feet which he mistook for that of a monkey), and, in his own

---

55 Metcalf 2005: 3.
56 Barrallier 1975: 4–5.
57 Barrallier 1975: 5.
58 Barrallier 1975: 8–9.

attempt to curry favour with Governor King, had them sent to him 'in a bottle of spirits'. That same night Gogy 'built for Barrallier a *very* large hut', perhaps as a reminder that before Bungin's arrival, he had a stronger friendship with the explorer.[59] These gifts and ostensible symbols of friendship were arguably strategic attempts on Gogy's behalf to exploit mutual needs, and induce mutual accommodation. Like Bennelong's gifts, they were intended to induce reciprocity: Gogy had adapted the supposed local custom of building a hut as a sign of friendship by building a hut for Barrallier, even though he was not in his own territory, as custom dictated, and outperformed his rivals by building a very large one.

Towards the end of the Blue Mountains expedition, Gogy seemed especially determined to show Barrallier that his own allegiance was to the French surveyor and not the Gandangara 'natives'. As Barrallier repeatedly doubled-back to the depot after each failed excursion to find a route over the mountains, he frequently found that his huts had been burnt down or destroyed by the Gandangara people. In response to this, and arguably as a sign of his loyalty to Barrallier, 'Gogy set the country over which [they] were passing on fire to avenge [themselves] on the natives who had burnt [their] huts'.[60]

Gogy's motive for fostering a close alliance with Barrallier, not to mention the four redcoats who accompanied the expedition, was to forge an alliance with the British against the Gandangara, much like Bennelong seemed to do with Phillip against the Cameragal. On 12 November, Bungin discovered a group of Gandangara men including Gogy's enemy Goondel sitting around a fire. Bungin approached them in a reassuring manner, 'telling them not to be frightened' and that the white men 'were travelling without any intention of doing them any harm'.[61] Gogy followed, but instead of placating the Gandangara men he 'held [Barrallier's] gun in his hand to show them he could make use of the [British] arms'.[62] This threatening demonstration of his superior weapon and allies was perhaps Gogy's main motivation for agreeing to guide Barrallier into the territory of the enemy he had previously fled. However, Gogy's aggressive

---

59   Barrallier 1975: 9 (my emphasis).
60   Barrallier 1975: 45.
61   Barrallier 1975: 15–16.
62   Barrallier 1975: 16.

performance did not elicit the reaction he intended: the men refused to speak to Gogy, and instead threw 'terrible glances at him' and deliberately excluded him from a share in their meal, a gesture that Gogy considered 'as the greatest insult'.[63]

Unable to create an alliance between himself and Barrallier against the Gandangara, Gogy changed tactic, and tried to prevent Barrallier from having further contact with Goondel and his men. He begged Barrallier not to camp near them, claiming that they would kill Gogy in his sleep despite the presence of armed sentries. Later in the expedition, whenever they happened upon Goondel or his men Gogy would 'insist that they must not disturb him' and encourage the expedition to move on. Towards the end of the journey, on 14 December, when they were in Gandangara country, Gogy exclaimed that they were about to enter the territory of a new tribe who 'were anthropophagi' and that 'they ought not to try and mix with them'.[64] Bennelong and other Port Jackson Aboriginal people had similarly launched exaggerated accusations against neighbouring Aboriginal people in order to dissuade the British from approaching them.[65] When Barrallier laughed at Gogy's apparently tall tale, he grew angry and retorted: 'Well master, you will see that I am not a liar.'[66] Yet the next day, instead of discovering the apocryphal tribe of cannibals as they ventured further into the mountains, they again happened upon Goondel.

Like Bennelong, Gogy's most shocking and perplexing performance was a violent assault on a woman, his wife. One month earlier, on 14 November, while they waited at the depot for their supplies, Gogy unexpectedly flew into a rage when his wife ate some 'morsels' of food given to his son. He suddenly 'took his club and struck his wife's head such a blow that she fell to the ground unconsciously'. Ignoring the others' attempts to pacify him, Gogy paced around, all the while 'abusing his wife', and then rushed back, stabbing her in the thigh

---

63 Barrallier 1975: 17.
64 Barrallier 1975: 47.
65 For instance Bennelong had told Phillip that the Botany Bay people 'always kill the white men', which eventually led 'Governor Phillip … to suspect, though very unwillingly, that there was a great deal of art and cunning in Bennelong', and the Port Jackson Aboriginal people reported to the British that the Botany Bay man 'Gòme-boak was a cannibal'. Phillip 1968: 327; Collins 1975, I: 342.
66 Barrallier 1975: 47n.

with his fishing spear several times, and then grabbed a musket and threatened to shoot her. After a short interlude in which Bungin attempted to calm him down, Gogy 'walk[ed] up and down in a great fury', everyone cowering in his wake. Finally, Gogy went to Barrallier and 'said he was almost certain one of [Barrallier's] people had seduced his wife'. The Frenchman replied that this 'was impossible' and it was only his 'state of anger which made him believe things that did not exist'. However, this did not placate Gogy and he again struck his wife, who then revealed that the seducer was 'Withington, one of [the] soldiers' and assured him that 'she had never responded to his advances'. Barrallier did not put much faith in her testimony, instead commenting that in general 'cruelty and laziness are two prominent characteristics of the natives'.[67]

Scholars have deplored Gogy's violent attack on his wife and, like Barrallier, construed it as an example of how male violence against women has been 'a feature for Aboriginal culture since long before the First Fleet'.[68] However, even though this was a shockingly brutal incident, it cannot be explained by the ostensibly violent nature of Aboriginal gender relations.[69] Again, Gogy's performance is reminiscent of Bennelong's protracted and violent attack on the young woman Boorong in front of the British officers and Governor Phillip, in retaliation of a crime committed against him by her father.[70] Both attacks appeared to have been flagrant and defiant aggressive acts performed in front of the colonists, whom in both instances claimed to pity the women but failed to intervene. Further, both Bennelong and Gogy demonstrated their power over women, perhaps to show the newcomers that they still exerted some authority within their own domestic polity in spite of the colonial authority of the governor and expedition leader. However, I suspect that Gogy's charge that one of white men had wronged him by seducing his wife was his attempt to make Barrallier beholden to him and allow him to demand retribution.

---

67   Barrallier 1975: 22–23.
68   Thomas 2013. See also Lhuedé 2003: 13. However, in response to similar charges made by Manning Clark, Macqueen points out that Bungin, Gogy's competitor for Barrallier's esteem, tenderly dressed Gogy's wife's wounds, and in the following days Gogy 'looked sorry for having ill-treated, his wife', and was 'very affectionate towards her'. Macqueen 1993: 96.
69   For a more detailed discussion of colonial tropes about Aboriginal gendered violence, see Konishi 2008.
70   See Konishi 2012: 60.

Conclusion: The parallel lives of two strategic brokers

In 1792 Phillip completed his term as governor and voyaged back to Britain. Bennelong accompanied him there, along with Yemmerawanne, and they were the first Australian Aboriginal people to venture to Europe. Bennelong stayed in Britain for two years; sadly, Yemmerawanne died after the first. During his stay Bennelong visited key sites of Britain's power, culture and history – the Houses of Parliament, St Paul's Cathedral and the Tower of London – but was determined to return home.[71] After his homecoming in September 1795, Bennelong was reported to have initially 'assumed the manners, the dress, and the consequence of an European', but ultimately 'returned to his old habits', living 'in the same manner as those who never mixed with the civilised world' until his demise in January 1813.[72] Yet after his return he no doubt had little interest in mixing with the 'civilised world' as he, Bennelong, continued to occupy a 'respected position in the Eora clan networks',[73] playing significant roles in gatherings of the Eora clans, and the ceremonial punishment of transgressors.

After failing to find a route through the mountains, Barrallier returned to Sydney, where he soon fell out of favour with Governor King and abruptly left the colony. Gogy remained an outlaw and continued to transgress Aboriginal law. He was ritually punished by Bennelong in 1805, receiving two seemingly mortal spear wounds which he remarkably recovered from (as described in the epigraph).[74] Unlike Bennelong, he continued to try to strategically attach himself to various colonists. Such endeavours served him well in 1816 during Governor Macquarie's punitive raids against the Gandangara, for his old friend John Warby and Charles Throsby protected Gogy from the soldiers who mistook Gogy for a 'hostile native', allowing him to flee to Botany Bay.[75] At this point he disappeared from colonial records, however, in February 1824 French explorer Dumont D'Urville observed a large gathering of the Eora clans from 'Parramatta, Kissing Point, Sydney,

---

71 Fullagar 2009: 31.
72 David Mann, *The Present Picture of New South Wales*, London, 1811, 46–47, cited in Smith 2009: 19.
73 Smith 2009: 22.
74 *Sydney Gazette and New South Wales Advertiser*, 17 March 1805, 7 April 1805.
75 Liston 1988: 52.

Liverpool, Windsor, Emu Plains, Broken Bay, Five islands, Botany Bay, and even from Hunter River etc. etc.' and observed that the 'Liverpool tribe [was] commanded by Coagai [Gogy]'. This time, as opposed to being the transgressor, Gogy was there to see the punishment of eight individuals who had killed an ally of his from the Windsor clan.[76] Thus, like Bennelong, Gogy also eschewed close contact with the British once he had managed to occupy an esteemed position within Aboriginal society.

Through a comparison with Bennelong, who is well recognised as political and strategic, I suggested motivations for Gogy's 'attachment' to Barrallier and re-read his behaviour as tactical, as opposed to erratic and obnoxious as previous scholars have claimed. I have also tried to tease out Bennelong's and Gogy's individual personalities, to show that Indigenous responses to the colonial presence were idiosyncratic. This was especially the case in the early stages of the colony, when the conditions still allowed for a nascent 'middle ground' to exist; that is a time when there was still a rough balance of power between Indigenous people and colonists, and intermediaries served important functions in negotiating their mutual needs and accommodation.[77] Such histories reveal that the early history of cross-cultural interaction in Australia was not just one of colonial oppression and Indigenous resistance, but shaped by myriad interpersonal encounters influenced by complex and individual relationships and interests. By considering the process of mediation in these early New South Wales encounters, this chapter provides insights into how Indigenous individuals such as Bennelong and Gogy saw the presence of the newcomers as an opportunity to remake themselves, and to attempt to elevate their status and power within their local Indigenous society.

References

Aboriginal Heritage Office 2015, *Filling a Void: A Review of the Historical Context for the Word 'Guringai'*, Aboriginal Heritage Office, North Sydney.

---

76 Dumont D'Urville 1987: 85.
77 White 2011: xii.

Barrallier, Francis 1975, *Journal of the Expedition into the Interior of New South Wales 1802, by Order of His Excellency Governor Philip Gidley King, by Francis Barrallier, Ensign, New South Wales Corps*, Marsh Walsh Publishing, Melbourne.

Clendinnen, Inga 2003, *Dancing with Strangers*, Text Publishing, Melbourne.

Collins, David 1975, *An Account of the English Colony in New South Wales*, B. Fletcher (ed.), 2 vols, A.H. & A.W. Reed in association with the Royal Historical Society, Sydney.

Cunningham, Chris 1996, *Blue Mountains Rediscovered: Beyond the Myths of Early Australian Exploration*, Kangaroo Press, Kenthurst.

Dictionary of Sydney n.d., 'Cameragal people', www.dictionaryof sydney.org/organisation/cameragal_people, accessed 1 February 2016.

Dortins, Emma 2009, 'The many truths of Bennelong's tragedy', *Aboriginal History* 33: 53–75.

Dumont D'Urville, Jules S.-C. 1987, *An Account in Two Volumes of Two Voyages to the South Seas by Captain Jules S-C Dumont D'Urville of the French Navy to Australia, New Zealand, Oceania 1826–1829 in the corvette Astrolabe and to the Straits of Magellan, Chile, Oceania, South East Asia, Australia, Antarctica, New Zealand and Torres Strait 1837–1840 in the corvettes Astrolabe and Zélée, Vol. 1: Astrolabe 1826–1829*, Helen Rosenman (trans. and ed.), Melbourne University Press, Carlton, 1987.

Fritsch, Kathrin 2009, '"You have everything confused and mixed up…!" Georg Schweinfurth, knowledge and cartography of Africa in the 19th century', *History in Africa* 36(1): 87–101.

Fullagar, Kate 2009, 'Bennelong in Britain', *Aboriginal History* 33: 31–52.

Kennedy, Dane 2013, *The Last Blank Spaces: Exploring Africa and Australia*, Harvard University Press, Boston.

King, Philip G. 1968 [1793], 'Lieutenant King's Journal', in John Hunter, *An Historical Journal of Events at Sydney and at Sea, 1787–1792, by Captain John Hunter, Commander H.M.S. Sirius, with further Accounts by Governor Arthur Phillip, Lieutenant P.G. King, and Lieutenant H.L. Ball*, John Bach (ed.), Angus and Robertson, Sydney.

Konishi, Shino 2007, 'The father Governor: the British administration of Aboriginal people at Port Jackson, 1788–1792', in *Public Men: Masculinity and Politics in Modern Britain*, Matthew McCormack (ed.), Palgrave Macmillan, Hampshire, 54–61.

—— 2008, '"Wanton with plenty": Questioning ethno-historical constructions of sexual savagery in Aboriginal societies, 1788–1803', *Australian Historical Studies* 39(3): 356–372.

—— 2012, *The Aboriginal Male in the Enlightenment World*, Pickering and Chatto, London.

Lhuedé, Valerie 2003, 'Francis Barrallier, explorer, surveyor, engineer, artillery officer, aide-de-camp, architect and ship designer: Three years in New South Wales (1800–1803)', *Explorations: A Journal of French-Australian Connections* 35.

Liston, Carol 1988, 'The Dharawal and Gandangara in colonial Campbelltown, New South Wales, 1788–1830', *Aboriginal History* 12(1): 58.

Macqueen, Andy 1993, *Blue Mountains to Bridgetown: The Life and Journeys of Barrallier, 1773–1853*, A. Macqueen, Springwood.

Metcalf, Alida C. 2005, *Go-Betweens and the Colonization of Brazil: 1500–1600*, University of Texas Press, Austin.

Phillip, Arthur 1968 [1793], 'Phillip's Journal', in John Hunter, *An Historical Journal of Events at Sydney and at Sea, 1787–1792, by Captain John Hunter, Commander H.M.S. Sirius, with further Accounts by Governor Arthur Phillip, Lieutenant P.G. King, and Lieutenant H.L. Ball*, John Bach (ed.), Angus and Robertson, Sydney.

Reynolds, Henry 1990, *With the White People*, Penguin Books, Ringwood, Vic.

Russell, Lynette 2001, 'The instrument brings on voices: Writing a biographical history', *Meanjin* 60(3): 142–151.

Smith, Keith Vincent 2009, 'Bennelong among his people', *Aboriginal History* 33: 7–30.

Sydney Gazette and New South Wales Advertiser.

Tench, Watkin 1979 [1789–1793], *Sydney's First Four Years: being a reprint of A Narrative of the Expedition to Botany Bay and A Complete Account of the Settlement at Port Jackson*, L.F. Fitzhardinge (ed.), Library of Australian History in association with the Royal Australian Historical Society, Sydney.

Thomas, Martin 2003, *The Artificial Horizon: Imagining the Blue Mountains*, Melbourne University Press, Melbourne.

Thomas, Tony 2013, 'The long history of Aboriginal violence – Part II', *Quadrant*, 7 May.

Turnbull, David 2009, 'Boundary-crossings, cultural encounters and knowledge spaces in early Australia', in *The Brokered World: Go-Betweens and Global Intelligence 1770–1820*, Simon Schaffer, Lissa Roberts, Kapil Raj and James Delbourgo (eds), Science History Publications, Sagamore Beach, MA, 387–428.

White, Richard 2011, *The Middle Ground: Indians, Empires, and Republics in the Great Lakes Region, 1650–1815*, Twentieth Anniversary Edition, Cambridge University Press, Cambridge.

3

'Race', intimacy and go-betweens in French–West Papuan encounters

Nicole Starbuck

From the early modern age of discovery to the nineteenth-century era of science, relations between European maritime explorers and Indigenous peoples grew easier and the gaze explorers cast over the bodies and behaviours of their 'native' hosts became far more focused; yet paradoxically, scholars observe, explorers' records of cross-cultural encounters increasingly obscured the agency and influence of local individuals. Particularly in the case of French explorers, who had an almost constant presence in Oceania from 1817 to 1840, this development has been largely accounted for by the nature of modern ethnographic knowledge production. By the nineteenth century, in order to facilitate and lend authority to their claims about human diversity, many French voyager-naturalists were distancing their reports from the 'messiness of locally tortuous wheeling and dealing' and particularly from the potential for 'failure, infection and leakage' caused by local go-betweens.[1] Certainly, they were also seeking more explicitly in their reports to advance existing theories in the nascent field of anthropology and, to that end, referring more to previous studies than to their own observations in the field:

---

1   See Schaffer et al. 2009: xxi–xxx.

the effects of accumulating knowledge were more pronounced and profound at this time than ever before. Yet, while the demands of scientific method, on paper, may have increased the distance between voyager-naturalist and ethnographic subject, during the encounter itself, as close observation necessitated some intimacy, they also placed a heightened significance on the cultivation of cross-cultural 'friendships'. Evidence of the voyagers' efforts to this end is found mainly in the expedition narratives – the *voyages historiques* – and, more sparsely, in manuscript journals and notebooks. These records demonstrate that it could certainly be a messy, even 'tortuous', venture and one, moreover, which shaped the formal ethnographies so silent about it.[2] At each encounter, voyager-naturalists entered dynamic zones of cross-cultural exchange, where the local interests competed with their own and where often they were not the first Europeans to land. Like them, though influenced by generations of their own knowledge and experience and driven by their own interests, the 'observed', too, sought both friendships and a sense of distance. While the visitor, for his own part, reached out to his host then later retreated, moving from the beach to his desk, from field observer to sedentary naturalist, the Oceanic go-between in turns drew in and withdrew from the visitor, endeavouring to limit the interaction to a particular space, to draw political, social and material benefits from it while preventing 'leakage and infection' in their community. It is this process, which in nineteenth-century French–Oceanic encounters is seen to have been so pronounced, so heavily, if inconsistently, papered over in expeditionary writings, and was in fact so shaped by accrued knowledge, that forms the main theme of this chapter.

One of the questions considered here is just how far nineteenth-century voyagers did neglect the role of local intermediaries in their records, in comparison to their predecessors on fifteenth- to eighteenth-century expeditions. The historiography of cross-cultural history has been even more silent on the relations between French explorers and Oceanic Islanders in the nineteenth century than have the voyage records themselves. Most of the key interrogations of European–Indigenous contact, and of the role of intermediaries in particular, have been set in the context of New World conquest. From various disciplinary angles and focusing on particular geographic regions, colonising

---

2   See Bronwen Douglas's discussions of countersigns. Douglas 2009a, 2009b.

nations and colonial periods, Stephen Greenblatt, Tzvetan Todorov, Mary Louise Pratt, Patricia Seed and Alida Metcalf unpack the cross-cultural encounter and lay out its many elements: the performances, exchanges, and negotiations; the tensions and bonds; the (mis)understandings and representations.³ It is such scholarship that has established the figure La Malinche as the quintessential model for the local go-between. La Malinche, or Malintzin, was a Nahua woman who acted as translator and political intermediary for Hernan Cortez during the Spanish conquest of the Aztec Empire. More clearly than most, La Malinche demonstrates the ways in which cultural boundaries were drawn, redrawn, manipulated and crossed by individuals – individuals who, in the historical narrative, had long remained indistinguishable amongst a supposedly powerless crowd. In the very rich body of eighteenth-century contact history, most particularly the British studies, Tupaia and Bennelong have followed in La Malinche's footsteps: Tupaia for some months contributing to the success of James Cook's *Endeavour* journey; and Bennelong, over a much longer period, moving in and out of British and Aboriginal worlds.⁴ Studies of these individuals reveal the complexity of that space where the worlds of the visitor and the local overlap, as new knowledge, practices and views emerge, and consequential imperial relations develop. In different contexts this space has been articulated as the 'contact zone' or 'middle ground'.⁵ Many New World and later contact studies recognise that go-betweens in this space emerged not only amongst the local people but also amongst the visitors. For example, Greenblatt and Metcalf argue that it is important to acknowledge that voyagers themselves acted effectively as envoys for the government, intellectual bodies and the public at home. In their ceremonial performances and their exchanges of objects and knowledge, they worked hard to translate French, Spanish, Dutch or British interests into a language that 'natives' might understand. They also mediated in the reverse direction, representing to the authorities and the public at home the lives, capacities and bodies of those same natives.⁶ It is the voyagers' own mediation, in fact, that scholars have most easily and fruitfully been able to study and they reveal that it has always tended to obscure local agency. As Todorov explains, for example, Columbus sees his

---

3   Greenblatt 1991; Seed 1995; Todorov 1999; Metcalf 2005; Pratt 2008.
4   See, for instance, Fullagar 2008: 211–237; Turnbull 1998: 126–31; 2009: 390–402.
5   White 1991; Pratt 2008.
6   Greenblatt 1991: 119–151; Metcalf 2005: 10–11, *passim*.

'Indian' acquaintances only as 'living objects', part of the landscape and without a right to their own will.[7] Similarly, Cortez shows more interest in the objects produced by the Aztec people than in the people themselves. He did not acknowledge them as 'human individualities', remarks Todorov.[8] From the 1760s through to the turn of the nineteenth century, captains Cook, Alessandro Malaspina and Nicolas Baudin and their men produced more objective and thorough accounts of Indigenous peoples, but theirs was not a golden era. Their reports are muddied, too, by colonial preoccupations, ideas of the 'noble savage', and desire to preserve their own safety and sense of superiority. On the whole, the presence and significance of local go-betweens are only inadvertently revealed in these records. Both this pattern of denial or blindness concerning local agency among European voyagers and the rich and varied methodology scholars have developed to elucidate the history of contact intermediaries – both Indigenous and European – need to be kept in mind when we turn our attention to the nineteenth century.

On the question of the relationship between 'race', intimacy and go-betweens during the final years of French–Oceanic exploration, the West Papuan encounters of 1819–1827 provide valuable insight. The expeditions of captains Louis Freycinet, Louis-Isidore Duperrey and Jules-Sébastien-César Dumont D'Urville visited Waigeo Island in the Raja Empat Archipelago and Dorey Bay on the Bird's Head Peninsula of New Guinea. They represented a new era in the history of France and French maritime exploration. Since the last French expedition had sailed for Oceania, slavery in the French colonies, abolished during the Revolution, had been introduced, the Napoleonic Empire had risen and fallen, and the Bourbon monarchy had been restored. Politically, the Restoration period itself was uneasy. A resurgent class of elites were calling for 'legitimacy' while, in the midst of a society thoroughly transformed by democratic revolution, a new bourgeois generation revived the writings of Rousseau and Voltaire and expressed increasing dissatisfaction with the Bourbon regime.[9] Culturally, this was a time when 'sentiment' was relegated to the female, private, sphere, while Frenchmen conducted themselves according to the deeply imbedded, if only recently democratised,

---

7   Todorov 1999: 41, 49, 34–50.
8   Todorov 1999: 129.
9   McPhee 2004: 113–119.

rules of honour.[10] The division of natural history into professionalised disciplines, further divided by sedentary and fieldwork roles, had been affected, and a shift from the 'natural history' to a 'science' of Man was well in progress. Reflecting these changes, the Restoration expeditions were markedly leaner and more disciplined machines than their predecessors: they carried only naval staff, pursued specific scientific questions, and kept to shorter and more circumscribed itineraries. In West Papua, they were each to gather data that would facilitate classification of 'les papuas'. Comparative anatomist Georges Cuvier had inquired with some sense of urgency: 'Are the Papuans [in fact] Negroes who may formerly have strayed across the Indian Ocean? We possess neither figures nor descriptions precise enough to allow us to answer this question.'[11]

Indeed, prior to the encounters of the Restoration era, Europeans in general and the peoples of New Guinea and the nearby islands had had only rare and, typically, very limited contact. That said, the inhabitants of Dorey Bay experienced an encounter of some weeks with Thomas Forrest, of the East India Company, and his crew in 1774, and even a short-lived British settlement led by John Hayes, a lieutenant in the Bombay Marine, in 1794–1795.[12] Forrest had also made a brief visit to Waigeo, and he was followed there by a French expedition led by Bruni d'Entrecasteaux in 1794. D'Entrecasteaux's botanist, Jacques-Julien de Labillardière, wrote favourably of the local peoples' hospitality and character and remarked, too, on the combination of Indonesian and Papuan cultures, the evidence of conflict between these inhabitants and the Dutch colonists further east, and the sophistication of local commerce.[13] Located on the trade route between mainland New Guinea and the archipelagos of Indonesia, the Waigeo Islanders were involved in vigorous networks of exchange in produce, objects and slaves while also entangled in a subservient and tense relationship with the Sultan of Tidore.[14] They would have had an interest in incorporating the Frenchmen into their trade networks

---

10 Nye 1998: 31–46, 127–147; Reddy 1997: 1–17, *passim*; Reddy 2001: 211–256.
11 Cuvier 1817: 99. See also Ballard 2008: 158–159.
12 Forrest 1780: 79–82, 93–114.
13 Labillardière 1800: 298–303.
14 Moore 2003: 86.

– indeed, leading that process was bound to enhance the status of local intermediaries – but particularly at Waigeo Island they also had reason to beware of potential exploitation.[15]

As a case study in cross-cultural history, this set of French–Papuan encounters has received little attention. Bronwen Douglas does argue, however, that the official ethnographic reports that resulted are especially illustrative of the emergent 'science of race' and of the influence of Indigenous 'countersigns' on voyagers' ethnographic reports.[16] Factors beyond the actual encounters undoubtedly played a strong part in this development: the drive for theoretical advances in Paris, the generational differences between captain Freycinet and his two successors,[17] and the voyager-naturalists' increasing focus on the knowledge that accumulated on paper rather than in the field. The voyagers' itineraries may have been influential as well for, as Chris Ballard suggests, trajectories from east to west, or vice versa, could influence what would later be recognised as Polynesian/Melanesian comparisons.[18] Freycinet approached Waigeo from the west, after visiting Western Australia and Timor, whereas Duperrey and Dumont d'Urville both sailed from the east, having visited Tahiti and New Zealand. These are all factors that bore particularly on the French explorers in their capacity as, to borrow from Metcalf, 'representational intermediaries'.[19] Yet, the actions and experiences of individuals in the particular spaces and moments of the encounters themselves are certain to have had a fundamental influence as well.

* * *

The Freycinet expedition weighed anchor and set up camp at Rawak Island off the north coast of Waigeo in 1818. It stayed only two weeks, but the conscientious Freycinet and his surgeon-naturalists, Jean René

---

15   See Rutherford 2009: 13, 16–18; Moore 2003: 69.
16   Douglas 2008: 116–124; 2009b.
17   Freycinet was born in 1779 and joined the navy as part of the new Republican officer corps during the height of the French Revolution, early 1794. Freycinet served as first-lieutenant on the Australian voyage of Nicolas Baudin (1800–1804) and completed the publication of the official account of that voyage. Duperrey was born in 1786 and joined the navy in 1802, during the Consulate era, while Dumont d'Urville, born 1790, joined the navy of the Napoleonic Empire in 1807. It was during the Restoration era that Duperrey and Dumont d'Urville sailed to Oceania for the first time. See Roquette 1843: 501–502; Vapereau 1870: 592; Collectif 1836: 701–702; Cormack 1995; Starbuck 2013: 46–47, 53–54.
18   Ballard 2008: 160.
19   Metcalf 2005: 10.

Constant Quoy and Joseph Paul Gaimard, wrote extensively about the local people.[20] The captain produced a history of the encounter brightly illustrated with anecdotes about moments of contact while Quoy and Gaimard focused on a largely physical analysis of the Papuans' human nature. Of all the West Papuan records from this set of encounters, Freycinet's voyage narrative gives by far the most detail about local intermediaries and their interaction with the Frenchmen. However, it was the surgeon-naturalists' reports that informed the later observations by Duperrey, Dumont d'Urville and their men.

Early in the Freycinet expedition's stay at Waigeo, local chiefs set the boundaries of the encounter, and they continued to manage these boundaries throughout the following two weeks. The local delineation of spaces – spaces for commerce with visitors, spaces for private everyday life, and spaces of danger – shaped French–Papuan relations during each of the expedition's sojourns in this region, but it is clearest in the accounts of the Freycinet expedition. It is probably not coincidental, for instance, that the most flattering, empathetic and detailed ethnographies were produced by the only one of the expeditions which anchored at an uninhabited island. Unlike the others, the Freycinet expedition did not directly intrude upon a community at Rawak but remained on the very fringe of their world.[21] Instead, it was left to the local chiefs to choose to set out in their canoes to make contact with the strangers. Srouane, from nearby Boni Island, was the first of two chiefs to approach the French ship. Having rowed out to the *Uranie* with some companions, early on the expedition's first morning at Rawak, he offered the captain fresh fruit and fish. Srouane wanted cotton cloth, not trinkets, in exchange for this produce but Freycinet, not prepared to sacrifice his precious supply of cloth, instead gave him a 'gift'. The chief then called him his 'friend', Freycinet explained, and thereafter became his most regular dinner companion. Srouane dined often at the captain's table and, from the day the Frenchmen's oven failed them, also shared his own meals with Freycinet and the officers.[22] This interaction took place almost entirely at Rawak Island, and the fact that that was what Srouane wanted became abundantly clear when officers Duperrey and Quoy approached Boni Island to explore his village. According to Quoy's

20 Freycinet 1829: 20–30; Quoy and Gaimard 1826: 27–38.
21 See Shellam 2009.
22 Freycinet 1829: 20–21.

account, reproduced in Freycinet's narrative, the chief met them on the water and deliberately delayed their progress so that by the time they had arrived the local women and children were safely hidden a short distance away in the forest. Only then did he allow them access to the village, himself as their guide.[23] The accounts by Freycinet and his officers clearly depict Srouane standing between his people and themselves during this sojourn. Moreover, they allude to the influence of his actions on the relationship: officer Louis Raillard, for example, noted that the 'naturally fearful' locals became much more relaxed after the 'rajah' of Boni Island had 'hazarded' to step aboard the *Uranie*.[24] It is clear that this encounter was limited, largely as a result of the efforts of this individual, to a space deemed relatively safe and neutral, to the exchange of particular products and knowledge available within that space, as well as to Srouane himself and the other Papuan men.

The second chief who approached Freycinet, according to the voyage narrative, was Moro, chief of one of the Ayu Islands. He travelled some distance from the island group north of Waigeo in order to establish a relationship with the French expedition, which would suggest that he was motivated rather more by the possibility of material, political and cultural benefits than by a sense that he needed to protect his community. Indeed, what stands out about Moro as an intermediary, by comparison to Srouane, is less how he managed this encounter than how he exploited it. Freycinet's narrative shows how Moro positioned himself as a 'transactional' go-between. It was Moro, 'who came to our observatory', 'asked a thousand questions' and, asserted the captain, seemed the most 'intelligent and witty' person met during this encounter. Although the local chiefs generally could speak Malay, Freycinet highlights that Moro spoke it 'fluently'; presumably, then, he was able to communicate more effectively with the French than other locals.[25] However, in his efforts to benefit from the encounter he also drew heavily upon flattery and humour. This approach undoubtedly did much to gain Moro a detailed inclusion in the voyage narrative and also encouraged Freycinet's praise for the Papuan people. As Gillian Beer and Vanessa Smith highlight, European voyagers appreciated being subjects of curiosity and tended to take offence when they were

---

23 Freycinet 1829: 25–27.
24 Journal de Raillard, ANF 5JJ68.
25 Freycinet 1829: 22.

not.²⁶ Such conduct could also significantly influence the course of the relationship itself and the degree of benefit drawn from it by the 'curious' individuals. For example, indicating to the voyagers that he would not be comfortable boarding their vessel until dressed like themselves, and with a good dose of theatricality along the way, Moro gradually acquired a complete French outfit. Later, by pretending to inhale a handful of pepper, an act that played on the tendency for amusement at native 'ignorance' which he surely observed during his interactions with the French, he deliberately provoked the captain's and officers' laughter at the dinner table. Freycinet's appreciation for this entertainment led to gift exchange and soon Moro had acquired the role of 'police officer' and 'commercial agent': he took on selling French knives to local people at a profit both to himself and to Freycinet. The captain noted Moro's 'industriousness' with a laugh.²⁷

Neither Moro not Srouane rate a mention in the scientific paper produced by Freycinet's surgeon-naturalists, 'Observations on the physical constitution of the *Papous*'. Actually composed by Quoy, though attributed also to Gaimard,²⁸ this paper was based on analysis by the naturalists themselves and phrenologist Franz Josef Gall of skulls taken from Rawak Island. Accordingly, it was produced within what Dorinda Outram describes as the sedentary naturalist's 'inner space';²⁹ that is, where the author, distanced from the intensity and activity of the field,³⁰ was free to examine the material before him 'at his leisure', to 'choose and define his own problems', 'bring together relevant facts from anywhere', and, ultimately, illuminate the material 'with every ray of light possible in a given state of knowledge'.³¹ Quoy's compartmentalisation between this inner space and the 'outer space' of the ethnographic field, however, was not absolute. His memories of contact – of physical appearances, conversation, the Boni Island episode described in Freycinet's narrative – seeped

---

26 Beer 1996: 40–41; Smith 2010: 40–41.
27 Freycinet 1829: 22–23.
28 Douglas 2009a: 182.
29 Outram 1996: 259–265.
30 See Chris Ballard's discussion of the 'excess of experience' and nineteenth-century field workers' efforts to omit it from their published accounts. Ballard 2008: 159.
31 Cuvier quoted in Outram 1996: 260–261.

into this paper, showing that, as he wrote, he had wandered back and forth between the observational and theoretical roles of the naturalist-intermediary.[32]

In both Quoy's paper and Freycinet's narrative, the Papuans are sometimes described in essentialist terms and at other times with optimism and even admiration. Quoy attributes to them a 'carnivorous instinct' and a 'disposition for theft', for instance, but concludes that with some 'education' they could achieve a 'distinguished rank among the numerous varieties of the human species'.[33] He and Freycinet both also describe these people as 'naturally fearful', even 'distrustful'. Quoy suggests that this trait is 'a sort of instinct in half-savage men', but also relates it to the Papuans' experience of the Moluccan slave trade. Freycinet adds too that they are 'intelligent' and 'kind'.[34] Finally, while several French accounts note the Papuans' interest in trade, they do so only in passing and without animosity. The locals had provided Freycinet and his men with plenty of fresh meat, fish, fruit and vegetables and the Frenchmen recorded no complaints about the commerce. As shall be shown, the subsequent expeditions' reports would take up and expand only upon the developing racialist threads and derogatory claims in these records, not the warmth of Freycinet's narrative or the touches of optimism and humanity in Quoy's scientific paper. Srouane and Moro are not mentioned again, at least they are not identified; indeed, there would be little more mention of go-betweens at all. One has to wonder whether relatively active and 'friendly' Papuans during Freycinet's sojourn influenced the more humane, less racialist accounts, or whether a more open attitude encouraged greater recognition of local agency.

* * *

The Duperrey expedition visited Waigeo for 12 days in 1823 and the following year spent a month at Dorey Bay. Duperrey's narrative of this stage of the voyage was not published;[35] however, according to the officers' journal entries as well as the ethnographies by his

---

32 Quoy and Gaimard 1826: 31, 36–38.
33 Quoy and Gaimard 1826: 38.
34 Quoy and Gaimard 1826: 37; Freycinet 1829: 52.
35 Only the first volume of the *Voyage Historique* was published: Duperrey 1826.

surgeon-naturalists, René-Primivère Lesson and Prosper Garnot,[36] the visiting and local intermediaries' behaviours during these encounters differed noticeably from those exhibited during Freycinet's stay in the region.

At Waigeo the expedition was received with still greater caution than Freycinet's had been. The locals waited a longer period, watching from a distance on the water, before making direct contact. Perhaps they were anxious because the *Coquille* was anchored at Waigeo Island itself. Sub-lieutenant Jules de Blosseville recorded that it was not until he and some of his men followed a group of Papuans ashore and presented them with 'some small presents' that relations were eventually established.[37] At Dorey Bay, by contrast, perhaps because it was further from the Moluccan slave traders and the Dutch colonists, the *Coquille* was approached without delay by a number of canoes and a large prau. Blosseville noted that he and his men had felt uneasy at first, but that the 'friendly dispositions' of the people, manifested in part by an eagerness to enter the French space of the ship, soon put them at ease.[38] Both episodes are recorded as encounters between two groups rather than as meetings initiated by local chiefs or other individuals. However, Blosseville does mention that during the first days at Waigeo a 'rajah' established a 'union' with his captain, and that a local chief at Dorey Bay came aboard to communicate or trade specifically with Duperrey.[39]

At Dorey Bay, local guides allowed the voyagers a little more access to their environment than they had been allowed at Waigeo. For example, they were allowed to explore local villages, though women and children first retreated into the surrounding forest. This time, however, the guides went unnamed in the records and their agency is barely reflected in the reports Lesson and Garnot published in the *Zoologie* volume of the *Voyage autour du monde*. The naturalists admitted they were still unable to provide precise detail about the

---

36   Lesson and Garnot authored different sections of the 1826 *Voyage autour du monde, Zoologie* volume. Lesson composed 'Considérations Générales Sur Les Îles Du Grand-Océan, Et Sur Les Variétés de l'Espèce Humaine Qui Les Habitent' and Garnot wrote 'Notes Sur Quelques Peuples du Mer Du Sud'. It must be noted too that Garnot was not with the expedition when it visited Dorey Bay (he had disembarked at the British colony at Port Jackson, New South Wales).
37   Journal de Blosseville, ANF SM 5JJ82.
38   Journal de Blosseville, ANF SM 5JJ82.
39   Journal de Blosseville, ANF SM 5JJ82.

peoples' lifestyle, and whereas Quoy and Gaimard's zoological report related specifically to 'the Papuan', this one covers the peoples of Oceania overall. On occasion, it refers broadly to the peoples of Waigeo and Dorey Bay, in reference to customs and industry, but it merges them with other inhabitants of New Guinea and nearby islands when it comes to the subject of character. Lesson wrote, 'the moral character of these peoples has attained a profound barbarity, this sombre and continual distrust, which renders them traitorous, perfidious and murderous'.[40]

In their journals, the other officers used milder terms – as Douglas states, Lesson and Garnot had written 'self-consciously' within the discourse of developing 'racial science'[41] – but they also strongly emphasise the supposedly distrustful and fearful nature of the Papuans. They also reflect a preoccupation with the material exchanges. While it had been with little further comment that Freycinet's officers noted the arrival of canoes at their ship and the products those canoes carried, the men travelling with Duperrey described with disgust the Papuans' zeal for trade, their daily presence alongside the *Coquille*, and their demands and high prices. In addition, although the officers occasionally and briefly noted visits by local chiefs, they did not explain how or if those individuals directed the marketplace around them.[42]

No doubt, chiefs at Waigeo still exercised some control over their peoples' exchanges with the French, and we might assume that at Dorey Bay local individuals also supervised the village and inland excursions, yet their presence in the records is barely perceptible. We might surmise that Papuan intermediaries would have been more visible in the captain's narrative. It is notable, though, that while that had indeed been the case with Freycinet's narrative it was not to apply later to Dumont d'Urville's. If we are to believe the officers' claims at Waigeo, then, it might be that with this visit the Papuans felt sufficiently familiar with the French to trade with a view more to their material advantage than to learning about and befriending the newcomers.

* * *

---

40 Lesson 1826: 100.
41 Douglas 2008b: 118.
42 See the journals of Blosseville, Jacquinot, Deblois, Lottin and Berard, ANF SM 5JJ82.

The people of Dorey Bay received their next group of French visitors three years later. The Dumont d'Urville expedition arrived towards the end of its voyage and stayed for 11 days. As Duperrey's men had described their arrival, Dumont d'Urville's voyage narrative presents the *Astrolabe* being met by a crowd, rather than by a single canoe and a local chief. And it suggests a sense of unease on the part of the captain, who was unable to recognise amid the throng any 'old friends'.[43] Contemporary documents, however, suggest that the people of Dorey Bay provided more assistance in the Frenchmen's natural history researches than they had during the *Coquille*'s visit. In his journal, for example, Quoy (now on his second Oceanic voyage) explained that the local men no longer abandoned their homes, as they had done previously, first hiding their women from the Frenchmen's view. This time, Quoy states, he and his fellow voyagers were able to observe the Papuans living in their villages and, more specifically, the local children, who were 'of interest in all countries'.[44]

That said, even here in his journal, Quoy does not go on to provide any illustrative accounts of these village encounters let alone to reveal the individual character, actions or appearance of the locals who guided him or of the children he was finally able to meet. As Douglas explains, Quoy's 'racial' representations of the Oceanic peoples he encountered typically oscillated depending on the nature of his experience in the field and the genre and discourse at hand.[45] Certainly, the language he uses in the journal is generally descriptive rather than 'scientific'. Quoy discusses certain physical differences between different peoples observed in the region of Dorey Bay but draws no comparisons between Papuans altogether and the inhabitants of other areas of Oceania. Furthermore, there is a touch of cultural relativism and, in such descriptors as 'sagacity' and 'finesse', some positive recognition of agency in his reference to local trading practices.[46] And yet, even when his 'guides' protect him during a frightening disturbance, no individuals are drawn from the crowd. It would appear that Quoy formed no relationship close enough, observed no individual conduct or character sufficiently important to the encounter, to warrant inclusion in the record. It is in his published report of the Papuan

---

43 Dumont d'Urville 1832: 578.
44 Quoy 1827, reproduced in Dumont d'Urville 1832: 743–744, 747.
45 Douglas 2009a.
46 Quoy and Gaimard 1830: 744.

'race' that Quoy eventually singles out one individual to illustrate a point: although these people were generally unattractive, he wrote, 'one could find an agreeable physiognomy among the young', for example, one of his guides, 'Manebou'.[47] Still, however, Quoy did not continue on to discuss or illustrate the young man's contribution to the encounter.

Indeed, although according to Quoy's journal entry the inhabitants of Dorey Bay showed greater trust during the *Astrolabe*'s sojourn and by all reports demonstrated an assertive approach to trade, their character was consistently described as 'simple and gentle', 'fearful' and 'distrustful'.[48] Dumont d'Urville himself referred to an 'innate' fearfulness, and asserted further that these peoples' 'poverty, dirtiness and profound ignorance prevents them from making effective friendly advances'.[49] This claim sits uneasily alongside his description of the *Astrolabe*'s enthusiastic welcome at Dorey Bay: 'a large number of canoes surrounded the corvette and the savages began immediately to communicate freely with us', he had remarked; 'several among them remembered the ship clearly and they interacted with us as with people they knew well'.[50] Dumont d'Urville also complains with particular bitterness about the trade practices of Dorey Bay's inhabitants, still without reference to any particular individuals. Whereas the Papuans had previously been 'enchanted' at receiving payment in tin-plate bracelets, writes Dumont d'Urville, this time they wanted 'only' Spanish piastres; and, to make matters worse, he claimed they gave him an insufficient supply of fresh food in return.[51] Dumont d'Urville would write very similarly, in a later chapter, of the people at Vanikoro, and, in analysing those comments, Douglas argues that a complex combination of preconceptions, prejudices (arising particularly from his knowledge about the fate of the La Pérouse expedition) and developing racial theories came together over the course of and following the conclusion of the voyage to significantly harden his attitude.[52] No doubt, his memory of events and his motivations altered over time. His representation of the traders of Dorey Bay

---

47 Quoy and Gaimard 1830: 31.
48 Quoy 1827, reproduced in Dumont d'Urville 1832: 744; Quoy and Gaimard 1830: 48; Dumont d'Urville 1832: 578.
49 Dumont d'Urville 1832: 578–579.
50 Dumont d'Urville 1832: 578.
51 Dumont d'Urville 1832: 579–581.
52 Douglas 2009a: 197–200.

would also have been influenced by the pressures to advance, and to a degree also confirm, ethnographic knowledge in a coherent narrative. In fact, by comparison, Quoy refers in his journal to the same trading preferences and skills but without any evident degree of rancour.[53] However, what the journal and the official narrative have in common, in their treatment of this subject is their generality: neither provides an anecdote or even fleeting reference to an individual trading partner to illustrate their points. Similarly, neither record indicates if there was a system in place by which the commerce was managed: where did the trading take place, did someone, either French or Papuan, play the role of 'commercial agent', as Moro had done at Waigeo? Since the *Uranie* had sailed in Oceania, the imperatives of classification had grown considerably stronger. The 'finesse' that Quoy could mention in his journal posed greater problems for official ethnographic reports.[54] In general, shrewd trading, such as that observed at Waigeo and Dorey Bay, had long tended to disturb the simple civilised/savage distinction with which European voyagers were typically most comfortable and which smoothed over evidence of accommodation and resistance. It appeared to indicate a rather more ambiguous state. As Emma Spary observes, European travellers tended either to be blind to or to deem dismissible certain types of Indigenous agency.[55] However, as the nineteenth century gathered pace, dismissals of laughter turned predominantly to denials expressed in silence.

In all, the people of Dorey Bay were evidently more familiar with Dumont d'Urville's expedition than they had been with Duperrey's. Guides had loosened boundaries and significantly facilitated the naturalists' research. From their own point of view, they had also advanced the commercial relationship. All the same, in the records – the unpublished as well as the published – local intermediaries again appeared only very fleetingly and then with scarce recognition of their agency or demonstration of their individuality.

Certainly, the Frenchmen were leaving intermediaries out of the picture in their published accounts as they worked on sharpening their claims about 'race'. Yet developments in the 'science of Man' alone are unlikely to have produced such a pronounced change

---

53   Quoy 1827, reproduced in Dumont d'Urville 1832: 744, 746.
54   Quoy 1827, reproduced in Dumont d'Urville 1832: 744.
55   Spary 2009: 381.

within just eight years. The near disappearance of local individuals and the hardening attitude of many of the voyager-naturalists in the expeditionary record also result largely from the evolution of the voyager–Islander relationship. Although, in comparison to their predecessors, the Restoration era voyagers sought more consciously to distance themselves from their subjects in their writing, they also sought greater intimacy during the contact itself.

Duperrey, Dumont d'Urville and their men assumed that as the Papuans became more familiar with them, they would also become more generous with the products they required, such as fresh fruit and meat, and more open about their daily lives, their customs and relationships. However, at Waigeo, the Papuans' welcome was not warmer for the Duperrey expedition than it had been for Freycinet and his men, and although the people of Dorey Bay did show more openness it clearly was not enough. For the people of Waigeo and Dorey Bay, repeated visits from French ships apparently indicated an extension of the local commercial network, more than an opportunity to admire, wonder at and host newcomers. With each encounter, the Papuans treated the French first and foremost as trade partners. They annoyed the Frenchmen as they became more assertive in their negotiations, offended them when they showed insufficient interest in their ways, and, ostensibly, confirmed earlier impressions of fearfulness when they kept themselves at some distance. Indeed, although a middle ground developed as familiarity increased, it was a discordant one, and both inconvenient and distasteful to the French. The balance of power felt different to the voyagers, when the flattery ceased and the acquirement of fresh supplies grew difficult, and the natives paradoxically seemed only more savage. Evidently, inclusion in the written record as an individual, with the capacity to influence events, was an award voyagers granted to locals largely in appreciation of both their assistance and their amusement.

Acknowledgements

My sincere thanks for their generous help and comments concerning this research to Bronwen Douglas and Chris Ballard, and for her encouragement and keen editorial eye to Shino Konishi.

References

Ballard, Chris 2008, '"Oceanic Negroes": British anthropology of Papuans, 1820–1869', in *Foreign Bodies: Oceania and the Science of Race, 1750–1940*, Canberra, ANU E Press, 157–201.

Beer, Gillian 1996, *Open Fields: Science in the Cultural Encounter*, Oxford University Press, Oxford.

Collectif 1836, *Encyclopédie des gens du monde, Répertoire Universel des Sciences, des Lettres et des Arts; Avec des Notices sur les Principales Familles Historiques et sur les Personnages Célèbres, Morts et Vivans; Par une Société de Savans, de Littérateurs et d'Artistes, Français et Étrangers*, tome 6, Librarie de Treuttel et Wurtz, Paris.

Cormack, William S. 1995, *Revolution and Political Conflict in the French Navy, 1789–1794*, Cambridge University Press, Cambridge.

Cuvier, George 1817, *Le Regne Animal distribué d'après son organisation, pour servir de base à l'Histoire naturelle des animaux et d'introduction à l'Anatomie comparé*, tome 1, Imprimérie de A. Belin, Paris.

Douglas, Bronwen 2008, '"*Novus Orbis Australis*": Oceania in the science of race, 1750–1850', in *Foreign Bodies: Oceania and the Science of Race, 1750–1940*, Bronwen Douglas and Chris Ballard (eds), ANU E Press, Canberra, 99–155.

—— 2009a, 'L'idée de "race" et l'expérience sur le terrain au XIXe siècle: science, action indigène et vacillations d'un naturaliste français en Océanie', *Revue d'Histoire des Sciences Humaines* 21: 175–209.

—— 2009b, 'In the event: Indigenous countersigns and the ethnohistory of voyaging', in *Oceanic Encounters: Exchange, Desire, Violence*, Margaret Jolly, Serge Tcherkézoff and Darrell Tryon (eds), ANU E Press, Canberra, 176–98.

Dumont d'Urville, Jules-Sebastien-César 1832, *Voyage de la Corvette l'Astrolabe, exécuté par ordre du Roi, pendant les années 1826, 1827, 1828, 1829, sous le commandement de M. J. Dumont d'Urville*, tome 4, J. Tastu, Paris.

Duperrey, Louis-Isidore 1826, *Voyage autour du monde: exécuté par ordre du Rois sur la Corvette de sa Majesté, La Coquille, pendant les années 1822, 1823, 1824 et 1825, Histoire du Voyage*, Arthus Bertrand, Paris.

Forrest, Thomas 1780, *Voyage aux Moluques et a la Nouvelle Guinee, fait sur la galera la Tartareen 1774, 1733, & 1776, par ordre de la Compaigne angloise*, Hotel de Thou, Paris.

Freycinet, Louis 1829, *Voyage autour du monde, entrepris par ordre du Roi, sous le Ministère et conformément aux instruction de S. Exc. M. le Vicomte du Bouchage, secrétaire d'état au département de la marine, exécuté sur les corvettes de S. M. l'*Uranie *et la* Physicienne, *pendant les années 1817, 1818, 1819 et 1820, Historique*, tome 2, partie I, Pillet Aîné, Paris.

Fullagar, Kate 2008, '"Savages that are come among us": Mai, Bennelong and British imperial culture 1774–1795', *The Eighteenth Century* 49(3): 211–237.

Greenblatt, Stephen 1991, *Marvellous Possessions: The Wonder of the New World*, Oxford University Press, Oxford.

Journal de Berard, Archives Nationales de France, Série Marine 5JJ82.

Journal de Blosseville, Archives Nationales de France, Série Marine 5JJ82.

Journal de Deblois, Archives Nationales de France, Série Marine 5JJ82.

Journal de Jacquinot, Archives Nationales de France, Série Marine 5JJ82.

Journal de Lottin, Archives Nationales de France, Série Marine 5JJ82.

Journal de Raillard, Archives Nationales de France, Série Marine 5JJ68.

Labillardière, Jacques-Julien Houtou de 1800, Voyage in Search of La Pérouse. Performed by Order of The Constituent Assembly, During the Years 1791, 1792, 1793 and 1794, and Drawn up by M. Labillardiere, vol. 2, John Stockdale, London.

Lesson, René-Primivère, 'Considérations générale sur les îsles du Grand-Océan, et sur les variétés de l'espèce humaine qui les habitent', in R. P. Lesson and P. Garnot 1826, *Voyage autour du monde, exécuté par ordre du Roi, sur la Corvette de Sa Majesté, La Coquille, pendant les années 1822, 1823, 1824 et 1825, Zoologie*, tome 1, partie I, 1–113, Arthus Bertrand, Paris.

McPhee, Peter 2004, *A Social History of France, 1789–1914*, Palgrave Macmillan, Basingstoke.

Metcalf, Alida C. 2005, *Go-Betweens and the Colonization of Brazil*, University of Texas Press, Austin.

Moore, Clive 2003, *New Guinea: Crossing Boundaries and History*, University of Hawai'i Press, Honolulu.

Nye, Robert A. 1998, *Masculinity and Male Codes of Honour in Modern France*, University of California Press, New York.

Outram, Dorinda 1996, 'New spaces in natural history', in *Cultures of Natural History*, Nicholas Jardine, James A. Secord and Emma C. Spary (eds), Cambridge University Press, Cambridge.

Pratt, Marie-Louise 2008, *Imperial Eyes: Travel Writing and Transculturation*, second edition, Routlededge, New York.

Quoy, Jean-René-Constant and Joseph-Paul Gaimard 1826, 'Observations sur la constitution physique des Papous qui habitent les îles Rawak et Vaigiou; Lues à l'Académie des Sciences de l'Institut, le 5 mai 1823', *Annales des sciences naturelles* 7 : 27–38.

—— 1830, *Voyage de découvertes de L'Astrolabe, exécuté par ordre du Roi, pendant les années 1826–1827–1828–1829, sous le commandement de M. J. Dumont D'Urville. Zoologie*, tome 1, J. Tastu, Paris.

Reddy, William 1997, *The Invisible Code: Honour and Sentiment in Post-Revolutionary France, 1814–1848*, University of California Press, Berkeley.

—— 2001, *The Navigation of Feeling: A Framework for the History of Emotions*, Cambridge University Press, Cambridge.

Roquette, Jean-Bernard-Marie Dezos de la 1843, 'Notices Historiques de les MM. Henri et Louis de Freycinet, lue à la séance générale de la Société de géographie du 15 décembre 1843', in *Bulletin de la Société de Géographie*, Tome 40 second series vol. 20. Paris: 501–539.

Rutherford, Danilyn 2009, 'Sympathy, state building, and the experience of empire', *Cultural Anthropology* 24(1): 1–32.

Schaffer, Simon, Lissa Roberts, Kapil Raj and Jame Delbourgo (eds) 2009, *The Brokered World: Go-Betweens and Global Intelligence, 1770–1820*, Science History Publications, Sagamore Beach, MA.

Seed, Patricia 1995, *Ceremonies of Possession in Europe's Conquest of the New World, 1492–1640*, Cambridge University Press, Cambridge.

Shellam, Tiffany 2009, *Shaking Hands on the Fringe: Negotiating the Aboriginal World at King George's Sound*, UWA Publishing, Perth.

Smith, Vanessa 2010, *Intimate Strangers: Friendship, Exchange and Pacific Encounters*, Cambridge University Press, Cambridge.

Spary, Emma 2009, 'Self-preservation: French travels between cuisine and industrie', in *The Brokered World: Go-Betweens and Global Intelligence, 1770–1820*, Simon Schaffer, Lissa Roberts, Kapil Raj and Jame Delbourgo (eds), Science History Publications, Sagamore Beach, MA, 355–386.

Starbuck, Nicole 2013, *Baudin, Napoleon and the Exploration of Australia*, Pickering and Chatto, London.

Todorov, Tzvetan 1999, *The Conquest of America: The Question of the Other*, second edition, University of Oklahoma Press, Norman.

Turnbull, David 1998, 'Cook and Tupaia: A cartographic méconnaissance?', in *Science and Exploration in the Pacific: European Voyages in the Southern Oceans in the Eighteenth Century*, Margarette Lincoln (ed.), Boydell Press in association with the National Maritime Museum, Woodbridge and Rochester, 117–132.

—— 2009, 'Boundary-crossings, cultural encounters and knowledge spaces in early Australia', in *The Brokered World: Go-Betweens and Global Intelligence, 1770–1820*, Science History Publications, Sagamore Beach, MA, 387–428.

Vapereau, Gustave 1870, 'Duperrey (Louis-Isidore)', in *Dictionnaire universel des contemporains*, fourth edition, Hachette et Cie, Paris.

White, Richard 1991, *The Middle Ground: Indians, Empires and Republics in the Great Lakes Region, 1650–1815*, Cambridge University Press, Cambridge.

4

Aboriginal guides in the Hunter Valley, New South Wales

Mark Dunn

On 21 March 1820, John Howe from Windsor sent a message to Governor Macquarie from his camp at Wallis Plains on the Hunter River, by his calculations approximately 132 miles (212 km) overland north-north-west from Sydney.[1] Howe wrote, 'I embrace the earliest opportunity to inform your Excellency that I reached the River on Wednesday last' and that 'in our way down the river we came through as fine a country as imagination can form'.[2] For his trouble, Howe and the free men in his company were granted land along the river they had 'discovered', establishing themselves on the alluvial flood plains around the future town of Singleton. This story of discovery is well known to scholars of the Hunter Valley's colonial history. What is less well known is that Howe's success came after at least two earlier attempts by others to find a route between the Hawkesbury district and the upper Hunter Valley, and that he would not have succeeded at all without the assistance of his Aboriginal guides, Myles, Mullaboy, Murphy, Whirle and Bandagran.

---

1 Travelling on the modern Putty Road, which closely follows Howe's route from Windsor to the Hunter Valley, the distance between Windsor and Maitland, formerly Wallis Plains, is 210 km.
2 Howe to Macquarie, 21 March 1820, SRNSW Reel 6049, 4/1744.

The trope of the European explorer overcoming the barriers of a hostile Australian environment through their own ingenuity and perseverance is common in traditional colonial history. More recently, historians including Henry Reynolds, Greg Blyton and Tiffany Shellam have recognised and explored the assistance provided to European parties by Aboriginal guides, yet this still remains largely overlooked in popular understandings of Australian exploration.[3]

Aboriginal people had worked alongside Europeans in a wide range of roles and capacities ever since Europeans formed the colony of New South Wales in 1788. Henry Reynolds has noted that in the colonial period the exchange of labour was one of the most important elements in the relationships between Aboriginal people and Europeans. However, the relationship was never equal, with Aboriginal people making profound cultural adjustments to adapt to the new and often dangerous circumstances they found themselves in. For those Aboriginal men who worked as guides, additional dangers were ever present as they led Europeans into the often unfamiliar territory of neighbouring peoples, where cultural transgressions or misunderstandings could end in confrontations and attacks. However, while the European explorer was central to the theme of a developing nation, there was 'no discursive room left for Black pioneers', despite Aboriginal guides having been part of the explorer and settler experience from the first days of the colony.[4]

This chapter explores the role of Aboriginal guides in the Hunter Valley between 1818 and 1830, covering the closure of the penal station at Newcastle and establishment of free settlement in the valley. During these years the overland expeditions from Windsor, on Sydney's western fringe, forged routes through the mountains between the Hawkesbury and the Hunter rivers and the occupation of the alluvial river flats and prime farming land by European settlers took place. Although there are few sources that offer the Aboriginal perspective, through close reading of the letters, journals and diaries of the first wave of Europeans in this area, the hidden story of the

---

3   For recent examples of re-examinations of the relationships between European explorers and Aboriginal guides, see Reynolds 2000; Blyton 2012; Smith 2010; Shellam 2009; Macqueen 2004; Flannery 1998; Baker 1998.
4   Reynolds 2000: 9.

Aboriginal guides can be partially recovered and the crucial role they played in these early years of the European presence in the Hunter can be examined.

European occupation of the Hunter Valley began in the first years of the nineteenth century, and Aboriginal people working as guides, interpreters and trackers were integral to it from the start. In 1801 the first official survey party of the Hunter River led by Lieutenant James Grant on the *Lady Nelson* included Bungaree, an Aboriginal man already well known in the colony for his skills as an interpreter and intermediary.[5]

Bungaree was what Reynolds refers to as a 'professional guide': someone who lived close to or in the European settlements and who was employed full time with an exploratory party. These guides derived their expertise through a combination of traditional knowledge and an understanding of European culture and language. These men – and they were most often men – retained important bushcraft skills such as tracking and hunting as well as path-finding, being able to read the landscape in unfamiliar territory and following the most desirable route. They could act as interpreters or intermediaries through their knowledge of neighbouring language or via an appreciation of traditional customs and diplomacy.[6] The translation of these skills back into a form that Europeans could understand and trust displayed an ingenuity and cross-cultural creativity that has often been overlooked in the history of European exploration.

Even before Bungaree, Aboriginal people were assisting Europeans in the Hunter region. In July 1796, the crew of a fishing boat wrecked north of the Hunter at Port Stephens walked into Sydney. They had been guided along a coastal path to the Hunter River and then from there onto connecting paths via Lake Macquarie and Broken Bay to the north shore of Sydney Harbour. While the account of this overland expedition as given by David Collins is short on detail, he does note that the men were accompanied by Aboriginal people for the greater part of the way.[7] The wrecked fishermen were probably

---

5   Bungaree had accompanied Matthew Flinders in 1798 to Norfolk Island and again in 1799 to Hervey Bay, where he had acted as an interpreter and intermediary. He is one of the most recognised Aboriginal men of Colonial Sydney. See Smith 1992: 46–49.
6   Reynolds 2000: 34.
7   Collins 1975: 489.

escorted through country before being handed on to new guides as they proceeded further south, ensuring their safe passage through neighbouring territories down the coast.

Between 1804 and 1822, Newcastle operated as a penal station, during which time it functioned as both a place of banishment and a place of industry. Convicts were employed in its coal mines, burning lime and cutting cedar and other timbers in the forests along the river, and the prevention or recapture of runaways was of primary concern to the authorities there. Aboriginal men were employed as guides and trackers by successive Commandants to discourage convicts from absconding throughout the operation of the penal station.[8] In August 1804 the then Commandant, Charles Menzies, paraded the recaptured runaway James Field in front of the convict population at Newcastle as a warning. Field, starved and wounded by spears, was the sole survivor of three who had absconded from Sydney.[9] The use of Aboriginal trackers at the penal station resulted in Aboriginal people being the subject of convict hostility, with a number of fatal encounters recorded in and around Newcastle.[10] However, Aboriginal men were also employed as guides to take official parties into the surrounding bushland on kangaroo hunts or fishing expeditions. In 1821 the former commandant James Wallis, in charge at Newcastle from 1816 until 1818, reminisced about his Newcastle friend and guide Burigon:

> There are scenes in all our lives to which we turn back to with pleasurable tho perhaps with a tinge of melancholy feelings and I now remember poor Jack (Burigon) the black savage ministering to my pleasures, fishing, kangaroo hunting, guiding me thro trackless forests with more kindly feelings that I do many of my own colour, kindred and nation …[11]

In this short passage, Wallis outlines the main reasons that Europeans employed guides, not least to guide them through the seemingly trackless forests, while also reflecting on the close personal bond that had grown between the two men. The 'trackless forest' was of course

---

8   An earlier attempt had been made to establish a penal station at the mouth of the Hunter River in July 1801. This was abandoned by February 1802. See Governor King Letters, Re: Newcastle 1801–1805, SLNSW MLMSS 582.
9   King to Hobart, 14 August 1804, *HRA* Series I, Vol. V: 111–115.
10 Blyton 2012: 94.
11 James Wallis, Album of original drawings ca1817–1818, SLNSW PXE 1070.

a misnomer, for while looking like a wilderness to most Europeans the bush was criss-crossed with pathways and tracks used by Aboriginal people to negotiate their way across the country.[12]

While the penal station operated, there was very little formal exploration of the Hunter Valley beyond the margins of the settlement. It was not in the interest of the commandants for the bush to become a known place to the convict workers hemmed in by it. Yet some convicts did become familiar with the bush: the convict timber gangs were, by the very nature of their work, exploring the bush and moving through the forests. Ironically, the timber gangs reported less runaways than the convict gangs working in the settlement. One reason given at the time by Commandant John Purcell in 1810, and again by James Morisset in 1819, was that they chose their most dependable convicts to work in these gangs. Although the work was hard, the convicts were away from the scrutiny of the settlement, which Morisset claimed they preferred.[13]

During the years of the penal station's operation, Aboriginal guides were used primarily to assist the guards recapture absconding convicts. However, with the closure of the station, their role shifted to assisting European explorers and settlers entering the Hunter Valley. This was the period beginning with the discovery of an overland route from Windsor by Howe in 1819–1820 and culminating in the allocation of land grants to European settlers.

John Howe is credited with the discovery of the overland route that linked the settlements on the Hawkesbury to the Hunter Valley. Howe made two journeys to the river, the first in October–November 1819, when he and his party reached the Hunter River close to the present-day village of Jerrys Plains, and the second in March 1820 when they emerged out of the mountains near what is now Singleton. On the first expedition, Howe did not know what river he had come across, and assumed he was further north, close to Port Stephens. Through a combination of lack of supplies, fatigue and concern over the possibility of Aboriginal attack, he turned back without exploring further. It was only when he followed the river downstream on the

---

12   Needham 1981: 4.
13   Purcell to Campbell, 6 July 1810, SRNSW Reel 6066, 4/1804. Morisset evidence to Commissioner Bigge, Bonwick Transcripts, Box 1: 459. Also Turner 1973: 59.

second trip and came across a convict timber-getting camp at Wallis Plains, working out of the Newcastle station, that he realised he was on the Hunter River.[14]

Howe was following in the footsteps of two earlier attempts to cross the mountains from Windsor, one by William Parr in November 1817 and another by Benjamin Singleton in April–May 1818. Both Parr and Singleton had set out with the intention of finding a new route from Windsor through the Blue Mountains to Bathurst, but had each headed north-west towards the Hunter. Parr set out without an Aboriginal guide and soon became disorientated in the steep valleys and mountains around the Putty area. His way was blocked by thick brush and bushfires, which, coupled with a shortage of rations, saw him abandon his expedition.[15]

Singleton did have an Aboriginal guide, but also turned back near the Putty area, around 100 kilometres from his start point. Although Singleton's party reached Putty in half the time of Parr, their journey beyond was similarly hampered by thick brush and a struggle to find water.[16] Singleton's guide was unnamed in his journal of the expedition, but the failure of the party to penetrate beyond Putty suggests that he may have been unfamiliar with the territory he was being asked to enter, deliberately misdirecting the party to avoid a confrontation or a sacred place, or unwilling to go further into another group's country. On the night of 5 May, Singleton's camp was attacked by a group of Aboriginal men. Singleton wrote:

> about 8 o'clock Disturbed by the Voices of Natives Cracking of Sticks and Rolling big rocks, stones down towards us every man of us arose and fled from the fire secreting ourselves behind trees with our guns and ammunition where we could have a view of the fire Doubting if we staid by the fire every Man was lost spent the Whole of the Night in that Condition Raining very Hard the Native whom we had with us was timid than any of us saying he was sure we should be killed.[17]

Despite these alarming events and the perceived threat, no attack followed. But the next morning as the party set off they encountered a group of more than 200 Aboriginal men, clothed in skins and armed

---

·14 Howe to Macquarie, 21 March 1820, SRNSW Reel 6049, 4/1744.
15 Parr, Journal, 1817, SRNSW Fiche 3271, 2/3623. Also Macqueen 2004: 63–79.
16 Singleton, Journal, 1818, SRNSW Reel 6047, 4/1740: 209–214.
17 Singleton, Journal, 5 May 1818, SRNSW Reel 6047, 4/1740: 212.

with spears. One of them, a man named Mawby, spoke some English, while the rest had never seen European men before. Through his Aboriginal guide, Singleton encouraged Mawby and four others to come forward and asked them if his party could advance westward. He was told it was impossible due to rocky country and a lack of water.[18]

With communications opened the conversation went both ways, as Mawby then enquired after Singleton's purpose and to where he was heading. Through his guide, Singleton said that they were trying to get to Bathurst or find good grazing land. Mawby told them that good grass land was two days to the north-east, beside a wide river that they could not swim across, nor could they drink the water of, and that this river flowed in both directions. Singleton took this to indicate a wide, tidal river, perhaps the one that ran into Port Stephens. Yet this was as far as the expedition went. Despite now having Mawby's directions to good land, the unexpected encounter with such a large body of men had unnerved the party, especially their own Aboriginal guide. Singleton decided not to proceed, fearing that the 200 men would follow and 'betray' them for their provisions. With only five in their party, they would not be able to defend themselves. He noted that their guide 'was more in dread' than themselves, and so they turned back for Windsor.[19]

It is not difficult to understand Singleton's decision to turn back at this point. He was low on water, effectively lost and had been confronted by a very large group of armed Aboriginal men. However, the exact nature of the encounter, while clearly tense, is now difficult to fully interpret. The night of the stone-rolling attack, Singleton noted that they had camped at the base of the largest mountain he had yet seen, Mount Monundilla in the Hunter Range. This mountain area includes rock art and shelter sites, now well-known and documented as part of the Wollemi National Park.[20] This may explain the large group of men in the area, and their rock attack may have been a warning to the party to stay away. Singleton's description of the men wearing skins, rather than having their bodies daubed in ochre or paint, suggests they were

---

18   Singleton, Journal, 6 May 1818, SRNSW Reel 6047, 4/1740: 212.
19   Singleton, Journal, 6 May 1818, SRNSW Reel 6047, 4/1740: 212.
20   There are over 120 recorded art sites in the Wollemi National Park. See 'Rock paintings in the Upper Hunter', www.workingwithatsi.info/content/rockpaintings1.htm, accessed 18 March 2013; Macqueen 2004: 87.

not heading to ceremony or combat and so may have been hunting or moving through the country.[21] Indeed, Mawby's English skills indicate previous, prolonged contact with Europeans, or at least long enough to pick up some language. Coupled with his description of the tidal river, which was almost certainly the Hunter, this suggests that Mawby had been in contact with the penal station at Newcastle or the outlying camps around Wallis Plains. Mawby and the men were using pre-existing connections and pathways known to Aboriginal people into and out of the Hunter that were there long before Europeans began to search for them. Singleton had missed his opportunity. With his own Hawkesbury guide acting as the intermediary in the encounter, Mawby was presenting him with a local's knowledge of the way through the country.

When Howe was presented with the same opportunity, he took it. His party left Windsor in October 1819, with eight Europeans and two Aboriginal guides. One of his guides was identified by the European name Myles and would have been well known to Howe, and probably the rest of his party.[22]

Howe was Chief Constable in Windsor and in 1816 had been involved in the suppression of Aboriginal attacks in the area. In July 1816, William Cox, the magistrate at Hawkesbury River, wrote a memorandum to Governor Macquarie outlining recent violence between Aborigines and settlers and set out a series of actions recommended to protect the settlement. Cox also named eight Aboriginal men whom he considered dangerous, four of whom he described as the most notorious. At the top of this list of four was a man named Miles.[23]

Acting on Cox's recommendations, Governor Macquarie made it known that following the attacks along the Hawkesbury and Nepean rivers, and despite the offer of clemency to those Aboriginal men who would surrender, 10 leaders were still urging their followers to commit attacks. The 10 were described as being 'far more determinedly hostile and mischievous, who by taking the lead have lately instigated their deluded followers to commit several further atrocious acts of barbarity

---

21 Attenbrow 2010: 110.
22 Howe to Macquarie, 15 May 1820, SRNSW Reel 6050, 4/1747.
23 Cox to Macquarie, 19 July 1816, SLNSW, DLADD 81: 187. Howe was also named in this report as one of the constables involved in escorting 'friendly natives' back to Sydney at the end of the action in November 1816: 193.

on the unoffending and unprotected settlers and their families'. These men were therefore to be apprehended by anyone who came across them. Or, if this proved too difficult, citizens of the colony, be they 'free men, prisoners of the crown or friendly natives', were at liberty to kill the men using such means as was in their power.[24] Myles was identified as one of these 10 men.[25]

By November several on the list had been killed or captured. Macquarie issued a second proclamation offering a pardon to those remaining men who surrendered. The inclusion of Myles in Howe's party suggests he was reconciled with and had been accepted by the Europeans. Presumably, he had come into the settlements sometime after Macquarie's proclamation and his bush skills, so feared during the attacks in 1815–1816, were now recognised as being a valuable and necessary inclusion in any exploratory party. Whatever nervousness existed among the Europeans travelling into the uncharted bush with an identified resistance leader, or indeed with Myles as he set off with men who had put his name on a death list, was seemingly put aside.

Myles guided the party beyond Putty, where it appears they ran into the same problems Parr and Singleton had encountered. Instead of blundering on, Howe sent Myles and another man out to search for a local guide. Unsuccessful the first day, he sent them again, writing in his journal that he had 'sent two Natives out for a Native guide as we could proceed no further in the direction I wanted to go'.[26]

By sending Myles out to find local guides, Howe was displaying a more nuanced understanding of the way Aboriginal cultural practice and bushcraft operated. As Singleton found out, not all Aboriginal people were familiar with country outside their own, nor were they necessarily welcome in it. Myles may have advised Howe of the fact that they needed a local connection, maybe as much for guidance as for right of passage. Henry Reynolds argues that local knowledge was

---

24   *Sydney Gazette and New South Wales Advertiser*, 27 July 1816: 1. It should be noted the change in spelling from Miles in Cox's report to Myles in the Government Notice. Myles remains the spelling in official reports and in Howe's letters to Macquarie.
25   The name Myles probably derived from the Sydney language Aboriginal word *Mi-yal* which meant a stranger, according to a word list compiled by David Collins in his *An Account of the English Colony in New South Wales* (Collins 1975: 507). See also Ford 2010: 75, 122. Ford shows from blanket distribution lists that Myles's Aboriginal name was Mioram and adds that the English version, Myles, was taken to mean 'wild' or undomesticated.
26   Howe, Journal, 1819, SRNSW Reel 2623, 2/8093.

one of the most valuable resources that European explorers could rely on, providing an intimate knowledge of the country through which they were passing.[27]

The local guide, Murphy, led the party through the mountains and out onto the flood plains of the upper Hunter River. However, the route was at times arduous and difficult: the packhorses had to be unloaded and there were lengthy detours around swamps and bogs. Further, the party did not penetrate far into the valley, as Myles and Murphy refused to go on after it was discovered they were under surveillance by a group of Hunter Valley men. On their return, they visited the Aboriginal camp that Murphy had come from. There an older Aboriginal man, Whirle, admonished Murphy for taking them the hard way and told Howe he knew a quicker and easier route.[28] Why two different routes were eventually shown to Howe is unclear, although a number of interpretations can be made. Maybe Murphy was deliberately trying to mislead Howe and his group or lead them away from sacred sites, or attempting to discourage future European excursions into the area by taking them on such a difficult path. Alternatively, he might have been taking a higher track to enable him to cautiously approach the neighbouring country, or he may not have even been aware of the route proposed by the older Whirle. It is unlikely Murphy did not know Whirle's pathway, which passes close by to Baiame's Cave, an important initiation and ceremonial site, and suggests that caution may have been the real reason.[29]

The advantages of having the Aboriginal guides are clear in these accounts. The guides enabled Howe to move more quickly through the country, warned him of the potential danger of being in another group's country, and resulted both in discovery and knowledge of an easier route.

Three weeks after their return to Windsor, in what appears to be a first for the colony, Myles, his brother Mullaboy and 'a small number of natives' were provisioned, equipped and armed with muskets by

---

27 Reynolds 2000: 25.
28 Howe, Journal, 11 November 1819, SRNSW Reel 2623, 2/8093; Howe to Macquarie, 27 December 1819, SRNSW Reel 6068, 4/1743. It is not known where the names Whirle and Murphy originated from, whether they were attributed by Howe or through previous encounters with Europeans.
29 Moore 1981: 397.

order of Governor Macquarie, and sent back out to meet Whirle and another man, Bandagran, and follow their track to the river.[30] Nineteen days later the all-Aboriginal exploring party returned and reported to Howe that they had followed an easier path through the mountains to the river. This was the path that Howe took on his second expedition in 1820, following Myles back through the ranges along the Aboriginal pathway of Whirle. The Putty Road, which today connects Windsor to Singleton, closely follows the route. For his efforts, Myles was presented with a breast plate and musket. Howe was given a grant of 700 acres on the banks of the Hunter River after claiming the discovery of the overland way as his own.[31]

Myles's rehabilitation in the eyes of the Europeans was complete. In the space of four years, he had gone from hunted rebel warrior to trusted guide and rewarded explorer. Howe's use of and trust in Myles speaks of the personal relationship that had developed between the two men that was necessary for the successful collaboration of explorer and guide. A high level of trust was needed on both sides for these forays into unknown territory.

While the advantages for Europeans of using guides is clear enough, why would Aboriginal men agree to go? Without the voice of the guides themselves, we can only speculate on their motivations, but the experience of Myles may offer some clues.

Myles had been, until recently, a wanted man. The very name he was given by Europeans suggests someone on the outer – Myles being a derivative of the Aboriginal word *Mi-yal*, meaning stranger in the Sydney language.[32] Gaining the confidence of Europeans via a successfully guided expedition would have been an advantage for Myles on the potentially volatile frontier where he lived. Being with an armed party of Europeans while heading into another group's territory may also have been a strong motivation. Tiffany Shellam's examination of the relationships formed between Europeans and the King Ya-nup in south-west Western Australia in the 1830s demonstrates the recognition that Aboriginal people had of the

---

30   Howe to Macquarie, 27 December 1819, SRNSW Reel 6068, 4/1743.
31   Governor Macquarie Correspondence, 18 September 1820, SLNSW CY1449 C330.
32   Collins 1975: 507. Similarly, the Wiradjuri word *mayol* was also translated as meaning wild Aborigine by John Fraser in 1892. See Fraser 1892: Appendix 1, 98.

potential advantages of working alongside European explorers.[33] Aboriginal guides recognised the advantage that new knowledge of distant country could have for them amongst their own people and their neighbours. Knowledge about new country and new people was a valuable commodity that could be traded and benefited from, and could elevate a person's status in the eyes of both their own kin and those of the Europeans.[34]

Outside of security and status, guiding provided access to European goods and weapons. Clothes, tobacco and food were routinely traded by European explorers to Aboriginal helpers and guides in return for their service and served as a strong incentive. In a few cases, as seen with Myles, some were rewarded with muskets which would have been a highly prized acquisition. Some local guides, like Murphy or Whirle, may also have been motivated to assist Europeans as a means of steering them away from local sacred sites or to facilitate their rapid movement through and out of their country.[35]

However, the role of the guide was also a transitory one. The guide was only useful at the edge of the frontier, at the point in time when Europeans were pushing beyond their known boundaries. On his return to Windsor after his second expedition, Howe blazed the trees, thereby marking a clear path for others to follow.[36]

Pathways made through the bush by Howe and others hastened the closure of the Newcastle penal station. Four months after Howe's expedition, the Commandant Morisset complained that four convicts in a cedar party had run from Paterson's Plains, following the path made by Howe.[37] Another track blazed by the Reverend George Augustus Middleton, known as the Parsons Road, also became a well-used escape route from December 1821.[38] Middleton had travelled overland to Newcastle with 173 head of cattle, guided by an unnamed Aboriginal companion.[39]

---

33   Shellam 2009: 139–141.
34   Shellam 2009: 141.
35   Reynolds 2000: 32.
36   Howe to Macquarie, 13 April 1820, SRNSW Reel 6049, 4/1744.
37   Morisset to Goulburn, 6 July 1820, SRNSW Reel 6067, 4/1807.
38   Morisset to Goulburn, 18 December 1821, SRNSW Reel 6067, 4/1807.
39   Blaxland n.d., SLNSW AR 39/5.

With tracks marked, the role of the professional guides was effectively finished for journeys to the Hunter, but in the valley itself a new role for local guides began to emerge. Europeans arriving in the Hunter Valley to take land grants after 1821 were as lost in the seemingly trackless wilderness as Wallis had claimed to be in 1816. Many of the emigrant farmers travelled to Newcastle via ship from Sydney, before heading upriver to take up their land.

For those whose grants were further inland, away from the settled areas, the bush was still a formidable barrier, through which they had to pass before they could establish themselves and begin farming. Although Howe had reported fine, open country where he had entered the valley, around the Wallis Plains and Paterson's Plains sections of the river, the bush was thick and impenetrable.[40]

One of the first emigrants was John Brown, who arrived in Newcastle around May 1822 with a grant of 2,000 acres. An Aboriginal guide took Brown to his grant. This man told him the name of the place was Bolwarra, which reportedly meant 'flash of light', and which Brown adopted as the name of his estate.[41]

Most settlers could get to Wallis Plains by boat, but from there further travel was overland. At this starting point, a local pool of guides appears to have operated for a short time taking new settlers inland. James Mudie, a settler in the Patricks Plains area, was guided from Wallis Plains in August 1822. Heading inland, Mudie wrote to the Colonial Secretary requesting that if the assistant surveyor would provide him with:

> the necessary particulars of that part of the country called St Patricks Plains, so as to enable me to proceed through the bush, I would make an attempt to find it by the assistance of some of the Natives.[42]

Yet, despite their reliance on these men, few Europeans detailed how they actually procured the services of the guides.

In mid-1823, the brothers Robert and Helenus Scott, who had recently arrived in the colony, travelled to the Hunter to claim their land grant. The brothers hired a horse from a Wallis Plains farmer named Morgan

---

40 Dangar, Survey Field Book No. 193, 1822, SRNSW 2/4837: 31.
41 *The Australian*, 28 February 1834: 3.
42 Mudie to Colonial Secretary, 25 January 1823, SRNSW R6067, 4/1809.

before heading inland towards their grant without a guide. On their first morning as they were preparing to pack up camp, a young Aboriginal boy appeared out of the bush. Scott's servant, also named John Brown, kept a journal in which he related the first meeting:

> we asked him what his name was and where he was going, he said the White men call me Ben Davis, and he was going along with us, for Binghi Morgan sent him, which we was very glad of for we had been trying to get one of the Blacks to go with us but none of them happened to be at the settlement at the time, and this boy happened to go there soon after we had left and Morgan had sent him after us.[43]

The guide, Ben Davis, had taken or been given the name of the convict farmer Benjamin Davis, one of the first Europeans to settle along the Hunter River around Wallis Plains. Davis had been allocated a small plot on the river in 1814 under Governor Macquarie's plan to encourage good behaviour amongst convicts at Newcastle and to make the penal station self-sufficient. Although Davis was still living at Wallis Plains on his farm in 1823, the guide was sent by Morgan. The best known Morgan at Wallis Plains at this time was the emancipist Molly Morgan, yet Brown identifies Morgan as an Englishman. He may have been associated with Molly Morgan, however, as her influence in the area was such that the unofficial name for the settlement in the first half of the 1820s was Molly Morgan's.[44] Whoever organised for Ben Davis to pursue the Scott party through the bush, the arrangement suggests a close collaboration between Aboriginal people and some Europeans in the Wallis Plains area.

The labour hire service apparently provided by Morgan and Ben Davis displays aspects of what Richard White has called the 'middle ground' in frontier cross-cultural relations. In his work on the north-west frontier of colonial America, particularly around the Great Lakes district, White proposed a period of coexistence between French fur traders and the different American native nations that lived in the area. White argues that for a period both Europeans and the American nations lived in a mutually comprehended and advantageous world

---

43   Anonymous diary by a servant of the Scott family, 8 August 1821–March 1824, SLNSW MLMSS 7808: 55-56.
44   Wood 1972: 243. It is also worth noting that the word *Binghi* used by Ben Davis to identify Morgan could be Brown's spelling of the local word *Biggai*, identified by the Reverend Lancelot Threlkeld as meaning elder brother or an affectionate form of address for brother. If so it may identify a closer relationship between Ben Davis and Morgan. See Fraser 1892: 203.

immediately behind the frontier of the European empire. While it was still a violent place, the middle ground was also a place where both sides cooperated to some degree to accommodate each other for mutual benefit.[45] A central aspect was the inability of either side to gain what they wanted through the use of force, thereby making it necessary to come to some arrangement to achieve each other's objectives. While they acted out of interests derived from their own culture, those operating in this space also had to convince people of another culture that any mutual action was fair and legitimate.[46] For Aboriginal guides, their work allowed an aspect of protection while also keeping them in contact with their country, while their skills and knowledge of the land helped Europeans move through it and could assist them in avoiding confrontations with other Aboriginal people met along the way. A middle ground was only possible when the two sides were evenly balanced, and so was short lived in the Hunter Valley. It appears that while Morgan was acting as an agent or a go-between for newly arrived colonists with no experience of the bush or any existing relationships with Aboriginal people, Aboriginal people in the area were also taking advantage of Morgan's position to secure employment as guides and gain access to European goods. A local economy had developed to serve the needs of settlers in the short period before the valley was mapped out and made known to Europeans.

Brown continues:

> We set of [sic] with Ben Davis as a guide and he seemed very much pleased, and kept talking all the way he went but we did not understand him but by what we could make out he was telling us about the country.[47]

Brown's description of Ben Davis telling the Europeans about country is a tantalising glimpse of what may have been said by Aboriginal people about their relationship to the Hunter Valley, as well as the misconception of the European view. Brown gives no further information on what he thought Ben Davis was telling them but, through physical descriptions of the land added by Brown as they travelled towards their grant, it is likely he took Ben Davis's account as just that,

---

45   White 1991: x.
46   White 1991: 52.
47   Anonymous diary by a servant of the Scott family, 1821–24, SLNSW MLMSS 7808: 56.

a simple, physical outline of their surroundings. However, country meant different things to Aboriginal people than it did to Europeans. Country was a complex idea, an interweaving of physical, territorial and cultural understandings of a place. While it could indeed refer to the physical landscape, country was more multidimensional as it also identified the people who lived in or managed an area, the animals, the waterways, the earth, the soil, the sky and the underground.[48] Everyone had a country, an area of land defined by their sites and knowledge and under the care and management of a particular group. In their own country, a person might see the landscape shaped through their understanding of the Dreaming and filled with sites and stories that explained the logic of the place.[49] It is possible therefore that, rather than simply giving a physical description of the land, Ben Davis was offering a narration of country, imparting some of the deeper connections and knowledge that helped him navigate physically and spiritually through the Hunter Valley.

Ben Davis stayed with the party three days, until they reached Patricks Plains (Singleton). He acted as an intermediary and interpreter on two separate occasions along the way and later accompanied Robert Scott kangaroo hunting. These roles reflect the actions of earlier guides like Bungaree and Myles who helped negotiate through other people's country but at a local level. On one occasion when Ben Davis acted as an intermediary, he acknowledged that he knew the Aboriginal man who led a group that had approached the party. Ben Davis remarked that the man, identified as Mytie, was a 'very good fellow' and Brown was soon on friendly terms with the whole group, digging yams and fishing in the river with them.[50] Mytie himself said he belonged to the 'Womby tribe', the people who lived in the mountains and valleys south of Patricks Plains, through which Howe had passed in 1820. This geographical positioning illustrates the interconnectedness of the Aboriginal groups in the lower Hunter Valley and surrounding

---

48   Rose 1996: 8.
49   Gammage 2011: 139.
50   Anonymous diary by a servant of the Scott family, 1821–24, SLNSW MLMSS 7808: 59–60.

mountains, as previously hinted at by Mawby. Mytie's group stayed several days, but when the Scotts moved onto their grant at Glendon, Mytie and Ben Davis left them.[51]

Brown left Glendon after 25 weeks, heading to Newcastle to pick up a ship back to Sydney and eventually to England. Making his way to Wallis Plains, he once again employed an Aboriginal guide to help him get to Nelsons Plains where he could board a boat downriver to Newcastle. Brown agreed to pay the man with tobacco when he arrived safely at his destination.[52]

Brown only employed a guide for the unknown portion of his return trip to Newcastle, between Wallis Plains and Nelsons Plains. The area between Wallis Plains and the farm at Glendon, where Ben Davis had guided Brown six months before, was no longer an unknown landscape to Europeans, as tracks made by settlers began to connect the farms and outposts.

The land around Nelsons Plains, however, with thick brush forest and swampy ground, remained an area that Europeans treated with caution. Brown's employer Robert Scott was still finding his way in the bush here as well. On 15 October 1823, he wrote in his journal:

> M & I agreed to walk to Nelsons Plains across the country if we could have got a Native to show us the way … [However,] it seems there is to be a grand Cabbra Feast somewhere in the neighbourhood and nothing in the world could induce them to be absent from such an entertainment … As we could not get a Native, Mitchell and I were afraid to trust ourselves in the forest, therefore we only walked to the same spot we disembarked last night …[53]

Scott's account gives us a glimpse not just at the need for guides on even short excursions in some areas, but also at the motivations of Aboriginal people to join or not join an expedition. In this case, the advantages of assisting Scott on what was a relatively small journey were not enough to outweigh the cultural benefits of the cobbra feast and associated gathering.

---

51   Anonymous diary by a servant of the Scott family, 1821–24, SLNSW MLMSS 7808: 55–61. Ben Davis stayed in the Hunter Valley around Wallis Plains. He was identified by his name Munnion in a blanket distribution list in June 1834 at Paterson on the Hunter River close to Wallis Plains. See Colonial Secretary's Correspondence, Special Bundles, SRNSW 4/6666B.
52   Anonymous diary by a servant of the Scott family, 1821–24, SLNSW MLMSS 7808: 65.
53   Scott, Journal, 15 October 1823, SLNSW MLMSS A2266.

As with professional guides assisting exploratory parties, the use of local men as guides, employed as required by settlers heading towards their grants was also a short-term proposition. Between 1822 and 1825, the Assistant Government Surveyor Henry Dangar was surveying the valley for settlers and grant holders. His survey work made the place increasingly familiar to Europeans and reduced the need for guides in the settled areas. There is no evidence that Dangar himself utilised the skills of Aboriginal guides during these surveys, as neither his field books nor the detailed letters to the Surveyor General regarding his progress make any mention of them. He may have deliberately omitted reference to them to enhance his own reputation as a surveyor; however, his description of a young Aboriginal guide in an expedition to find a passage from the upper Hunter Valley to the Liverpool Plains in October 1824 suggests he was not averse to recognising their assistance.[54] Guidance was not as essential in his survey work, where he was mapping the land and marking his path as he progressed.

Dangar's surveys led to increased European penetration of the Hunter Valley. In 1828, he published a guide for emigrants, including a map compiled from his survey work that outlined the type of country in different parts of the valley and the various agricultural purposes it was suited to. Dangar, looking to profit from the emigrant market, wrote:

> I trust that the Map, with the Index ... will enable persons of all descriptions to proceed to any part of the country there delineated, and there to describe with accuracy the position they wish to select.[55]

Dangar's map effectively ended the need for Aboriginal guides in the Hunter Valley. Nevertheless, those wishing to travel beyond the settled districts or, in some cases, even between those areas that were less frequently visited, still needed guiding, even with Dangar's map or his surveys. In the year Dangar published his map and index, some visitors to the Hunter were still employing Aboriginal guides to assist them within areas Dangar had covered. Roger Oldfield, editor of the short-lived periodical *South-Asian Register*, wrote of a visit to the Hunter in 1828:

---

54   Surveyor General Letters Received 1822–55, SRNSW Reel 3060, 2/1526.1; Dangar Survey Field Book No. 221, 1824, SRNSW 2/4861.
55   Dangar 1828: v.

> In the course of our progress along the Hunter, we engaged a black fellow to be our guide, in which capacity the blacks are of a most essential service. A map and compass are useful: but the local maps, which are obtained directly or indirectly from the Colonial Surveyors, have very few natural boundaries laid down, for the guidance of a stranger; and the compass, is a very uncertain benefit, when standing on the margin of an extensive morass, or when fixed in the dilemma of a thicket.[56]

While the use of guides to take Europeans inland to their land was in decline by the late 1820s, Aboriginal men continued to be employed in the Hunter Valley throughout the 1830s and into the 1840s to take Europeans on hunting or fishing expeditions, as well as running messages across country and acting as guides for botanical and natural history collectors.[57] Although strangers and visitors still employed Aboriginal guides into the 1830s for collecting trips or more remote journeys, the role of the guides was beginning to wane.

This chapter demonstrates that the use of guides for the exploring parties and later for settlers was widespread in the Hunter Valley, as it was throughout colonial Australia. Although their role has been largely forgotten or overlooked in colonial histories, Aboriginal assistance had been essential for the exploration as well as the economic development of the region, and was actively sought out by Europeans arriving in the valley. By re-examining the journals, letters and reports of the first wave of Europeans, the story of the guides, intermediaries and interpreters that they relied on can be resurrected. As Greg Blyton has noted, these Aboriginal men while advancing the invasion of their country were also realists, responding to the opportunities presented by the European's needs, and using their traditional knowledge and skills to maximise their own chances of survival in a rapidly changing environment.[58]

---

56 Oldfield 1828: 107.
57 Gunson 1974: 144.
58 Blyton 2012: 105.

References

Anonymous diary by a servant of the Scott family, 8 August 1821 – March 1824 (written after 1825), with notes, 1832, State Library of NSW [SLNSW] MLMSS 7808 (Safe 1/403).

Attenbrow, Val 2010, *Sydney's Aboriginal Past: Investigating the Archaeological and Historical Records*, second edition, UNSW Press, Sydney.

Baker, Don 1998, 'Exploring with Aborigines: Thomas Mitchell and his Aboriginal guides', *Aboriginal History* 22: 36–50.

Blaxland, John de Marquet, n.d., 'Discovery of the road to Coal River', SLNSW AR 39/5.

Blyton, Greg 2012, 'Aboriginal guides of the Hunter region 1800–1850: A case study in Indigenous labour history', *History Australia* 9(3): 89–106.

Brown, John 1821–24, Anonymous Journal of a Servant of Robert Scott, SLNSW MLMSS 7808.

Collins, David 1975 [1798], *An Account of the English Colony in New South Wales*, vol. 1, Brian Fletcher (ed.), A.H. & A.W. Reed, Sydney.

Colonial Secretary's Correspondence, Special Bundles, SRNSW 4/6666B.

Cox, William to Governor Macquarie, 19 July 1816, Documents relating to Australian Aborigines 1816–1853, William Dixon Collection, Mitchell Library, SLNSW DLADD 81, p187.

Dangar, Henry 1822, Surveyors Field Book, No. 193, State Records Authority of NSW (SRNSW) 2/4837.

—— 1824, Surveyors Field Book, No. 221, SRNSW 2/4861.

—— 1828, *Index and Directory to Map of the Country bordering upon the River Hunter; the lands of the Australian-Agricultural Company; with the ground-plan and allotments of King's Town, New South Wales*, British Library Historical Print Collection, London.

Flannery, Tim 1998, *The Explorers*, Text Publishing, Melbourne.

Ford, Geoff 2010, *'Darkingung* Recognition: An Analysis of the Historiography for the Aborigines from the Hawkesbury-Hunter Ranges Northwest of Sydney', MA (Research) thesis, School of Philosophical and Historical Inquiry, Department of History, University of Sydney.

Fraser, John 1892, *An Australian Language: As spoken by the Awabakal, the people of the Awaba or Lake Macquarie; being an account of their language traditions and customs by L.E Threlkeld; re-arranged, condensed and edited with an appendix by John Fraser*, Government Printer, Sydney.

Gammage, Bill 2011, *The Biggest Estate on Earth: How Aborigines Made Australia*, Allen & Unwin, Crows Nest, NSW.

Governor King Letters, Re: Newcastle 1801–1805, SLNSW, MLMSS 582.

Governor Macquarie Correspondence, SLNSW, CY1449 C330.

Gunson, Niel (ed.) 1974, *Australian Reminiscences and Papers of L.E. Threlkeld: Missionary to the Aborigines 1824–1859*, Australian Institute of Aboriginal Studies, Canberra.

Howe, John 1819, Journal of John Howe Expedition from Windsor to the Hunter River in 1819, NSW Surveyor General Field Books, SRNSW Reel 2623, 2/8093.

Howe, John to Governor Macquarie, 27 December 1819, Colonial Secretary's Correspondence, SRNSW Reel 6068, 4/1743.

—— 21 March 1820, Colonial Secretary's Correspondence SRNSW Reel 6049, 4/1744.

—— 13 April 1820, Colonial Secretary's Correspondence, SRNSW Reel 6049, 4/1744.

—— 15 May 1820, Colonial Secretary's Correspondence, SRNSW Reel 6050, 4/1747.

King, Governor to Lord Hobart, 14 August 1804, *Historical Records of Australia*, Series I, Vol. V: 111–115.

Macqueen, Andy 2004, *Somewhat Perilous: The Journeys of Singleton, Parr, Howe, Myles & Blaxland in the Northern Blue Mountains*, A. Macqueen, Wentworth Falls, NSW.

Moore, David R. 1981, 'Results of an archaeological survey of the Hunter River Valley, New South Wales, Australia: Part II Problems of the lower Hunter and contacts with the Hawkesbury Valley', *Records of the Australian Museum* 33(9): 388–442.

Morisset, James T., Commandant to Frederick Goulburn, 6 July 1820, Colonial Secretary's Correspondence, SRNSW Reel 6067, 4/1807.

—— 18 December 1821, Colonial Secretary's Correspondence, SRNSW Reel 6067, 4/1807.

Mudie, James to Colonial Secretary, 25 January 1823, SRNSW Reel 6067, 4/1809.

Needham, William J. 1981, *Burragurra: Where Spirit Walked: The Aboriginal Relics of the Cessnock-Wollombi Region in the Hunter Valley of NSW*, Bill Needham, Cessnock, NSW.

Oldfield, Roger (ed.) 1828, *The South-Asian Register*, No. 2, January 1828: 107.

Parr, William 1817, 'Journal and Station Book of a trip to the westward (Hawkesbury Valley)', Colonial Secretary's Correspondence, Special Bundles, Logs, Diaries and Journals of Exploration, SRNSW Fiche 3271, 2/3623.

Purcell, John to John T. Campbell, 6 July 1810, Colonial Secretary's Correspondence, Special bundles-Newcastle, SRNSW Reel 6066, 4/1804.

Reynolds, Henry 2000, *Black Pioneers: How Aboriginal and Islander People Helped Build Australia*, Penguin Books, Ringwood, Vic.

Rose, Deborah Bird 1996, *Nourishing Terrains: Australian Aboriginal Views of Landscape and Wilderness*, Australian Heritage Commission, Canberra.

Scott, Robert 1823, Journal describing a voyage from the Hunter River to Sydney in company with Rev. Middleton, Mr Bowman and Mr Dixon, vol. 7, SLNSW MLMSS A2266.

Shellam, Tiffany 2009, *Shaking Hands on the Fringe: Negotiating the Aboriginal World at King George's Sound*, UWA Publishing, Perth.

Singleton, Benjamin 1818, Journal, Colonial Secretary's Correspondence, SRNSW Reel 6047, 4/1740.

Smith, Keith Vincent 1992, *King Bungaree: A Sydney Man Meets the Great South Pacific Explorers, 1799–1830*, Kangaroo Press, Kenthurst, NSW.

—— 2010, *Mari Nawi: Aboriginal Odysseys*, Rosenberg Publishing, New South Wales.

Surveyor General Letters Received 1822–55, Henry Dangar Letters, March 1822–August 1824, SRNSW Reel 3060, Item 2/1526.1.

Sydney Gazette and New South Wales Advertiser.

The Australian.

Turner, John (ed.) 1973, *Newcastle as a Convict Settlement: The Evidence before J.T. Bigge in 1819–1821*, Newcastle History Monographs No. 7, Newcastle Public Library, Newcastle.

Wallis, James, Album of original drawings ca1817–1818, SLNSW PXE 1070.

White, Richard 1991, *The Middle Ground: Indians, Empires and Republics in the Great Lakes Region 1650–1815*, Cambridge University Press, New York.

Wood, Walter Allan 1972, *Dawn in the Valley: The Story of Settlement in the Hunter River Valley to 1833*, Wentworth Books, Sydney.

5
Guided by her: Aboriginal women's participation in Australian expeditions

Allison Cadzow

I was compelled in a great measure to be guided by her. She was acquainted with all their haunts and was a native of Port Davey, belonging to this tribe and having a brother and other relatives living among them, [Low. Ger Nown] was her native place. Though I knew she intended sojourning with them, yet there was no alternative but to follow her suggestions ...

George Augustus Robinson discussing Dray's guiding in Tasmania (6 April 1830)

Our female guide, who had scarcely before ventured to look up, stood now boldly forward, and addressed the strange tribe in a very animated and apparently eloquent manner; and when her countenance was thus lighted up, displaying fine teeth, and great earnestness of manner, I was delighted to perceive what soul the woman possessed, and could not but consider our party fortunate in having met with such an interpreter.

Thomas Mitchell discussing Turandurey's guiding in New South Wales (12 May 1836)

The Aboriginal women mentioned above are clearly represented as guides and appear in plain view; they are not in hiding. While women did hide from white expedition members – for good reason considering the frequent violence of white people towards them – this was not the only reaction they had. Historians have largely ignored Aboriginal women's involvement in exploration expeditions, though there are some notable exceptions in the work of Henry Reynolds, Lyndall Ryan and Donald Baker. Some other authors who have attended to them, such as Philip Clarke, imply that women were invariably hidden away during encounters, suggesting they were not actively involved in expeditions.[1] Even when women did hide, this was not necessarily the end of the story, as they sometimes re-emerged after assessing the situation. Some women reputedly approached expedition members, aware that they were a group of men without white women present, as the accounts of Charles Sturt, Daniel Brock and Thomas Mitchell show, though such comments from expedition participants need careful consideration.[2] Other women, like Dray of Tasmania and Turandurey in New South Wales as shown above, acted as guides and interpreters.

This chapter will argue that while it is vital to maintain awareness of accounts of women in hiding, we also need to look at representations of women's involvement in expeditions and to consider their contributions, motivations and interests in guiding explorers through country. The chapter will briefly discuss historiographical material on women's agency in expeditions and how women's presence in exploration journals has been obscured or ignored in histories of exploration. It then focuses on close reading of two major expedition accounts, rather than trying to cover a full range of Aboriginal women's participation in expeditions. By bringing together examples that tend to be discussed separately, it is possible to see connections across different expeditions and to begin to interpret the women's actions in their own social and cultural contexts. The accounts of missionary George Robinson's Tasmanian Port Davey expedition of 1830 with Dray, Trugananner, Pagerly and others (one of six expeditions), and NSW Surveyor General Thomas Mitchell's 1836 expedition in New South Wales and Victoria where Kitty and Turandurey guided are examined.

---

1   Clarke 2008: 22.
2   See, for example, Tcherkézoff's (2009) cautionary discussion of representations of Polynesian women giving themselves 'freely' to the expeditioners. Brock 1975: 45, 135; Sturt 1965 [1849]: 295–296. See also Thomas Mitchell cited in Baker 1997: 65–66. Daniel Brock, bird collector and gunsmith on Sturt's inland expedition of 1844, noted that Nitebook, their Aboriginal guide, teased him about his wife Delia's absence. He hid behind bushes and called out 'Brock Lubra Delia', to surprise Brock. Brock 1975: 41.

These examples offer opportunities to consider how women were involved in expeditions, the skills they demonstrated and a chance to read their actions and statements for signs of their motivations and perspectives.

Historians and women guides

Henry Reynolds has included brief coverage of women such as Toodyep in Western Australia within accounts of Aboriginal intermediaries and their involvement in expeditions. In other publications, he has also considered Trugannaner and Dray's political role in Robinson's expedition (discussed further later in this chapter) and the importance of their cultural and language skills to the expedition's progress.[3] Lyndall Ryan has closely examined George Robinson's expeditions in Tasmania and the involvement of Trugananner, Dray and others in her histories of Aboriginal Tasmania,[4] while Donald Baker has discussed the work of specific women guides within an examination of Thomas Mitchell's relations with Aboriginal people and expeditions.[5] These works, however, are not primarily focused on Aboriginal women and exploration, nor do they tend to examine women's involvement in expeditions comparatively, so further examination of Aboriginal women's guiding is warranted.

Further afield, the work of anthropologist Johannes Fabian and historian Dane Kennedy on African women and expeditions offer insights on the importance of women to exploration. As Fabian has noted, the significance of their work was rarely acknowledged. His work has shown that the women travelled with their husbands, and often children too.[6] They were central to food collection and preparation, diplomacy, influencing the mood of the party, relationships – intimate and otherwise – and were involved in dance and trade. Fabian discussed accounts recorded by Belgian and German explorers which recognised that women were especially adept at finding out information from others. Furthermore, Dane Kennedy's recent work includes discussion of intimate relationships between

---

3   Reynolds 1980, 1990.
4   Ryan 2012; also covered extensively in her earlier work Ryan 1981, 1986.
5   Baker 1993, 1997, 1998.
6   Fabian 2000: 32–33, 40. Also see chapter 4; Rockel 2000.

John Speke, Kahala and Meki, during Speke's 1862–1863 expedition to locate the source of the White Nile in Africa. Mentions of these relationships survived only in proofs and were not included in Speke's published expedition account. This suggests erasure and silences around women's intimate involvement, which can be difficult to trace in published expedition accounts; not only have women's experiences been hidden from history, they have been actively deleted.[7]

Historians have also unearthed the experiences of the guide Sacagewea who assisted the Lewis and Clark expedition in North America, and in South America the crucial role of Doña Marina has been discussed by Stephen Greenblatt. Doña Marina, fluent in Aztec, Mayan and Spanish languages was central to cross-cultural communication for Cortez in Mexico. Greenblatt notes that her gender was a significant factor in Marina becoming a go-between. She had been 'exchanged' by her own family as a girl, then enslaved and by necessity (and talent) she became skilled at negotiation, with an agenda of both revenge and survival. Cortez was reliant upon her for 'her linguistic ability, strategic information and for her grasp of MesoAmerican reality'. As Greenblatt explains it, Marina became 'at once his tongue and ears' and his mistress too.[8] Alida Metcalf draws attention to Doña Marina, but also Damiana da Cunha who assisted on multiple expeditions and Margarida who initiated contact between Alvaro Rodriguez, the Aimore people and the Portuguese in seventeenth-century Brazil. Metcalf argues that Margarida's language skills, mobility and knowledge of both cultures made her an effective go-between.[9] Such international scholarship offers useful comparative examples where women's guidance, especially in terms of their language and negotiating skills, can be seen. They suggest ways to explore the significance of Aboriginal women's participation in Australian exploration.

Rather than simply showing that 'women were there too', it is worthwhile considering *how* they vanished from view in histories. Part of the reason women have been excluded is related to the way some exploration histories have been written about, as solo heroic journeys of the expedition leader, as if there were no cooks, crews, intermediaries or anyone else there. As Fabian has remarked succinctly:

---

7   Kennedy 2013: chapter 7, especially: 195–198, 208, 223.
8   Greenblatt 1991: 141–145 and the rest of chapter 5.
9   Greenblatt 1991; Metcalf 2005: 1–2, 270–271.

'Solitary explorers never travelled alone.'[10] Felix Driver and Lowri Jones, and D. Graham Burnett have shown that expeditions were a collective act, with women as well as children involved. Indeed, on some occasions the men refused to travel without their female partners.[11] In early Australian histories such as Ernest Favenc's *History of Australian Exploration*, masculinity and the figure of the explorer are intricately linked. Exploration is represented as white men's work alone, again obscuring women from view. In 1888, for example, Favenc described Australian exploration as 'the spectacle of one man pitted against the whole force of nature', and a few years later, Albert Calvert wrote of the explorers as a 'noble band of brave and devoted men'.[12] Charles Long claimed to cover 'some of the exploits of those dauntless men, who took the chief part in opening up the continent'.[13] Even some more recent works can give the impression expeditions were an all-male enterprise, with remarks such as '[e]xploration parties always consisted of a team of men'.[14] Some histories which quote extensively from explorer journals have noted the presence of women, if briefly, but the absence of women both Aboriginal and non-Aboriginal is persistent in many histories, nonetheless. It was less common for women to be involved in expeditions, so it follows that they feature less in exploration histories, but women did join and contribute significantly to some expeditions. While Aboriginal men's involvement in expeditions as guides and participants has been obscured in histories, Aboriginal women's guidance has been even more hidden.

Another reason women may have vanished from view is that Aboriginal women do not seem to have been hired 'officially' at the outset as guides. Women tended to join expeditions along the way, so they appear less often in expedition member lists, for example. Yet expedition work and participation was often more elastic than such lists suggest. Often the Europeans sought advice and assistance along the way and this tends to be when Aboriginal women's guidance comes into the picture. This is seen in the accounts of Thomas Mitchell,

---

10   Fabian 2000: 29.
11   Driver and Jones 2009: 13; Burnett 2000: 23; 2002: 29–30.
12   Favenc 1888: vi; Calvert 1895: preface.
13   Long 1903: 219.
14   Cathcart 2001: 234.

Charles Sturt and Robert Hoddle in eastern Australia, where women provide information on country ahead and the location of water to either Aboriginal guides or the explorers themselves.[15]

Historians also bring presumptions about Aboriginal women, their authority and their agency to the sources, which can block the women from view. As Kay Schaeffer has noted, using Mary Louise Pratt's idea of the contact zone (a space in which colonised and coloniser interact and where power dynamics are not always clear cut): 'Women both white and Aboriginal have been consistently left out of considerations about the nature of ... contact zone experience.'[16]

When Aboriginal women are included in exploration histories they are not widely represented as adventurous, skilled communicators or even as expert travellers.

Selective and repeated use by historians of accounts where Aboriginal women are portrayed as victims of 'savage' violence, without careful consideration of other coexisting representations, continues to influence analyses, as Ann McGrath and Shino Konishi have shown.[17] Violence happened, and should be recognised, but it was not the only experience women had. Aboriginal women as well as Aboriginal men may have sought to develop what Tiffany Shellam has described as 'travelling knowledge': information gained through expeditions about distant people and country as well as colonists, which could be used to increase their status within their own community and beyond.[18] Heather Roller notes that Amerindian crew members who joined

---

15   Charles Sturt noted that women approached the expeditioners camp on the Darling and enjoyed some tea with them (Sturt 1965 [1849]: 133). Robert Hoddle, travelling towards the Shoalhaven, New South Wales, in 1827, recorded that 'On the evening of the 19th Friday, I met with two native black women, with two children who shewed me the water holes', cited in Colville 2004: 110. During Mitchell's 1845 expedition, two women told Mitchell's guide, Piper, where permanent water could be found around Nyngan, NSW, and beyond (Mitchell 1848, 17 January 1845: 36). An older woman advised Edmund Kennedy, NSW Assistant Surveyor General, of the course of the Balonne River (in Mitchell 1848: 357). The singing and dancing of women is also remarked upon by Mitchell in this entry.
16   Schaeffer 2001; Pratt 1992: 7. Assumptions also exist in relation to white women and expeditions, though since the 1990s especially several studies have addressed this such as Birkett 1989; Mills 1991; Blunt 1994 and others.
17   Konishi 2008; McGrath 1990.
18   Shellam 2009: 138–153.

collecting expeditions in the Amazonian Sertão may have sought opportunities to travel and to visit relatives; Aboriginal women may have pursued chances to do the same.[19]

Traces of Aboriginal women's roles in expeditions can be found in some explorers' published journals, if not always in exploration histories. The journals are problematic sources for a study of Aboriginal women's participation, being representations by white men who may have downplayed women's actions and the accounts were not written from the women's perspectives. Often Aboriginal women are unnamed, making the tracing of their histories harder. Yet, sometimes the journals contain reported speech and accounts of their actions, which can be read 'against the grain' to provide at least some sense of creative Indigenous responses to expedition encounters.[20] Bronwen Douglas has argued 'countersigns' – indications of local agency and strategy within foreign/coloniser representations of local people – can be teased out in such accounts. As she explains it, 'the presence and agency of Indigenous people infiltrated the writings and pictures produced by sailors, naturalists and artists … and left ambiguous countersigns in the very language, tone and content of their representations'.[21] Such traces can point to moments where women's agency was shown, even if it is perhaps a fraction of what they did. Much activity by guides also remained unremarked in journals until conflict or problems occurred, as Burnett has shown.[22]

Mentions of Aboriginal women's guidance on Australian expeditions can be found in the published accounts of James Grant, Thomas Mitchell, Robert Hoddle, Edward Eyre, George Augustus Robinson, George Fletcher Moore and, later, William Hann and David Carnegie. The latter took women hostage to show him where water was in northern Australia – a reminder that not all participation in expeditions was voluntary.[23] These were a few of the explorers who wrote about women and expeditions. Aboriginal women's leadership

---

19 Roller 2010: 467.
20 Reynolds 2006: 4.
21 Douglas 2014: 21–22; Douglas 2009: chapter 6.
22 Burnett 2002: 7, 29. See also Kennedy 2013: 163–164 and Wisnicki 2010 regarding the impact of non-Western dynamics and events on published and unpublished expedition accounts.
23 Carnegie 1898. Leichhardt's 1844–1845 journal mentions that the male Aboriginal guide Gnarrangan 'intended to take his wife with him' on the expedition, Leichhardt 1847, 10 December 1845: 523.

of informal expeditions is occasionally mentioned in non-Aboriginal women's accounts too. Amateur anthropologist Ethel Hassell wrote about Aboriginal women taking her on bush explorations in south-west Western Australia in the 1870s, for example. Botanical painter Ellis Rowan wrote of a trip up Mt Macmillan in Queensland where Aboriginal women carried provisions and laughed at the bumbling movements of the white people.[24]

Trugannaner, Pagerly, Dray, Timemedene and George Augustus Robinson's Port Davey expedition, Tasmania, 1830

Aboriginal women as well as men provided guidance for missionary George Augustus Robinson in the initial expedition to 'conciliate' Aboriginal Tasmanians in 1830 to Port Davey and the west.[25] Before the expedition commenced, Robinson proposed to Governor Arthur a program of conciliation, to bring in Aboriginal people for their own safety, to civilise and covert them to Christianity. Robinson stated that he had discussed the trip with the people living on Bruny Island, where he had been overseer since March 1829. Some of these people were from Port Davey originally, and had come to stay on the island for a while. Reynolds, however, argues that the group regarded the expedition as a regular seasonal journey to the West Coast and that they happened to agree to take Robinson with them.[26] Other circumstances probably influenced their decision to travel with him also.

The expedition took place after much illness on Bruny Island and the ongoing violence of the Black War in Tasmania. Aboriginal people were being shot at in areas pastoralists were occupying, and in the north-west islands some sealers had kidnapped women. As Lynette Russell has shown, Aboriginal people's relationships with sealers were far more complex and varied than the simple uniform story of

---

24   Hassell 1975, also cited in Reynolds 1990; Rowan 1898: 119–124.
25   Aboriginal women worked as guides for John Batman in Tasmania (1830) also, to assist with 'bringing in the tribes'. Batman 1830: n.p.
26   Reynolds 2012: 71–72. See also Burnett regarding Amerindians in British Guiana's possible consideration of the traveller Schomburgk as 'their temporary passenger'. Burnett 2002: 29.

kidnapping that Robinson's account suggests.²⁷ Either way, retaliatory violence was rife and pressures upon Aboriginal Tasmanians were increasing, which may have influenced their decision to join Robinson.

Robinson, his son Charles, Tom, Robert, Dray, Pagerly and Trugananner, Woorraddy (Trugananner's partner) and his sons set off from Recherche Bay overland to Port Davey on 3 February 1830, amidst blustery southerly winds.²⁸ Robinson referred to their route as the 'track of the natives', and claimed that 'no person had ever attempted it'.²⁹ They were a party of 14, including six convicts as well as support vessel staff who dropped food and supplies to key points on the coast. They spent four months away in the west of Tasmania, an area that is still remote and rugged today.

The focus of most work on this expedition and Robinson's account (first published in 1966) has been on Trugananner, rather than the other women involved. Much work debates her participation in moral terms: Did she betray her people? Was she emotionally entangled with Robinson? Or was she a survivor? Lyndall Ryan has examined such representations and debates closely, drawing out culturally contextualised and historicised readings of Trugananner's involvement. Ian Anderson has reflected upon the way Trugannini has been represented symbolically, in ways which have denied Tasmanian Aboriginal identities, survival and histories.³⁰ Henry Reynolds has also critiqued moralistic and sexually preoccupied accounts of Trugananner's participation and argued the case for Trugananner acting politically in assisting Robinson. He argued that women were crucial negotiators and he recognised the contribution of Dray and others.³¹ His interpretation centres mostly on Aboriginal people's political action and treaty making, but other reasons for participation are worth considering more closely too.

---

27 Russell 2012.
28 Robinson 2008, 3 February 1830: 143. See also pages 142–144, Plomley's summary on pages 154-155.
29 Robinson 2008, 3 February 1830: 143. See also pages 142–144, Plomley's summary on pages 154–155.
30 Anderson 1995, 2008.
31 Ryan 2012; Reynolds 1995.

Trugannaner was aged around 17 at the time of the expedition. In 1876 she stated that her 'fiancé' Paraweena had been killed by sawyers in 1828, her sister Moorina was 'taken away' by sealers, her other sister shot, her mother stabbed to death by men who came onshore, while her father was shot by a soldier.[32] After such loss, amidst illness and frequent deaths on Bruny Island, it may have seemed to her that she had little left to lose by leaving. She had relatives in the area they were heading to, which was likely to have influenced her decision to go.[33]

Dray was a widow, around 30 years old, and her child had become ill and died on Bruny Island not long before the expedition started. She had chosen to stay with sealers and had avoided Robinson at times.[34] She was from Port Davey originally and Robinson took her as a guide because this was her country and language group so he anticipated she would prove helpful with translations and introductions. Robinson recorded her motivation: 'One of the women named DRAY said she should now see her brother.'[35] Visiting family and country seem likely motivations for joining forces with Robinson.

Another guide mentioned was Pagerly who was from the south-east region of Tasmania and was living on Bruny Island. She was approximately 18 years old at the time the expeditions began. Less is known about her background. Other women such as Sall were involved in subsequent Robinson expeditions as guides.

Before the expedition party did much negotiating or interacting with local Aboriginal people, they encountered difficult travel conditions in thickly forested areas with swift-running rivers. The women, as well as the men, worked to clear and recut the path through the forest, and advised of the best way through, literally making the way forward.[36] Robinson soon found that their European provisions were almost exhausted. It was the Aboriginal women and men who kept Robinson and the convicts from starvation. Robinson survived on mussels, roots, berries and fish that they procured.[37] He noted that

---

32   Graves 1876: 3; Robinson 2008: 49.
33   Ryan 2012; Miller and Cameron 2011.
34   John Freake (a convict), 27 November 1829, in Robinson 2008: 122, n. 49; Robinson 2008, 11 September 1830: 81.
35   Robinson 2008, 30 January 1830: 115.
36   Robinson 2008, 11 March 1830: 156.
37   Robinson 2008, 19 February 1830: 151.

the women fished and collected crayfish and that they brought him wild duck eggs too. They had specific skills in hunting and gathering, which enabled his survival. Trugananner and Pagerly also collected and carried provisions and heavy gear according to Robinson.

Importantly, the Aboriginal women were part of groups who tracked local people and initiated discussions with them, brokering between Robinson and the local people and mediating on behalf of Robinson. He described how this was done:

> [A]fter observing for some time the movements of the natives they stripped themselves of their European clothing and went in quest of them. At 7pm Trugananner, Pagerly and Woorrady returned and informed me that they had been with the Port Davey natives and that the other woman DRAY had stopped behind, having met with her brother. They further stated that they had made the Port Davey natives understand the nature of my mission to them, and said the Port Davey natives was anxious I should come to them in the morning.[38]

What was actually said remains unknown, though the women clearly used this as an opportunity to reconnect with family and share information. It was the Aboriginal women and men, not Robinson, who brokered contact.

Dray returned the next day with two young Port Davey women. Robinson 'performed' at their initial meeting; he tried to charm them by playing the flute, and encouraged them to try novel food such as biscuits. Yet they were assessing him as much as he was them. He sent them in quest of others – but they returned saying they could not find them. Considering their skills in tracking, the women may have chosen not to locate them, or the others may have decided to avoid him.

The significance of women in keeping watch and alerting others to danger is also apparent in Robinson's account. Dray and Wooraddy tracked a group after spotting their abandoned fire and meal. They found around 15 women and children, whom Dray asked to come out of hiding. Again, Robinson sat by the fire, offered food, beads and trinkets, and noted 'the women began to hoot a signal for the men to

---

38 Robinson 2008, 16 March 1830: 162.

come home'.[39] Here, the women assessed the situation and advised the men that it was safe for them to return to camp. Still, they refused to camp with Robinson and they departed overnight.[40]

Five days later, the explorers followed local people to a river Robinson described as a 'rendezvous for the natives'. The camp that Robinson's group joined later was located near plenty of ripe kangaroo apples, which suggests this was likely to have been a key time for gathering to feast on them. The expedition's camps possibly had other meanings for the women and men, for example, the timing coinciding with their own social and cultural calendar of movements. A celebration on the reuniting of relations followed at the 'Friendly River' camp:

> The evening was spent with great conviviality, singing and dancing until a late hour, make the woods to echo with their song. The song they call Lun.Ner.Ry and the dance True.De.Cum. My blacks danced and sung in their turn.[41]

Gatherings like these over subsequent nights suggest the social and family connections were key considerations for Aboriginal people in the party and those they were visiting or returning home to. Aside from the dancing and singing, other clues indicate they were trying to bring Robinson into their world: 'At the request of the natives had my face painted black. The natives continually painting themselves.'[42] The symbolism is hard to miss.

Shortly after the feasting evening, the women's finely honed observation skills were shown. One of the Port Davey women alerted the others to the pistols in Robinson's knapsack and was appointed to guard him, taking on an important role of protection:

> The circumstances of these pistols induced them to place a watch before my hut and this duty was assigned to one of the young females, I suppose from being less likely to excite suspicion. This woman never left her post, whatever the weather might be. Frequently the rain fell in torrents, yet she remained firm to her duty.[43]

---

39 Robinson 2008, 18 March 1830: 163.
40 Robinson 2008, 19 March 1830: 163–164.
41 Robinson 2008, 25 March 1830: 168. March is when kangaroo apples tend to ripen, though this varies depending on seasonal conditions.
42 Robinson 2008, 28 March 1830: 171.
43 Robinson 2008, 26 March 1830: 168–169.

5. GUIDED BY HER

So much for Robinson's claims of his peaceful, unarmed negotiation. The women often acted as lookouts and watched him as he slept; their skills clearly valued by their own people and, when used for his purposes, by Robinson too.

Dray played a key role in providing explanations of the Aboriginal people's behaviour to Robinson – or at least explanations that she thought he could accept. She explained to him why the people they met were afraid, not only of the white men but also some of the male Aboriginal guides who had been in roving parties, which had captured Aboriginal people. He wrote, revealingly, '[they] called all my blacks Num viz white people', suggesting the suspicion that their prior behaviour and 'new' ways caused.[44]

Dray educated Robinson about negotiating with her people, insisting that he waited until she had spoken to them first, taking on a leading role. As Henry Reynolds has argued, these negotiations were Aboriginal ones, pursued by them rather than Robinson and for their own purposes it would seem.[45]

Dray and her Port Davey group left the camp at the Little Rocky River area before dawn without telling Robinson, which he regarded as a betrayal.[46] He does not appear to have considered that they may have had their own reasons for moving on, even though numerous people came and went and would not stay constantly with him. Such episodes where guides vanished or unexpectedly departed an expedition can reveal that intermediaries had their own agendas and terms of interaction, as Kennedy has shown.[47]

The women were also essential to the expedition because of their swimming abilities. The Aboriginal men built vessels from bark, which Robinson described as 'catamarans' in order to cross the numerous rivers in the region, but it was often the women who swam ahead and steered them across. Aboriginal women were the expert swimmers and divers in their communities, responsible for collecting abalone, mussels and crayfish, these skills being adapted to expedition purposes. This was especially important as Robinson could not swim

---

44   Robinson 2008, 30 March 1830: 172.
45   Reynolds 1995: 139.
46   Robinson 2008, 7 April 1830: 176–177.
47   Kennedy 2013: 187.

and would not have been able to get far without them.[48] Trugananner, Dray and two Port Davey women who joined them, Timmedenne and Wyyerer, made sure all the luggage was safely transported over and then the children were taken across. They made several trips across the river, in chilly water.[49]

Figure 5.1: George Augustus Robinson, Aboriginal women and men taking Robinson across the river, 10 June 1830.
Source: George Augustus Robinson, Journal Van Diemen's Land, 10 June 1830, Vol 6, A7027, Cy reel 266, Mitchell Library.

The women's swimming skills were also useful in attempted negotiations when they reached areas where sealing communities lived, such as Green Point. Some of the women fled into the sea in a desperate attempt to escape the white men (either having being shot at, raped or kidnapped before, or highly aware of this as a possibility). Dray and Trugananner swam out to them and attempted to talk with them.[50]

The Aboriginal women were important also in gaining the confidence of some of the sealing community women who told them of being captured. They provided testimonies about massacres and cruelties

---

48 Robinson 2008, 25 and 26 March 1830: 167–168.
49 Robinson 2008, 26 March 1830: 170.
50 Robinson 2008, 19 April 1830: 186.

that they had experienced at the hands of sealers and pastoralists. Robinson used this information to build his case for further expeditions and intervention in the communities, devising a case for removing women from the sealers. It is not clear whether he made this purpose explicit to Dray, Trugananner and Pagerly. The responses of some of the sealing women on Robbins Island to the arrival of the women suggests again that reuniting with relatives and people such as 'Jack' and 'Maria' was an important part of the expedition for those visited: 'the sealer women appeared remarkable fond of my aboriginal females, caressing them and kissing them incessantly. As they were eastern women my aborigines could converse with them.'[51]

By the time the expedition made it to George Town on the mouth of the Tamar River in northern Tasmania, after travelling inland to the Hampshire and Surrey Hills, non-Aboriginal people were being incited to take up arms and join in the Black Line. From this point, the expeditions increasingly seemed to be about the capture and removal of people from country for Robinson, rather than negotiation, which was his original stated intention. As Lyndall Ryan, Henry Reynolds and James Boyce have all noted, Robinson's journals show him becoming more forceful (and arrogant, presuming he could out-track Aboriginal people, for example) after this. He ultimately allowed force to be used to have people sent to Flinders Island – a major change in approach from this initial Port Davey expedition.[52]

Kitty, Turandurey and Ballendella and Thomas Mitchell's expedition in New South Wales and Victoria, 1836

On the much drier mainland, in 1836, Aboriginal women and men acted as guides in the third and final journey of Thomas Mitchell's expeditions as Surveyor General of New South Wales, in eastern Australia. The expedition was instructed by the governor to finish the survey of lower Darling River where it joined the Murray River, though

---

51 Robinson 2008, 21 and 24 June 1830: 212–217.
52 Ryan 1981; Reynolds 1995; Boyce 2008.

it also ventured into the 'Australia Felix' (Victoria). The underlying aim, however, was to seek and find land suitable for grazing cattle and white occupation.

Mitchell's published account of 1839 clearly described Turandurey as a guide.[53] Nineteenth-century historians William Pridden and William Howitt mentioned Turandurey and Kitty in their histories, and more recently Dane Kennedy has mentioned Turandurey briefly.[54] Donald Baker's work on Mitchell and his relationship with Aboriginal guides brought Turandurey and Kitty to the fore, noting their language skills, knowledge of country and gender protocols around meetings. However, Baker occasionally treats Mitchell's account as literal truth, rather than representation, overlooking alternative readings of behaviour and actions of Aboriginal participants.[55]

Mitchell's party of 23, complete with a cook, bird collector, medical assistant, butcher and others met at the preparation camp near Bathurst in 1836.[56] The waterholes were low and the country parched by drought when Piper, an Aboriginal man, approached Mitchell to assist the expedition, on the condition he was fed, clothed and had a horse.[57] While he was referred to by Mitchell as an interpreter and brokered others guiding, he was effectively the main guide for the expedition. Mitchell's account shows that several men, such as Barney, and women also provided guidance along the way. One of these women was Kitty, who joined Piper near Lake Cargelligo/Cudjàllagong in Wiradjuri country after he temporarily left the expedition party to 'marry' her. Piper had spoken of 'obtaining a gin' in the area as a motivation for heading there.[58] Mitchell introduced Kitty: 'a good strong woman marched behind him into our camp, loaded with a new opossum-skin cloak, and various presents that had been given to Piper with her.'[59]

---

53 Mitchell 1839: 40. *Athenæum*, September 1838, also published excerpts from the text which mentioned Turandurey as a guide.
54 Howitt 1865: 294, 298; Pridden 1843: 180–184.
55 Baker 1997.
56 The camp was in the 'Valley of Canobolas' in Mitchell's terminology.
57 The overseer Alexander Burnett knew Piper and suggested to Mitchell that he come with them.
58 Mitchell 1839, 15 April 1836: 37.
59 Mitchell 1839, 15 April 1836: 37.

5. GUIDED BY HER

Mitchell presumed Kitty was from a 'strange' tribe, little known to Piper while Granville Stapylton, the second-in-command (whose journal was first published in 1986), represented the marriage as an act of abduction: 'In one short space Piper talks to them in a conciliatory mood and in another robs them of a daughter.'[60] That Piper conversed with them at length and that Kitty had been given a cloak and gifts suggests that their union was organised and communicated between Kitty and Piper's people well ahead of Piper's arrival. The timing of this marriage may even have been central to Piper joining the journey at this point, as well as the material benefits.

Kitty proved a valuable guide, both with Piper and independent of him, informing the party of where they would find water, such as at Combèdyega.[61] She appeared regularly throughout Mitchell's narrative as part of negotiations with groups they encountered. She was with the party when it was negotiated that Turandurey, a widow aged about 30, join the expedition with her young daughter. This occurred after they reputedly 'surprised' an Aboriginal group. Two children remained by the cooking fire after the expedition group had retreated, watching. The rest of the group re-emerged and exchanges commenced soon after:

> An old man came up to the fire afterwards, with other children. He told us the name of the water-holes between that place and the Murrumbidgee, but he could not be prevailed on to be our guide. Subsequently, however, a gin who was a widow, with the little girl above-mentioned, whose age might be about four years, was persuaded by him to accompany us.[62]

Mitchell did not discuss Turandurey's possible reasons for joining the expedition with her daughter Ballandella, but he noted the considerable assistance she provided to the party. Turandurey gave directions on which way to head, where to find water and where to camp – an expert on her country, the Lachlan Plains. She shared guiding responsibilities with Piper and Kitty.[63]

---

60   Stapylton 1986, 14 May 1836: 61.
61   Mitchell 1839, 2 May 1836: 60.
62   Mitchell 1839, 2 May 1836: 60.
63   Mitchell 1839, 6 May, 7 May 1836: 60–61.

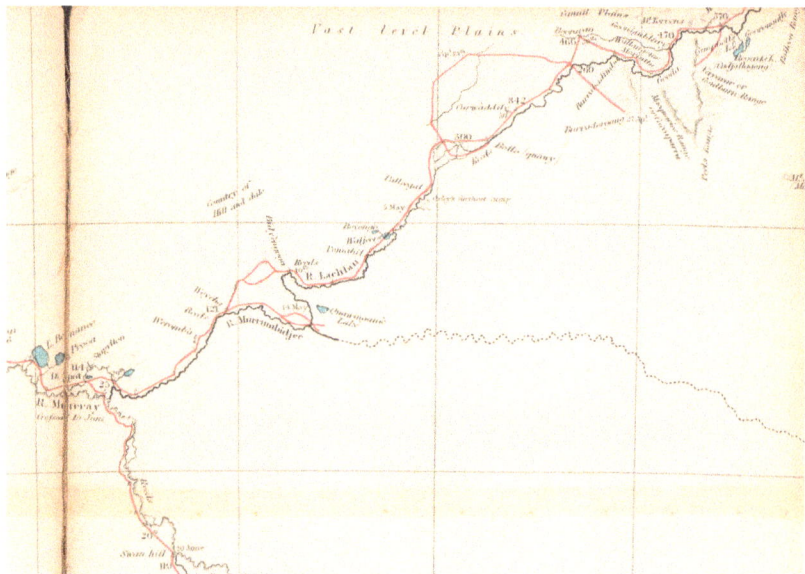

Figure 5.2: Detail from map by Thomas Mitchell, 'The south eastern portion of Australia showing the routes of the three expeditions and the surveyed territory', 1838, which noted the camp and the name of the waterhole, Pomabil, that Turandurey guided Mitchell's party to.
Source: Thomas Mitchell, *Three Expeditions in the interior of Australia*, 1838, MAP NK 1476, National Library of Australia.

At first glance, some of the women's guiding appears to be a straightforward response to Mitchell's requests – for example, he asked them to locate the furthest point John Oxley's 1817 exploration party reached on the Lachlan River. The women showed him this site, but they also pointed out that one of Oxley's men nearly drowned there and that they rescued him. They mentioned three white men on horseback and their canoes (boats) on the Murrumbidgee. Such specific, located memories reveal just how keenly observed 'strangers' in country were, offering a view back from people who lived on this country. Perhaps this was intended to remind Mitchell that he was being watched too.[64] The women's accounts drew attention to the assistance they provided to the expeditions and could also be seen as an assertion of their knowledge and ownership of place.

---

64   Mitchell 1839, 5 May 1836: 62–64.

Figure 5.3: Portraits of Turandurey (the female guide), and her child Ballandella, with the scenery on the Lachlan (10 May 1836).

Source: Thomas Mitchell, *Three Expeditions in the interior of Australia*, 1839: 68–69 (Plate 34), National Library of Australia.

Later, in a move reminiscent of Dray's actions in Tasmania, Turandurey pursued and talked with a family. While Mitchell wanted Piper to ask the elderly man of the Murrumbidgee group questions, he remained silent. Neither Piper nor the man would look at each other, or speak, as protocol demanded. Turandurey intervened:

> The female, however, became the intermediate channel of communication, for both spoke alternately in a low tone to her … by slow degrees, they got into conversation. We were then informed that water was to be found a mile or two on, and the old man agreed to guide overseer Burnett and Piper to the place.[65]

She negotiated Mitchell being able to travel through this country. Further along the Murrumbidgee, Turandurey proved a crucial intermediary for the party and, later still, she initiated discussions with a group on the riverbank, before Mitchell caught up. He saw this as a gendered skill she brought to the expedition, though it may have been shaped by her status/relationship to the speaker in other ways too:

> it appeared that while some diffidence or ceremony always prevents the male natives, when strangers to each other, from speaking at first sight, no such restraint is imposed on the gins; who, with the privilege of their sex, are ever ready to speak …[66]

The guides appeared to have enjoyed appearing worldlier than the group they spoke with, the women laughing at the Aboriginal men's request to have the 'wild' sheep and horses sent away.[67]

In this case, Turandurey played a significant role in opening up communication for the party and ensuring her own safe passage through the area. Turandurey and Kitty were sent ahead by Mitchell at various points to negotiate. In addition to this ability to be a conversation conduit, women were perhaps seen as less threatening to 'strangers'.

---

65 Mitchell 1839, 7 May 1836: 68.
66 Mitchell 1839, 12 May 1836: 76.
67 Mitchell 1839, 12 May 1836: 76.

Turandurey also appears to have had a talent for entertaining the party, impersonating Mitchell's 'explorer' activities in the field: 'I was informed that the widow could also amuse the men occasionally — by enacting their leader, taking angles, drawing from nature, &c.'[68]

While only a fleeting mention, it alludes to a different perspective on exploration and provides a sense of how odd the practices of Mitchell and others may have looked to her. On other expeditions some similar revealing moments were recorded. For example, in George Fletcher Moore's account of an expedition north of the Swan River in Western Australia, Toodyep questioned why he walked so much in the bush and she mimicked Moore's words of wisdom, to the amusement of the other Aboriginal people present.[69] As Simon Ryan has argued, 'mimicry is the best possible method of indicating that the explorers are subject to Aboriginal surveillance'.[70]

Turandurey and Kitty answered Mitchell's queries and provided cultural explanations when grave sites were encountered. When Mitchell noted a shelter and asked about it, the women imparted information connected to child rearing that the Aboriginal men either would not comment on. They reputedly told Mitchell 'it was usual to prepare such a bower for the reception of a new-born child'.[71]

Their commitment to the expedition was not always unwavering. Turandurey and Kitty wanted to leave, which Mitchell stated was due to Turandurey being beyond her own area and worried that he would take her daughter from her.[72] Her daughter, Ballandella, had a broken leg from a cart accident earlier in May, and they had waited for it to heal after the expedition's medical attendant, John Drysdale, treated her. The ever-suspicious Stapylton saw signs of 'collusion' between the 'wild' tribes and Turandurey.[73] She may have merely sought information to ensure her way back was safe. They left,

---

68 Mitchell 1839, 27 September 1836: 277.
69 Moore 1836a: 692, 693; Moore 1884: 387. Moore noted they were surprised at the collections of shrubs by the botanist Ludwig Preiss, and 'are very curious to know what he does with them', questioning the premise of botanical collecting. Imbat asked a starving George Grey in north Western Australia why he did not stay where there was food and he could be fat and handsome. Grey in Howitt 1865: 387.
70 Ryan 1996: 187–190.
71 Mitchell 1839, 7 September 1836: 251–252.
72 Mitchell 1839, 3 July 1836: 162–163.
73 Stapylton 1986, 23 May 1836: 74.

swimming across the Millewa/Murray River, Turandurey pushing Ballandella ahead of her on a bark sheet, but they ultimately returned. The Aboriginal people on the opposite bank, angry on seeing her fire, asked who went there. Turandurey and Ballandella retreated through the frosty night.[74] This episode suggests the precariousness of the guide's position. Alliances with white explorers could also open up the potential for conflict between groups, making it a risky role to take on.

Turandurey and Ballendella remained at the depot camp, beyond the junction of the Murray and Lachlan, with Stapylton and others. However, Kitty continued with Mitchell after Piper argued the case for her joining them.[75] They travelled on to the junction of the Murray where Mitchell came face-to-face with the daughters of the woman his party had killed on his Darling River expedition a year earlier. They had travelled down to confront him, according to Piper. Though reputedly filled with regret about the death, Mitchell managed to observe that the younger of the two daughters was attractive. His interest noted, the 'chief' offered Mitchell intimacy with her in exchange for a tomahawk. Perhaps Mitchell had misunderstood and 'the chief' was explaining that Mitchell had obligations to provide for the daughter, being connected with the killing of her mother.[76]

During this tense time, Kitty was represented as an important scout for gossip and intelligence, faithfully reporting back to Mitchell.[77] He does not seem to have considered that she may have been tipping them off. With Piper, Kitty watched and explained to Mitchell the tactics of a group that shadowed them, and then pulled back. He noted that they were:

> strong men, <u>neither women nor boys being among them</u>; and although we had little to fear from such an attack, having arms in our hands, the scheme was very audacious.[78]

---

74 Mitchell 1839, 6 July 1836: 162, 165. According to Stapylton, Piper tracked them: 124–125.
75 Stapylton 1986, 2 July 1836: 125.
76 Mitchell 1839, 24 May 1836: 93.
77 Mitchell 1839, 24 May and 1 June 1836: 94, 112.
78 Mitchell 1839, 1 June 1836: 111–112 (my emphasis).

Mitchell and other explorers read a lack of women and children's presence among Aboriginal groups as a sign of hostility toward the expedition.[79] Even when women were not actively involved in guiding expeditions, some explorers considered their presence or absence attentively.

Kitty proved valuable to the party again when violence erupted. It was likely to have been a response to previous violent encounters on the Darling River with Mitchell's party in 1835. Local Aboriginal people told Daniel Brock, gunsmith and bird collector on Charles Sturt's inland expedition in 1844, that convict members of Mitchell's party had raped and killed a woman and then killed her child there.[80] As Mitchell represented the situation, the Darling people had followed them and approached them with spears and one of his men fired on them. Seven Aboriginal people died as the rest of the party opened fire. Mitchell named the place 'Mt Dispersion'. During this chaos, Kitty became an impromptu guard, watching over the horses and cattle, gear and provisions that the men had abandoned. Mitchell celebrated her quick thinking.[81]

Women were knowledgeable about places and could read country and cues from the environment, having been schooled in this from childhood. Mitchell recognised that the women guides' directions and assistance were important:

> [the] native party usually explored the woods with our dogs, for several miles in front of the column. The females kept nearer the party, and often gave us notice of obstacles, in time to enable me to avoid them. My question on such occasions was, *Dāgo nyōllong yannāgary?* (Which way shall we go?) to which one would reply, pointing in the proper direction, *Yalyāi nyōllong-yannār!* (Go that way.)[82]

---

79   Mitchell 1839, 24 May 1836: 94; Sturt 1849: 133–134.
80   Brock 1975, 16 October 1844: 50–51. In Brock's account, Topar, an Aboriginal expedition guide, showed Brock where he witnessed the killing, the marks of the shots on the tree and the graves. Sturt mentioned an 'unhappy occurrence that took place between them and Sir Thomas Mitchell during a former expedition', Sturt 1965 [1849]: 99.
81   Mitchell 1839, 27 and 28 May 1836: 103.
82   Mitchell 1839, 19 June 1836: 135.

It is likely they were carefully leading him in particular ways, managing the presence of the party so that key powerful places were avoided. As in Tasmania, the women knew how to steer craft across rivers and assisted Mitchell with transporting his specimens and papers safely across to the riverbank.[83]

It was through Piper, Kitty and Turandurey's interactions with local people that Mitchell was able to find names for his maps, water, and route advice, often from families. This is a reminder that it was a domestic landscape that the explorers were moving through, a place of families; not just men, but women and children too. In a valley near the Wando River in western Victoria this was clearly shown:

> I perceived at length two figures at a distance … as the female saw us, she began to run. I presently overtook her, and with the few words I knew, prevailed on her to stop, until the two gins of our party could come up; for I had long been at a loss for the names of localities. This woman was not so much alarmed as might have been expected; and I was glad to find that she and the gins perfectly understood each other. The difference in the costume on the banks of the Wándo, immediately attracted the notice of the females from the Lachlan. The bag usually carried by gins, was neatly wove in basketwork, and composed of a wiry kind of rush. She of Wándo carried this bag fastened to her back, having under it two circular mats of the same material, and beneath all, a kangaroo cloak … The boy was supported between the mats and cloak.[84]

The guide's curiosity about other women's appearance and practices are evident here, showing some of the different experiences that participation in an expedition might bring for guides, possibly increasing knowledge of people distant from their usual travel routes.

---

83 Mitchell 1839, 3 November 1836: 336.
84 Mitchell 1839, 10 August 1836: 212.

Figure 5.4: 'Female and child of Australia Felix'.
Source: Thomas Mitchell, *Three Expeditions in the interior of Australia*, 1839: 210–211 (Plate 44), National Library of Australia.

The woman that the party stopped stated that the main river was called 'Temiángandgeen' and that the country to the east was similar: downs and valleys, to Mitchell's delight. When they came to a major river crossing, he thanked her by gifting her a tomahawk. The Aboriginal women interpreted for him, demonstrating its use, showing their knowledge of white people's ways and goods. Mitchell noted that 'she seemed still at a loss to conceive the meaning of *a present*', perhaps wondering what terms of exchange or trade had taken place.[85]

Finally, when the party was returning to Sydney and reached the Murrumbidgee River, Turandurey left the group.[86] She reputedly left her daughter Ballandella in Mitchell's care, the mother's and daughter's faces painted white for mourning, according to Mitchell. Yet Mitchell had noted earlier that 'the mother seemed uneasy under an apprehension that I wanted to deprive her of this child', so why would she have changed her mind?[87] Turandurey may have intended that grandparents or relatives care for Ballandella. Even Mitchell acknowledged that she was under the immediate care of Kitty, rather than him. She might not have thought she was delivering her to Mitchell permanently. Stapylton described Ballandella as being 'kidnapped away' to a station 10 miles from them, raising questions about the arrangement.[88] Mitchell presumed in his account that Turandurey gave her daughter to him so that she might escape the 'wretched state of slavery to which the native females are doomed' and be raised in a western way. He reached this conclusion even though Turandurey had just acted relatively independently, guiding him around her country and beyond.

Turandurey left to 'marry' King Joey of the Murrumbidgee, according to Stapylton and 'proceeds with him to her friends'.[89] The timing of the expedition passing through may have aligned with her own plans to travel to the area for this alliance. Perhaps this was what was discussed with the senior man before Turandurey and Ballandella joined the expedition? The gift of the expedition to her, according

---

85   Mitchell 1839, 10 August 1836: 211 (original emphasis).
86   Mitchell 1839, 19 September 1836: 162.
87   Mitchell 1839, 3 July 1836: 163.
88   Stapylton 1986, 7 November 1836: 235. For other theories regarding what may have happened to Turandurey and her daughter after the expedition, see Brook 1988.
89   Stapylton 1986: 235; Mitchell 1839: 335, citing Stapylton's report of 11 November, near Guy's station on the Murrumbidgee.

to Stapylton, was a couple of leftover blankets. While this may seem small recompense for her efforts, the blankets may have proved useful to her for trading or had symbolic importance.

In his Port Davey expedition journal, Robinson wrote a revealing passage about one of the women guides:

> Followed my female companion through wood sand morasses, over hills &c for about five miles. On ascending a hill my guides descried a smoke at considerable distance rising out of a thick forest … In a short time she called out *Too gee borer* [black man's fire]. Asked me if I did not see it? Said no. Took the glass and just discerned a small smoke rising out of a wood.[90]

Sometimes we need guidance to see more, to assess from other perspectives, to have our attention drawn to a wisp in the distance. Trying to find out about Aboriginal women's involvement in expeditions is something like this kind of looking. They are not always obviously present, but if we look hard and do not presume they are always in hiding or absent, we may see glimpses of them.

That Aboriginal women provided crucial guidance for some expeditions is clear. Close examination of some explorer accounts reveals some indications of the range of work they did and suggests possible readings of their reasons for involvement. In the cases discussed, the Aboriginal women guides were represented as providing vital provision support, directions to water, the names of places and geographical details. Their services in translation, guarding, diplomacy, humour and care for members of the party are also evident. In the Tasmanian examples particularly, their ability as swimmers and divers was crucial to the expedition's progress. In both cases, the women's knowledge of country, observation skills and their ability to communicate and negotiate proved important to the very movement of the expedition. The women's talents in managing cross-cultural relationships, etiquette and negotiation appear to have been particularly valued by these expedition leaders. It may have been the case that as women, there was less chance of their presence being interpreted as a threat by groups that the expeditions approached, especially those in dispute with each other. Harder to locate are the women's reasons for engaging in the expeditions, though some hints

---

90 Robinson 2008: 175.

can be found. Seeing family and relations appears to have been a key motivation for many of them and the journeys may have been familiar rituals for some of them at least. Visiting country for seasonal resources and for marriage/inter-group arrangements seem likely reasons for men and women alike to have been travelling in particular areas, dovetailing with expedition timing. Gaining new experiences, knowledge and status may have been significant too. The search for the smoke and fire of their stories needs to continue.

Acknowledgement

Many thanks to Tiffany Shellam for her constructive criticism and suggestions.

References

Anderson, Ian 1995, 'Reclaiming TRU-GAN- NANER: Decolonising the symbol', in *Speaking Positions: Aboriginality, Ethnicity and Gender in Australian Cultural Studies*, Penny Van Toorn and David English (eds), Department of Humanities, Victoria University of Technology, Melbourne: 31–42.

—— 2008, 'The people with no history?', in *Reading Robinson: Companion Essays to George Augustus Robinson's Friendly Mission*, Anna Johnson and Mitchell Rolls (eds), Quintus Publishing, Hobart.

Baker, Don 1993, 'John Piper: Conqueror of the interior', *Aboriginal History* 17(1): 17–37.

—— 1997, *The Civilised Surveyor: Thomas Mitchell and the Australian Aborigines*, Melbourne University Press, Carlton, Vic.

—— 1998, 'Exploring with Aborigines: Thomas Mitchell and his Aboriginal guides', *Aboriginal History* 22: 36–50.

Batman, John 1830, John Batman's Diary, from 3 March 1830, National Library of Australia.

Birkett, Deborah 1989, *Spinsters Abroad: Victorian Lady Explorers*, Basil Blackwell, Oxford.

Blunt, Alison 1994, *Travel, Gender and Imperialism: Mary Kingsley and West Africa*, Guilford, New York and London.

Boyce, James 2008, *Van Diemen's Land*, Black Inc., Melbourne.

Brock, Daniel George 1975, *To the Desert with Sturt: A Diary of the 1844 Expedition*, Kenneth Peake-Jones (ed.), Royal Geographical Society of Australasia, South Australian Branch, Adelaide.

Brook, Jack 1988, 'The widow and the child', *Aboriginal History* 12: 63–78.

Burnett, D. Graham 2000, 'Exploration, performance, alliance: Robert Schomburgk in British Guiana', *Journal of Caribbean Studies* 15(1&2): 11–37.

—— 2002, '"It is impossible to make a step without the Indians": nineteenth-century geographical exploration and the Amerindians of British Guiana', *Ethnohistory* 49: 3–40.

Calvert, Albert 1895 *The Exploration of Australia*, George Philip and Son, London, Liverpool.

Carnegie, David W. 1898, *Spinifex and Sand*, C. Arthur Pearson, London.

Cathcart, Michael 2001, 'Exploration by land', in *The Oxford Companion to Australian History*, Graeme Davison, John Hirst and Stuart MacIntyre (eds), revised edition, Oxford University Press, Melbourne.

Clarke, Philip 2008, *Aboriginal Plant Collectors: Botanists and Australian Aboriginal People in the Nineteenth Century*, Rosenberg Publishing, Dural, NSW.

Colville, Berres Hoddle 2004, *Robert Hoddle: Pioneer Surveyor 1794–1881*, Research Publications, Vermont, Vic.

Douglas, Bronwen 2009, 'In the event: Indigenous countersigns and the ethnohistory of voyaging', in *Oceanic Encounters: Exchange, Desire, Violence*, Margaret Jolly, Serge Tcherkezoff, Darrell Tryon (eds), ANU E Press, Canberra.

—— 2014, *Science, Voyages, and Encounters in Oceania, 1511–1850*, Palgrave Macmillan, New York.

Driver, Felix 2012, 'Hidden histories made visible? Reflections on a geographical exhibition', *Transactions of the Institute of British Geographers* 38(3): 420–435.

Driver, Felix and Lowri Jones 2009, *Hidden Histories of Exploration: Researching the RGS-IBG Collections*, Royal Holloway, University of London in association with the Royal Geographic Society and IBG, Kensington Gore, London.

Fabian, Johannes 2000, *Out of Our Minds: Reason and Madness in the Exploration of Central Africa*, University of California Press, Berkeley.

Favenc, Ernest 1888, *History of Australian Exploration from 1788 to 1888 compiled from state documents, private papers, and the most authentic sources*, Griffith, Farran, Okeden & Welsh, London; Turner & Henderson, Sydney.

Grant, James 1973, *The narrative of a voyage of discovery, performed in His Majesty's vessel The Lady Nelson, of sixty tons burthen, with sliding keels, in the years 1800, 1801, and 1802, to New South Wales*, Libraries Board of South Australia, Adelaide.

Graves, J. W. 1876, 'Trucanini's story of herself', letter to the editor, *Mercury* (Hobart), 6 June 1876: 3.

Greenblatt, Stephen 1991, *Marvelous Possessions: The Wonder of the New World*, University of Chicago Press.

Hann, Frank Hugh 1998, *Do Not Yield to Despair: Frank Hugh Hann's Exploration Diaries in the Arid Interior of Australia, 1895–1908*, Mike Donaldson and Ian Elliot (comps and eds), Hesperian Press, Carlisle, WA.

Hassell, Ethel 1975, *My Dusky Friends*, C.W. Hassell, Fremantle, WA.

Howitt, William 1865, *The History of discovery in Australia, Tasmania and New Zealand: from the earliest date to the present day; with maps of the recent explorations, from official sources*, Longman, Green, London.

Kennedy, Dane 2013, *The Last Blank Spaces: Exploring Africa and Australia*, Harvard University Press, Cambridge, MA.

Konishi, Shino 2008, '"Wanton with plenty": Questioning ethnohistorical constructions of sexual savagery in Aboriginal societies', *Australian Historical Studies* 39(3): 356–372.

Leichhardt, Ludwig 1847, *Journal of an expedition to the interior from Moreton Bay to Port Essington, a distance of upwards of 3000 miles, during the years 1844–1845*, T. & W. Boone, London.

Long, Charles R. 1903, *Stories of Australian Exploration*, Whitcombe and Tombs, Melbourne.

McGrath, Ann 1990, 'White man's looking glass', *Australian Historical Studies* 24(95): 189–206.

Metcalf, Alida C. 2005, *Go-Betweens and the Colonization of Brazil: 1500–1600*, University of Texas Press, Austin.

Miller, Linn and Patsy Cameron 2011, 'Telling Places in Country (TPIC): Historical Biographies', Australian Institute of Aboriginal and Torres Strait Islander Studies and University of Tasmania, www.utas.edu.au/telling-places-in-country/historical-context/historical-biographies.

Mills, Sara 1991, *Discourses of Difference: An analysis of women's travel writing and colonialism*, Routledge, London.

Mitchell, Thomas 1838, 'Three expeditions into the interior of Eastern Australia &c.', *The Athenæum*, 6 October, 571: 725–728.

—— 1839, *Three expeditions in the interior of Australia With Descriptions of the Recently Explored Region of Australia Felix and of the Present Colony of New South Wales*, vol. 2, T. & W. Boone, London.

—— 1848, *Journal of an expedition into the tropical interior in search of a Route from Sydney to the Gulf of Carpentaria*, Longman, Brown, Green and London.

Moore, George Fletcher 1836a, 'A new river discovered by the Hon. G. F. Moore, Esq on a recent excursion to the northward', *The Perth Gazette and Western Australian Journal*, Saturday 14 May 1836, 692–693.

—— 1836b, 'A new river discovered by the Hon. G. F. Moore, Esq, on a recent excursion to the northwood', *The Sydney Monitor*, 13 August 1836, 3.

—— 1884, *Diary of ten years eventful life of an early settler in Western Australia and also a descriptive vocabulary of the Language of the Aborigines*, M. Walbrook, London.

Pratt, Mary Louise 1992, *Imperial Eyes: Travel Writing and Transculturation*, Routledge, London.

Pridden, William 1843, *Australia: Its History and Present Condition*, J. Burns, London.

Reynolds, Henry 1980, The Land, the Explorers and the Aborigines, *Historical Studies* 19 (75): 213–226.

—— 1990, *With the White People: The Crucial Role of Aborigines in the Exploration and Development of Australia*, Penguin, Ringwood, Vic.

—— 1995, *Fate of a Free People*, Penguin, Camberwell, Vic.

—— 2006, *The Other Side of the Frontier: Aboriginal Resistance to the European Invasion of Australia*, revised edition, UNSW Press, Sydney.

—— 2012, *A History of Tasmania*, Cambridge University Press, Port Melbourne.

Robinson, George Augustus 2008, *Friendly Mission: The Tasmanian Journals and Papers of George Augustus Robinson, 1829–1834*, N. J. B. Plomley (ed.), Queen Victoria Museum and Art Gallery, Launceston; Quintus, Hobart.

Rockel, Stephen J. 2000, 'Enterprising partners: Caravan women in nineteenth century Tanzania', *Canadian Journal of African Studies* 34(3): 748–778.

Roller, Heather F. 2010, 'Colonial collecting expeditions and the pursuit of opportunities in the Amazonian *Seratao* c. 1750–1800', *The Americas* 66(4): 435–467.

Rowan, Ellis 1898, *A Flowerhunter in Australia and New Zealand*, Angus & Robertson, Sydney.

Russell, Lynette 2012, *Roving Mariners: Australian Aboriginal Whalers and Sealers in the Southern Oceans, 1790–1870*, State University of New York Press, Albany.

Ryan, Lyndall 1981, *The Aboriginal Tasmanians*, University of Queensland Press, St Lucia.

—— 1986, 'Aboriginal women and agency in the process of conquest: A review of some recent work', *Australian Feminist Studies* 1(2): 35–43.

—— 2012, *Tasmanian Aborigines: A History since 1803*, Allen & Unwin, Crows Nest, NSW.

Ryan, Simon 1996, *The Cartographic Eye: How Explorers Saw Australia*, Cambridge University Press, Cambridge.

Schaeffer, Kay 2001, 'Handkerchief diplomacy: E.J. Eyre and sexual politics on the South Australian frontier', in *Colonial Frontiers: Indigenous–European Encounters in Settler Societies*, Lynette Russell (ed.), Manchester University Press, Manchester: 134–50.

Shellam, Tiffany 2009, *Shaking Hands on the Fringe: Negotiating the Aboriginal World at King George's Sound*, UWA Publishing, Perth.

Stapylton, Granville 1986, Stapylton with Major Mitchell's Australia Felix expedition, 1836, largely from the journal of Granville William Chetwynd Staplyton, Andrews, Alan E. J. (ed.), Blubber Head Press, Hobart.

Sturt, Charles 1965 [1849], *Narrative of an expedition into Central Australia, 1844, 1845, 1846*, vol. 1, facsimile edition [T. & W. Boone, London].

Tcherkézoff, Serge 2009, 'A reconsideration of the role of Polynesian women in early encounters with Europeans: supplement to Marshall Sahlins' voyage around the islands of history', in *Oceanic Encounters: Exchange, Desire, Violence*, Margaret Jolly, Serge Tcherkezoff and Darrell Tryon (eds), ANU E Press, Canberra.

Wisnicki, Adrian 2010, 'Rewriting agency: Samuel Baker, Bunyoro-Kitara and the Egyptian slave trade', *Studies in Travel Writing* 14(1): 1–27.

6

Bobby Roberts: Intermediary and outlaw of Western Australia's south coast

Clint Bracknell

Reinterpreting and juxtaposing a variety of colonial accounts from the south coast of Western Australia reveals particular Aboriginal individuals as active agents engaged in cross-cultural exchange motivated by their own interests, albeit with increasingly limited options.[1] The story of Bobby Roberts may be viewed as an example of such Aboriginal agency exercised in the early colonial context. A Noongar man from the south coast region of Western Australia,[2] Bobby assisted colonial interests as a guide and, later, a 'native constable'. However, colonial authorities also knew him as a brazen criminal.[3]

His former employer, the Surveyor General of Western Australia John Septimus Roe, once lauded the 'instinctive sagacity' of his 'sable friend'.[4] However, it may be argued Bobby's services were not proffered from naivety or 'instinct', but in the calculated hope of advancing his

---

1   Shellam 2009.
2   A term used to describe Aboriginal people and language from the south-west of Western Australia, see Douglas 1976: 5; Collard and Bracknell 2012; Bracknell 2013.
3   Scott and Brown 2005; *Inquirer*, 7 May 1851; 2 July 1851.
4   Roe 1852: 37.

position and authority in the emerging cross-cultural arena. Although clearly a complex and talented man, impressively improvising within a brutal historical context,[5] mention of Bobby's name is largely omitted from colonial records and he remains a controversial and tragic figure in Noongar oral histories.[6] Comparing the oral and written sources suggests a narrative of Bobby's early engagement with colonial interests, his subsequent resistance to and conditional accommodation of colonial authorities, and his growing disillusionment.

While he was reportedly the son of a man named 'Jerrymumup',[7] Bobby's great-granddaughter Hazel Brown (née Roberts) explains to her nephew Kim Scott, '[w]e don't know his Noongar name; we only know the name the police gave him. Old Bobby worked with the police ... and he went with the explorers'.[8] While it may *dance* around specific details, as most good stories do, Brown's oral accounts of her ancestor provide a Noongar ideological framework to guide the analysis of colonial source material. Her perspective enriches archival references to Bobby Roberts, providing contextual information and impressions of what colonists and Noongar thought of him:

> Bobby, he went with ... Roe, and they made him a good man. He done a stealing but they forgave him ... they pardoned him, after he been in trouble. He was like a boss-man, he kept the Noongars intact, and kept law and order, you know.
>
> Daddy used to say that great-grandfather was a good man, and the white people liked him because he helped the white people a lot, but he said most Noongar people hated the sight of him, because he used to go and grab the people what did wrong.[9]

Brown certainly conveys the impression of Bobby as a complicated, conflicted figure on the frontier.

---

5   Gifford 2002.
6   *West Australian*, 1936; Scott and Brown 2005.
7   *Perth Gazette and Independent Journal*, 4 January 1850.
8   Scott and Brown 2005: 32.
9   Scott and Brown 2005: 49–50.

Bobby the intermediary

John Septimus Roe is responsible for the earliest written accounts of Bobby, recorded in his expedition journal as they travelled together along the south coast of Western Australia, from Cape Riche to Cape Arid from late 1848 until early 1849. The writing of Australian explorers, argues Simon Ryan, was informed by 'pre-existent discourses' and, 'filled with pre-formed tropes, which ingest and normalize that which is seen on explorations'.[10] In light of this, as described by Henry Reynolds, Aboriginal people were subsequently cast in two apparently contradictory roles in the saga of Australian exploration.[11] The construct of Australian explorers engaged in a 'great war with the forces of nature'[12] relied not just on the wild and inhospitable environment, but also on the imminent threat of attack from the 'still wilder and more miserable savage'.[13] Conversely, the other typical Aboriginal trope was that of the explorer's guide, his 'loyal and faithful servant – Forrest's Windich, Eyre's Wylie, Kennedy's Jacky-Jacky – who illustrated the benign consequences of acculturation'.[14] However, despite the power relationship writers often impose upon their guides, Bobby is neither a silent nor benign presence in Roe's journal.

J. S. Roe remained in the role of Surveyor General until 1871, his impressive networks and political position making him especially influential in opening up Western Australia to pastoral interests.[15] Roe completed an array of expeditions, including some in the south coast region, around Albany in 1831 accompanied by Nakina, 'chief' of the Albany tribe, and in the vicinity of Doubtful Island Bay (including West Mount Barren) in 1835 with the Noongar guide Manyat.[16]

In his final expedition journal, describing country including the Fitzgerald, Ravensthorpe, Esperance and Cape Arid regions of south coast Western Australia from September 1848 to February 1849,

---

10   Ryan 1996: 17.
11   Reynolds 1980.
12   Murdoch 1929: 129.
13   Eden 1875: 2.
14   Reynolds 1980: 214.
15   *Inquirer and Commercial News*, 1 February 1871.
16   Shoobert 2005.

Roe mentions Bobby, who accompanied him from 2 October to 7 January, more often than any of the 'Aboriginal guides' he employed on that or any prior expedition.

Roe's paternalistic tone is typical of the era, although his growing respect for Bobby is revealed over the course of the journal. He concedes that he 'deferred to the native's judgement' when deciding which path to take up the Philips River. Furthermore, and based on 'the authority of our native',[17] he describes where a major branch of that river originates. Roe's use of the term 'authority' indicates his respect for Bobby's superior geographical knowledge and perhaps reveals Roe's impression of Bobby's high standing in both the Noongar and colonial communities. Later, when Bobby offered advice on the difficulties of travelling up river through the Fitzgerald region, Roe writes 'I learnt from our native … this changed my first intention … and induced me to proceed next day in the opposite direction'.[18] By this stage of the journey, Roe is more actively including information about Bobby's impact on the navigation process, signifying growing respect for his guide. In Roe's account, although a relatively young man, Bobby displays confidence and knowledge over a vast expanse of country, indicating impressive networks and influence of his own.

Roe's introduction of 'Bob' seems to suggest he had a considerable reputation among colonists even before joining the expedition party:

> I have succeeded in engaging … an intelligent native lad of this district, known as 'Bob,' from whom I expect to derive valuable information as to the nature of the country as far as it is known to him.[19]

Roe wrote this from Cape Riche where he was the guest of entrepreneur George Cheyne. Cheyne had arrived to 'take up land' at Albany in 1831 when the site, initially established as a British military camp in 1826, was gradually becoming a base for colonial expansion. Shortly after arriving, Cheyne claimed that he was on 'friendly terms' with Noongar, although he acknowledged the apparently frequent need to use 'coercive measures' to maintain his 'rights'.[20] After selling some of his property to Captain J. Hassell in 1840, Cheyne moved

---

17 Roe 1852: 26, 35.
18 Roe 1852: 45.
19 *Perth Gazette and Independent Journal*, 28 October 1848.
20 Scott and Brown 2005: 36–37.

east to make Cape Riche the centre of his pastoral and sandalwood enterprises, while providing an alternative port for the increasing number of whaling and sealing vessels in the region. His apparent recommendation of Bobby for Roe's expedition party signals the continuation of similar 'friendly', albeit 'coercive' relationships with Noongar in the Cape Riche area.

Prior to Roe's expedition, contact between Noongar and visitors to the area east of Cape Riche had been mostly limited to various interactions with crew from American, French and British ships travelling along the coast.[21] In 1841, Edward Eyre and the young Noongar guide Wylie, journeyed westward via the southern coast from Fowler's Bay in South Australia to Albany, meeting 'very few natives, and those for the most part … timid but well disposed'.[22] In his expedition report, Eyre provided an early description of the eastern extremity of the Noongar language region:

> The language spoken by them [Aboriginal people encountered] is exactly similar to that of the natives at King George's Sound [Albany] as far as the Promontory of Cape 'Le Grand,' and similarly may probably extend to the commencement of the Great Cliffs, in about longitude $124\frac{1}{2}$ degrees E [Cape Arid]. A little beyond this point the language is totally different, and the boy 'Wylie' could not understand a word of it.[23]

Bobby's various interactions with other Aboriginal people encountered on the journey with Roe confirms the accuracy of Eyre's observations about the eastern limits of Noongar language at Cape Arid.

Roe described Bobby confidently attempting to initiate communication with local Noongar over the duration of the expedition. However, only two instances of actual conversation were documented: Roe stated that information about the interior was obtained from 'some natives we fell in with' around Esperance Bay;[24] and, on an earlier occasion, that Noongar from all along the south coast met the expedition:

---

21 Gibbs 2003.
22 *Perth Gazette*, 7 August 1841.
23 *Perth Gazette*, 7 August 1841.
24 Roe 1852: 23.

> While at the camp, a Cape Riche native known as 'Bob', who had been engaged to form one of our party to the eastward, was visited by several of his friends from Doubtful Island Bay, and other parts, including two who had walked with him from what he represented to be the neighbourhood of Middle Island.[25]

'Middle Island' is the largest island of the Recherche Archipelago, off the coast of Cape Arid, at the eastern extremity of the Noongar language region. Bobby was clearly an important link to the geography, language and people of the country Roe intended to 'explore'.

In light of this, Roe also indicated that he already considered Bobby more reliable than other potential informants, for he 'could gather from them nothing more as to the nature of the interior country than "Bob" himself was able to communicate'.[26] He affirmed his confidence in Bobby, admitting that he 'did not regret [his] inability to engage the proffered services of one of the two who offered to accompany' him.[27] This guide had previously accompanied two geologists who had surveyed the Fitzgerald region prior to Roe's expedition in an unsuccessful attempt to find a 'supposed coal field' he had told them about.[28] Roe's confidence in his principle guide was rewarded, as Bobby 'assured' him that he knew the exact location where 'his friends had told him' they had witnessed a French whaler procuring coal.[29] After almost a week travelling west, 'all former toils and sufferings were amply rewarded by the discovery of extensive beds of coal, occupying the lowest levels in the channel of the river'.[30] Thanks to Bobby's guidance, Roe reported the existence of coal near Cullham Inlet on the Phillips River.[31]

This episode displays Bobby's intricate knowledge of not only his country but also what was happening within it, no doubt due to close communicative relationships across the coastal region. However,

---

25 Roe 1852: 3.
26 Roe 1852: 3.
27 Roe 1852: 3.
28 '… a native who told us he had been on board a French ship lying at anchor … east … of Doubtful Island Bay … [H]e said, they had met with a seam of black stuff of the banks of the river, which they conveyed in bags on board the ship, and it turned out to be coal of the same description as he, the native, had seen at Sydney and Hobart Town.' *Perth Gazette and Independent Journal*, 29 July 1848.
29 Roe 1852: 32; *Inquirer*, 7 February 1849.
30 Roe 1852: 36.
31 *Perth Gazette and Independent Journal*, 10 February 1849.

as Roe led his party of colonists further inland, seemingly in areas where the local people had not yet encountered British colonists, Bobby Roberts's ability to communicate with other Aboriginal people was not always so effective. For instance, on one occasion north-east of Esperance, Roe reported:

> [We] came suddenly upon a small fire, which had just been abandoned by some natives. The embers were under my feet before they were discovered and the country was so thick that I did not immediately perceive near them several long bark baskets, tied up at the extremities, and filled with honey flowers, which the natives had been employed in collecting. Their retreat was so hasty that they had even left behind two carved and well-greased 'womeras,' used in discharging their spears, nor could hey be induced by loud calls and invitations of our native to return and give us an interview. We therefore placed some biscuit in their baskets, left everything as we found it and proceeded on our way, Bob being divided in opinion that they would either have taken us for devils and would never venture near the spot again, or that they were concealed at the time within a few yards of it.[32]

It was not uncommon for explorers to describe arriving at places only to find that the Aboriginal people appeared to have made a hasty retreat. Yet it did not mean that they had left and were not there, but rather, as Reynolds and Hallam point out, they would often track and observe the interlopers, communicating their movements to neighbouring Aboriginal groups via smoke signals.[33] Roe reflected the unease that this practice instilled in the explorers:

> We had on several occasions reason to suppose that the natives were aware of our vicinity as we passed through the country, and were even watching our movements, but we saw none of them … although we … observed their signal smokes rise suddenly up within a mile and a half of us soon after we had passed.[34]

This incident occurred as the party travelled eastward toward the Russell Ranges, which lie inland from Cape Arid.[35] Due to this location constituting something of a linguistic boundary,[36] it is possible that the Aboriginal people encountered primarily spoke

---

32 Roe 1852: 15.
33 Reynolds 1982; *Hallam* 1983.
34 Roe 1852: 15.
35 *Inquirer*, 7 February 1849.
36 Bracknell 2014.

Ngadju, the neighbouring Aboriginal language to the eastern extent of the Noongar language region. However, given the multilingualism prevalent among Aboriginal people,[37] it is equally as likely these people understood Bobby's calls and were too overawed and cautious to actively respond.

Roe's journal indicates that most local Aboriginal people encountered on the expedition preferred to observe rather than be observed. At Young River, he observed that '[t]racks and fires of the natives were numerous in this vicinity, but none showed themselves'.[38] Furthermore, exploring the upper branches of the Phillips River, he had:

> reason to believe that our repast was overlooked by a party of natives from the rising ground above, whose suppressed voices reached the acute and practiced ears of Bob, but whose presence could be nowhere discovered on our searching and calling out.[39]

However, it is entirely plausible that local Aboriginal people had opportunities to converse with Bobby unbeknownst to the rest of the expedition party. On numerous occasions, Roe trusted Bobby to scout ahead of the party or left him alone to tend the horses.[40] After all, Bobby was not a stranger in this country.

Scratching a small hole in the sand

Henry Reynolds observes, 'While they remained on traditional land, Aborigines retained an unmatched knowledge of their environment, related expertise and a resulting self-confidence which Europeans found hard to understand'.[41] Reynolds has described explorers relying on Aboriginal knowledge of the environment, resources, languages and diplomacy, although McLaren and Cooper have argued that because of the extremely local nature of this knowledge, Aboriginal guides were less useful to explorers the further they travelled from their home region.[42] Tellingly, Roe gave more credit to Bobby as the journey

---

37 Dixon 1980.
38 Roe 1852: 27.
39 Roe 1852: 33–34.
40 Roe 1852: 19, 39, 43.
41 Reynolds 1980: 225.
42 McLaren and Cooper 1996.

progressed, increasingly impressed by his ability to locate water and well-grassed country the further they travelled from Cape Riche, where he initially joined the party. Near Culham Inlet, Roe wrote:

> Bob remembered to have drunk fresh water from a well amongst good feed for the horses ... we reached it and were afforded another proof of the unerring memory and instinctive sagacity of our aboriginal native, in thus being able in so intricate a part of the country, almost totally unknown to him, to walk direct to a small water-hole, entirely concealed from view amongst tufts of grass.[43]

In assuming the Culham Inlet area was 'almost totally unknown' to his guide, Roe seems to have underestimated how well travelled and informed Bobby already was before their expedition together. Indeed, the knowledge of country he shares indicates familiarity with the whole south coast region, from Albany to Cape Arid.

Over 150 kilometres west of Culham Inlet at Mt Barren, Bobby again displayed intricate knowledge of country: 'We found most tempting little pools of fresh-water in the pure sand amongst the limestone rocks and our native said that good water was always procurable here by scratching a small hole in the sand.'[44]

Roe's account of Bobby reveals that the knowledge he shared went beyond the environmental and resource information Aboriginal guides shared with explorers elsewhere in Australia, as discussed by Reynolds and Hallam.[45] Bobby displays a full awareness of the recent history and goings-on across the south coast region from Albany to Cape Arid. When Roe's party encounters a skeleton near the coast, Bobby knew the story of how it got be there:

> Our native immediately explained they were the remains of one of three seamen who had quitted a Hobart Town whaler some 18 months ago in the vicinity of Middle Island for the purpose of walking to Albany, a distance fully 350 miles at the shortest ... they became much distressed for fresh water, and at length separated to search for it more inland ... but they never did so re-join or see each other ... The natives seemed to have been fully aware of the death ... and ascribe it to actual starvation and exhaustion, disclaiming most strongly having used any

---

43 Roe 1852: 37.
44 Roe 1852: 42.
45 Reynolds 1982; Hallam 1983.

personal violence, but on the contrary, having endeavoured to assist the only one of them they saw before his death, who had, however, though fear or distrust invariably pointed his gun when any of the natives offered to approach him. The unfortunate man now before us was said to be one of them, the other lying somewhere in the sandhills to the E., in a spot which our native did not profess to know.[46]

Reflecting on the disturbing incident, Roe remarked that the death might have been avoided if the unfortunate party had known that water was 'in abundance within a stones throw, by scratching a small hole in the sand'.[47] Roe's reiteration of Bobby's instructions reveals the significant impression his guide has made.

A place called Jerramungup

Bobby was clearly more than a navigator and go-between, as he also provided Roe with valuable information on both the potential for mining and farming in the area. Roe named the best-grassed river system Bobby led him to after Western Australia's governor, Fitzgerald, as it was 'more important than any they had fallen in with during their researches, and capable of conferring the greatest benefits on the colony'.[48] He named various landmarks after prominent colonial officials and members of the expedition party, even naming 'Mount Ney', north-west of Esperance, after his favourite horse. Yet Roe did not name anything after his Noongar guide. While his descriptions of Bobby reveal Roe's respect for the knowledge he provides, it seems that Roe either did not hold particular sentimental affection for his guide, or simply assumed that Bobby was too naïve of the practice to appreciate having a place named after him.

One of the few areas for which Roe recorded a geographical name of Noongar origin happened to be 'beautiful country as richly grassed as any that is known in the colony'.[49] Roe writes, 'We were gladdened by the view of a large tract of good grassy country to the N.E., lightly timbered, and at this time well-watered by a river and its numerous

---

46   Roe 1852: 49.
47   Roe 1852: 50.
48   *Inquirer*, 7 February 1849.
49   *Inquirer*, 7 February 1849.

branches. It is known to the natives as Jeer-a-mung-up'.⁵⁰ As he was the only Noongar in the expedition party, one can assume that Bobby informed Roe as to the 'native' name for what arguably proved to be the most important 'discovery' of the expedition. Asserting a name for this particular place arguably indicates Bobby's growing awareness of colonial land values and is an attempt at undermining or subverting Roe's colonisation of the landscape with his own language.

An 1850 news report names Bobby and his father 'Jerrymumup', the 'headman' of the local 'tribe' of the Fitzgerald region.⁵¹ In other reports from this era, Hassell's station is also reported as being called 'Jerrymumup', likely an alternate spelling of the 'Jeer-a-mung-up', originally recorded by Roe. It is unusual for Noongar geographical nomenclature to be derived from the names of individuals.⁵² Supplying Roe with the name is perhaps a sign of Bobby recognising the new power dynamics after the British arrival, indicating the place discussed was his father's territory and making a new strategic claim for himself.⁵³ Furthermore, Bobby would have been privy to the conversations Roe and his party engaged in when deciding to name rivers, mountains and other geographical features after each other, or respected colonial authorities. Bobby may even have seized upon this imported British practice and emulated it, naming the most 'beautiful country' in the region after its custodian, a respected figure in the community, the 'headman', his father.

By the time the party return to Cape Riche, Roe has grown dependant upon the advice and assistance of his guide.⁵⁴ After a few days respite, Roe proposed to commence the journey back to Perth via Albany, but on 7 January 1849:

> it was then found that our native had become tired of the service on which he had been engaged, and had gone to re-join his tribe. Finding it impossible to replace him without much loss of time, I had

---

50   Roe 1852: 5. Jeer-u-mung-up, later to be officially spelled Jerramungup, is translated as *yira-mo-up*, literally 'up high, yate tree, place' in Forrest and Crowe 1996. It could just as likely be *yira-mangart*, 'up high, jam tree'. *Mangart*, or the jam tree – *Acacia acuminata* – is referred to in Scott and Brown 2005.
51   *Perth Gazette and Independent Journal*, 4 January 1850.
52   Collard and Bracknell 2012.
53   Konishi (2012) describes Bennelong making similar strategic claims in the Port Jackson area.
54   Scott and Brown 2005.

to abandon my intentions of taking a new route ... as all the parties agreed in assuring me that fresh water was then extremely scarce along that line, and could only be found by the aid of a native.[55]

Despite the prejudices of the time, Roe seemed to have been particularly impressed by this particular Noongar guide. However, he still underestimated Bobby Roberts.

On 19 January 1849, travelling back to Perth, he witnessed 'Mr. Hassell transferring his principal station to the fine country we had discovered on the 22nd of October, at Jeer-a-mung-up, on the Fitz-Gerald'.[56] Hazel Brown explains, 'Bobby was the one that took Hassells to Jerramungup and showed them the place there'.[57] It seems Bobby may not have left the expedition 'to re-join his tribe' because he was 'tired'; he left to inform the shipping merchant and emerging pastoralist Captain J. Hassell about good grazing land at the place he told Roe was called 'Jeer-a-mung-up'.[58] Clendinnen and Konishi have discussed instances where Aboriginal people elsewhere in Australia have been effective at repeatedly misleading the British to achieve their own ends because of inherent colonial assumptions that Aboriginal people would be too naïve to operate so strategically.[59] Roe wrote nothing to indicate he recognised that Bobby had abandoned him to assist Hassell claim Jerramungup, perhaps indicating similar underestimation of his guide's judicious thinking.

Hassel had been cultivating relationships with Noongar intermediaries for some time, says Hazel Brown:

> See, Hassells went looking for Aboriginal people. Well, for land I s'pose it was. They made friends with people from Bremer Bay, and some of them were camped up at Hunter River. That was Grandfather Bobby; he was there, old Grandfather Bobby Roberts. (His son Pirrup was also called Bob.) They made friends with him ... and he went away on an expedition looking for property for Hassells ... Well, when they came back they settled for Jerramungup. Bobby was only a young man then.[60]

55　Roe 1852: 53.
56　Roe 1852: 54.
57　Scott and Brown 2005: 57.
58　Scott and Brown 2005: 43–44.
59　Konishi 2012; Clendinnen 2003.
60　Scott and Brown 2005: 49.

As a young man, Bobby was making alliances. He was travelling to the eastern extremity of his language region and strengthening networks along the south coast, perhaps accruing a powerful reputation among locals via his association with Roe's expedition party. As Hazel Brown also explains, 'They were all taking womans back in those days, and dumping them, bringing another woman back'.[61] As Captain Hassell's daughter-in-law would later document, marriages between people from distant locations were common and preferable among Aboriginal people in the south coast region.[62] Bobby exploited his position as an intermediary to further his own interests, likely using his journeys eastward to facilitate and maintain relationships of the *most* intimate nature. Even though Roe may have respected Bobby, he seems to have assumed that his guide was simply happy to help, that the assistance he provided was 'instinctive'.[63] In an era of rapid change, Bobby was looking for strategic partnerships.

On 19 May 1849, A. C. Gregory reported again finding coal at Culhum Inlet accompanied by a 'native', named 'Bob'. As their supplies became scarce, they discharged Bobby and returned to Cape Riche. Hoping to set out again, they were told Bobby was at 'Polyungup Spring, thirty miles distant'. After following his track 75 miles without overtaking him they gave up pursuit and returned to Perth.[64] This abandoned expedition seems to have constituted a turning point for Bobby. By disrespectfully dismissing his 'guide' when supplies became scarce, Gregory may have inadvertently impacted on Bobby's willingness to provide assistance to newcomers and provided impetus to actively resist their encroachment onto his country.

'Cape Riche Bobby' the outlaw

On 30 November 1849, John Williams, a shepherd working around Jerramungup on the Fitzgerald River, where Hassel had since 'formed extensive sheep stations', claimed three men, 'Jerrymumup and his

---

61 Scott and Brown 2005: 57.
62 Hassell 1936, 1975.
63 Roe 1852: 37.
64 *Perth Gazette and Independent Journal*, 1 June 1849.

son Bobby, and Bulliah, a very large native',[65] arranged for a young boy to steal his ammunition and subsequently stole his sheep. Having fled the Fitzgerald region to Albany, Williams stated:

> I saw a native with my gun in his hand ... and I have every reason to believe that all the other party are murdered ... The natives were making smokes all the way down the coast, which I understand to be calling the natives together.[66]

On 14 December, a messenger arrived at Albany with news that two of the shepherds had been accidentally wounded in the ensuing panic, but that the Aboriginal 'thieves' had not injured the shepherds, just scared them away and taken possession of their huts.

While 'Jerrymumup' or 'Jerramungup' is described as the 'headman' of the 'tribe', his son Bobby seems to be have been at the forefront of the emerging resistance in the Fitzgerald region. On 16 April 1951, a report from Albany stated:

> The natives have had so much of their own way lately, that half measures will not do with them now; for instance, a party of them came to one of the stations on the Salt River a few days ago, and they were driving away about 20 of the sheep; the shepherd pointed a gun that he had at them to frighten them, but instead of which, they came all round him with their spears fixed, and told him if he did not put it down, they would spear him; he put the gun down, and one that goes by the name of Cape Riche Bobby, and who is leader of a strong party of the natives, took hold of the gun, and took out the flint; returned the ramrod, and sprung it in the barrel; finding there was nothing in the gun, he said to the shepherd 'that gun nothing in him; you cannot shoot him; all the same [as a] piece of wood', and then threw the gun away from him ... Cape Riche Bobby was considered to be an intelligent and well behaved native, and I believe Mr. Roe found him very useful when exploring to the eastward, but there is no dependence to be put in them; the more they find out our ways, the more daring they get to misbehave ...[67]

This account saw 'Roe's Bob', the intelligent and loyal guide, transformed into the outlaw 'Cape Riche Bobby'. While the *Inquirer* asserts that the two Bobs are one and the same, Aboriginal oral histories

---

65 *Perth Gazette and Independent Journal*, 4 January 1850.
66 *Perth Gazette and Independent Journal*, 4 January 1850.
67 *Inquirer*, 7 May 1851.

complicate their identities. Hazel Brown uses the name 'Cape Riche Bobby' to refer to two local contemporaries of her ancestor: a man who was killed and from whom Bobby Roberts stole a promised wife; and an 'old blind man'.[68] However, archival records suggest that these 'Bobbys' Brown mentions are likely to be 'Doubtful Island Bobby' who was murdered in 1859,[69] and 'Candyup Bobby', an old man also known as 'Blind Bobby', who died in 1898.[70] Such discrepancies are a consequence of the fact that Noongar names were seldom recorded in the nineteenth century. An overwhelming number of Aboriginal men were variously referred to as 'Bobby', 'Jacky' and 'Billy' in this era, which increases the difficulty of tracking a single individual through the archives.[71] Nonetheless, in June 1951, the same 'Cape Riche Bobby' was reportedly captured:

> Three of the tribe of natives who have been carrying on a system of sheep and cattle stealing at the Salt River district have been apprehended; they were brought in last week and are now in Albany gaol ... The authorities are in possession of the names of upwards of 40 members of the same tribe who have been concerned in these stock robberies. One of the captives was formerly a policeman in Albany, and is known as 'Cape Riche Bobby' ...[72]

It is possible that immediately after departing Roe's expedition party in January 1849, Bobby showed the Jerramungup area to Hassell, who established extensive pastoral interest there. He was then engaged as a guide for Gregory in May and could also have been employed as a 'native constable' in Albany some time that year, on the recommendation of Roe or Hassell, both of whom he assisted. After his arrest in June 1951, and despite numerous escape attempts, Bobby was in custody at Albany and later Perth, sentenced to 15 years' imprisonment, though he was given a pardon in 1853.[73] While Bobby was imprisoned, his father Jerramungup, described as an old man

---

68 Scott and Brown 2005: 55.
69 Green 1997: 111.
70 *Albany Advertiser*, 9 August 1898.
71 Parry (2007) has written about similar complications arising from colonists' habit of bestowing nicknames on Aboriginal people elsewhere in Australia.
72 *Inquirer*, 2 July 1851.
73 Green 1997: 97.

and with his name spelt various different ways, was reported stealing sheep in his son's absence with a group of Noongar in the Fitzgerald region in 1852 and 1853.[74]

Bobby the 'native constable'

On 18 January 1853, Mr Arthur Trimmer was been appointed as 'Sub-Protector of Natives' at Albany.[75] Shortly after his appointment, Trimmer asked that 'Cape Riche Bobby' be pardoned, as he was regarded as having a good influence on the 'Aborigines of the Jerramungup district and would make a very good policeman'.[76] Trimmer was proven right, as in 1854 he commended Bobby for apprehending three escaped Aboriginal prisoners.[77]

Historian Peter Gifford considers it probable that by this point in frontier history, some Noongar 'had formed the conclusion that there was no defeating the European invaders and that it would be best to take their side rather than continue sporadic resistance which was always met with bloody retribution'.[78] However, there was negligible remuneration or respect for Western Australia's 'native constables' of this era. Bobby was no doubt poorly rewarded for his services to colonial authorities, especially as they would have compromised his relationships and standing in the Noongar community. Upon viewing a nineteenth-century photograph depicting Aboriginal prisoners in chains, Hazel Brown reflects on her ancestor Bobby's role as a 'native constable':

> They gave him the Blucher boots and the britches, they gave him a hat and a gun, they give him a stockwhip. They made him a police tracker. I reckon that's really sad, to think that those [Aboriginal] people in chains ... they reckon that those people were Bobby's own relations.[79]

---

74 Green 1997: 140–141, 171.
75 *Inquirer*, 12 January 1853.
76 Green 1997: 97.
77 Green 1997: 92.
78 Gifford 2002: 41.
79 Scott and Brown 2005: 49–50.

Few traces of Bobby exist in the archives after 1854. He may have been the unnamed 'native' with whom Charles and William Dempster surveyed the area from Bremer Bay to Cape Arid in April 1863,[80] or the 'native constable' lauded as 'hero of the day' in the Fitzgerald region a year later, capturing a notorious escaped convict who had boasted that 'no policemen should take him alive'.[81] Going 'undercover', without a uniform, the 'native constable' made 'friends' with the convict and at one point offered to shoot an emu. However, once armed, the 'hero' turned the gun on his new 'friend' and secured the arrest in a manner certainly reminiscent of Bobby's confidence and wit. 'Cape Riche Bobby' is recorded again as a witness to the 1870 murder of an Aboriginal man at Jerramungup station,[82] and he could also be, 'Bob, a native constable, who was engaged as a tracker … and … gave his evidence in a very intelligent manner' in an 1874 trial for murder at Narrogin.[83]

On 3 June 1882, a 'Cape Ritchie Billy' (likely to be Cape Riche Bobby) deserted the service of the Hassells of Jerramungup station.[84] As the moving frontier extended east from Jerramungup, we could assume that Bobby travelled across the south coast.[85] While there is scant evidence as to what became of Bobby after 1882, he left a conflicted legacy. Reflecting on her ancestor's conditional complicity in 2005, Hazel Brown exclaimed:

> I hate the people who put the gun in my grandfather's hands, so they could get control over Noongars, and gave him the chains, so he could chain them up … He used to work from Bremer and out to Jerramungup, and from Jerramungup he used to go to Ravensthrope and bring the prisoners back.[86]

---

80 *Perth Gazette and Independent Journal*, 25 September 1863.
81 *West Australian Times*, 14 April 1864.
82 Green 1997: 97; *Inquirer and Commercial News*, 13 July 1870.
83 *Inquirer and Commercial News*, 11 March 1874.
84 As recorded in the *Police Gazette*, 14 June 1882.
85 Scott and Brown (2005) consider it likely that Bobby arranged for his son to later marry two young women from around the Ravensthorpe district (Ngurer/Monkey and Karbian/Emily Dabb). These women are said to be among the few survivors of frontier violence in the region during the 1880s, as also documented by Grey Forrest 2004.
86 Scott and Brown 2005: 47.

Conclusion

A pivotal figure in the history of Western Australia's south coast, Bobby Roberts assisted Roe's expedition and helped 'open up' the south coast for pastoral development.[87] He was a well-travelled young man in the middle of the nineteenth century and provided conditional assistance to colonists for the likely purpose of expanding his own networks and influence amongst Noongar and newcomers in the region. Soon after, Bobby was one of many Noongar of the era to engage in a type of economic warfare that consisted of attacks on colonial livestock and supplies, and which frequently held back colonisation in other parts of Australia.[88] However, as the colony expanded and his options decreased, he became involved in the enforcement of imposed colonial laws, before perhaps meeting his end as isolated colonists in the region reverted 'to savagery' in the 1880s.[89] A significant, complex and undoubtedly conflicted intermediary, Bobby Roberts was intelligent, talented and somewhat ruthless. Nevertheless, he would have struggled to retain a sense of agency and maintain relationships on both sides of the moving frontier.

Acknowledgements

Thanks to Hazel Brown, Kim Scott, Aileen Walsh, Olivia Roberts, Iris Woods and Shino Konishi for their assistance in reviewing and making suggestions for this chapter.

References

Albany Advertiser 1897–1950, *The Albany Advertiser*, Albany, WA.

Bracknell, Clint 2013, 'The Wirlomin project: Sustaining Aboriginal language and song', *The International Journal of Sustainability in Economic, Social and Cultural, Context* 9(1): 45–55.

---

87 Scott and Brown 2005; Green 1997; Roe 1852.
88 Reynolds 1982.
89 Sheldon 1944: 299.

—— 2014, 'Wal-Walang-al Ngardanginy: Hunting the Songs (of the Australian Southwest)', *Australian Aboriginal Studies* 1: 3–15.

Clendinnen, Inga 2003, *Dancing with Strangers*, Text Publishers, Melbourne.

Collard, Leonard and Clint Bracknell 2012, 'Beeliar Boodjar: An introduction to Aboriginal history in the city of Cockburn, Western Australia', *Australian Aboriginal Studies* 1: 86–91.

Dixon, Robert M. W. 1980, *The Languages of Australia*, Cambridge Language Surveys, Cambridge University Press, Cambridge.

Douglas, Wilfred 1976, *The Aboriginal Languages of the South-West of Australia*, Australian Institute of Aboriginal Studies, Canberra.

Eden, Charles Henry 1875, *Australia's Heroes: being a slight sketch of the most prominent amongst the band of gallant men who devoted their lives and energies to the cause of science and the development of the fifth continent*, third edition, Society for Promoting Christian Knowledge, London.

Forrest, Roni and Stuart Crowe 1996, *Yarra-mo-up Place of the Tall Yate Trees: A Report on the Noongar Social History of the Jerramungup Region*, Australian Government Publishing Service, Canberra.

Gibbs, Martin 2003, 'Nebinyan's songs: An Aboriginal whaler of the South West', *Aboriginal History* 27(1): 11–20.

Gifford, Peter 2002, *Black and White and in Between: Arthur Dimer and the Nullarbor*, Hesperian, Carlisle.

Green, Neville 1997, *Aborigines of the Albany Region 1821–1898*, UWA Publishing, Nedlands.

Grey Forrest, Roni 2004, *Kukenarup – Two Stories: A Report on Historical Accounts of a Massacre Site at Cocanarup near Ravensthorpe W.A.*, Department of Indigenous Affairs, Perth.

Hallam, Sylvia J. 1983, 'A view from the other side of the western frontier: Or "I met a man who wasn't there …"', *Aboriginal History* 7(2): 134–156.

Hassell, Ethel 1936, *Notes on the Ethnology of the Wheelman Tribe of South-Western Australia*. St Gabriel-Mödling, Wein.

—— 1975, *My Dusky Friends*, C. W. Hassell, Fremantle.

Inquirer 1840–1855, *The Inquirer: a Western Australian journal of politics and literature*, Perth.

Inquirer and Commercial News 1855–1901, *The Inquirer and Commercial News*, Perth.

Konishi, Shino 2012, *The Aboriginal Male in the Enlightenment World*, Pickering and Chatto, London.

McLaren, Glen and William Cooper 1996, 'Aboriginal involvement in Australian exploration: The enduring myth', *Northern Perspective* 19(2): 32–40.

Murdoch, Walter 1929, *The Making of Australia: An Introductory History*, Whitcombe and Tombs, Melbourne.

Parry, Naomi 2007, '"Hanging no good for black fellow": Looking into the life of Musquito', in *Transgressions: Critical Australian Indigenous Histories*, Ingereth Macfarlane and Mark Hannah (eds), ANU E Press and Aboriginal History Inc., Canberra: 153–176.

Perth Gazette 1833–1847, *Perth Gazette and Western Australian Journal*, Charles Macfaull, Perth.

Perth Gazette and Independent Journal 1848–1864, *The Perth Gazette and Independent Journal of Politics and News*, Perth.

Police Gazette 1876–1900, *The Police Gazette of Western Australia*, Perth.

Reynolds, Henry 1980, 'The land, the explorers and the Aborigines', *Historical Studies* 19(75): 213–226.

—— 1982, *The Other Side of the Frontier: Aboriginal Resistance to the European Invasion of Australia*, Pelican Books, Ringwood.

Roe, John Septimus 1852, 'Report of an Expedition under the Surveyor-General, Mr. J. S. Roe, to the South-Eastward of Perth, in Western Australia, between the Months of September, 1848, and February, 1849', *Journal of the Royal Geographical Society of London* 22: 1–57.

Ryan, Simon 1996, *The Cartographic Eye: How Explorers Saw Australia*, Cambridge University Press, Cambridge.

Scott, Kim and Hazel Brown 2005, *Kayang and Me*, Fremantle Arts Press, Fremantle.

Sheldon, H. D. 1944, 'Characteristics of colonial cultures', *Pacific Historical Review* 13(3): 298–302.

Shellam, Tiffany 2009, *Shaking Hands on the Fringe: Negotiating the Aboriginal World at King George's Sound*, UWA Publishing, Nedlands.

Shoobert, Joanne (ed.) 2005, *Western Australian Exploration 1826–1835 Volume 1*, Hesperian Press, Carlisle.

West Australian 1897–2014, *The West Australian*, Perth.

West Australian Times 1863–1864, *West Australian Times a political and literary journal*, Richard Pether, Perth.

7

Mediating the imaginary and the space of encounter in the Papuan Gulf

Dario Di Rosa

Writing about the 1935 Hides–O'Malley expedition in the Highlands of Papua New Guinea, the anthropologist Edward Schieffelin noted that Europeans 'had a well-prepared category – "natives" – in which to place those people they met for the first time, a category of social subordination that served to dissipate their depth of otherness'.[1] However, this category was often nuanced by Indigenous representations of neighbouring communities, producing significant effects in shaping Europeans' understanding of their encounters. Analysing the narrative produced by Joseph Beete Jukes,[2] naturalist on Francis Price Blackwood's voyage of 1842–1846 on HMS *Fly*, I demonstrate the crucial role played by Torres Strait Islanders as mediators from afar of European encounters with Papuans along the coast of the Gulf of

---

1   Schieffelin and Crittenden 1991: 5.
2   Jukes 1847. As Beer (1996) shows, the viewing position of on-board scientists during geographical explorations was a particular one, led by their interests (see, from a different perspective, Fabian (2000) on the relevance of 'natural history' as episteme of accounts of explorations). This is a reminder of the high degree of social stratification within the 'European' micro-social community of the ship's crew, a social hierarchy that shaped the texts available to the historians. Although he does not treat the problem of social stratification as such, see Thomas 1994 for a well-argued discussion about the different projects that guided various colonial actors. See also Dening 1992 for vivid case of power relations in the micro-social cosmos of a ship.

Papua in 1845. I focus predominantly on this particular text because it became a canonical reference for later explorations of the Gulf of Papua. I highlight two specific aspects of Torres Strait Islanders' mediation: a linguistic mediation which proved vital for the actual encounters; and the projection of certain stereotypes of Papuans which impinged on European imaginaries of 'the Natives'.[3]

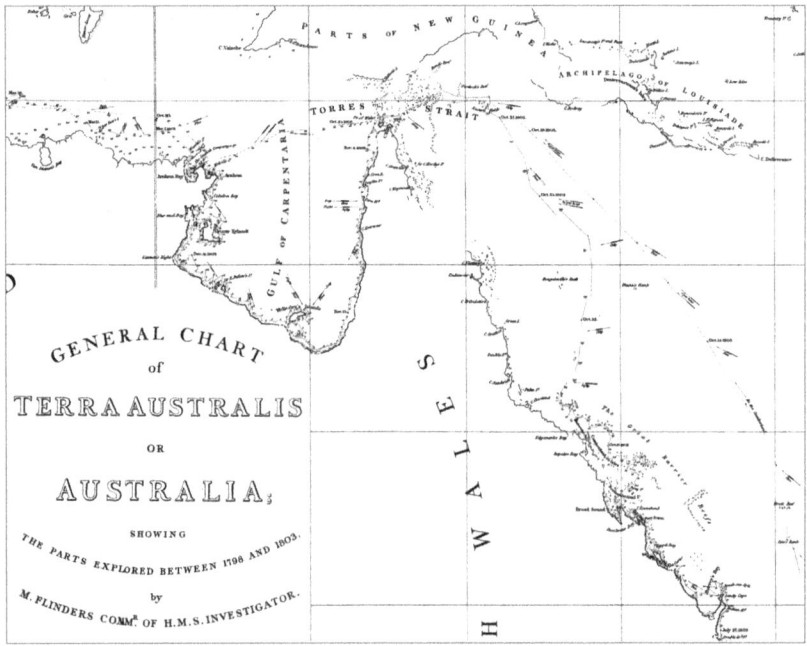

Figure 7.1: Detail of 'General Chart of Terra Australis or Australia: Showing Parts Explored Between 1798 and 1803 by M. Flinders Commr. of H.M.S. Investigator', 1822 [1814].
Source: National Library of Australia, MAP RM 1777.

By the 1840s, the seas of Torres Strait were regularly scoured by boats from Australia trying to reach Asian ports more quickly than was permitted by the longer and yet no safer passage north of New Guinea.[4] However, those reef-strewn waters were dangerous and the

---

3   In using the term 'stereotype', I follow Michael Herzfeld's analysis of the performative construction of what he terms 'cultural intimacy' (2005 [1997]: especially chapter 9).
4   For a discussion of the available routes 'from the South Pacific to the Indian Ocean', see Jukes 1847, I: 305, note. In this paper, 'New Guinea' refers to the whole island now divided into the Indonesian provinces of Papua and West Papua and the nation of Papua New Guinea. I deal here with the western portion of what became the British Protectorate of New Guinea and, subsequently, the Australian Territory of Papua.

cause of frequent shipwrecks, through which Torres Strait Islanders had already experienced sustained engagement with ships' crews. Lying between the Torres Strait and the northern passage through the Louisiade Archipelago at the eastern tip of New Guinea, the south coast of New Guinea was still poorly charted (Figure 7.1).[5]

The *Fly* sailed from England to the South Pacific in 1842. In August, the vessel reached Australia and spent over a year surveying its coasts. In 1845, Blackwood and his crew surveyed the Great Barrier Reef, Torres Strait, and the Gulf coast of New Guinea, a task that took more than a month (Figure 7.2). They spent several days at Darnley Island, known locally by the name of Erub. Interactions with Torres Strait Islanders were peaceful and oriented toward exchanges, particularly of food and 'curios' for iron tools. These exchanges produced a linguistic engagement and progressive acquisition of a vocabulary, mostly with the people of Erub.[6] Here the English crew engaged particularly with two figures, named Mammoos and Seewai, who seemed to have been 'two of the most influential men of the island'.[7] Preparing to leave for the south coast of New Guinea, and inquiring about their next destination, the English learned that Erubians called that place 'Dowdee' and regarded it as a vast land full of cuscus, a kind of possum. Information collected by Oswald W. Brierly, painter on board HMS *Rattlesnake* between 1848 and 1850, suggests that 'Dowdee' was part of a regional social geography created by chains of exchanges, which stretched from Cape York to the southern coast of New Guinea, encompassing the Torres Strait islands:

> Natives of the islands that lie between Cape York and the coast in that neighbourhood, have a general idea that there are two large countries, one of which they call Mugee Daudthee – New Guinea to the near northward … [They] have no direct communication with New Guinea, but hear about them and see ornaments, feathers etc. from the country through the Badthoos [Badus] who belong to a group of islands intermediate between the islands on this side of the straits and the

---

5 The most recent map available to Blackwood and his crew was Flinders' *General Chart of Terra Australis or Australia Showing Parts Explored Between 1798 and 1803* (1814), updated in 1822. In this map, the New Guinea coastline has many blanks, while the Torres Strait portion is very detailed.
6 Published as an appendix in Jukes 1847, II: 274–310.
7 Jukes 1847, I: 173.

natives of another island or islands whom they call the Gamulaga-garkadjie ... who, it would appear, communicate immediately with the natives of New Guinea.[8]

Dowdee was inscribed on the map in Figure 7.2. Other place names learned at Erub, such as Keewai (Kiwai), Mowat (Mawata), or Baigoo (Boigu), are easily recognisable as referring to places located either in the contemporary Western Province of Papua New Guinea or in Torres Strait.

Figure 7.2: Detail of 'Chart of the northern part of the Great Barrier Reef including Torres Strait, & y.ᵉ adjacent Coast of New Guinea', 1847.
Source: Joseph Beete Jukes, Narrative of the Surveying Voyage of the H.M.S. Fly, 1847, National Library of Australia.

---

8 Moore 1979: 201, see also 171, 204.

The *Fly* went on to explore the south-west coast of what is now Papua New Guinea and, near what seems to be the mouth of the Fly River, the Europeans' newly acquired linguistic competence enabled peaceful relations centred on exchange. Three canoes came close to the ship: 'They approached us very cautiously, and only one came within hail. We then tried them with Eroob words, such as "poud" (peace), "boonarree" (cocoa-nuts), "toorce" (iron), which they appeared to understand.'[9] Other encounters with Indigenous people on this portion of the coast were less friendly and were avoided, '[n]ot wishing to shed blood unnecessarily'.[10]

As the expedition proceeded eastward, Erubian words were increasingly ineffective for communication and this affected European interactions with local people. Due to the navigational difficulties, the pinnace *Midge* and a gig were sent to survey the coast with provisions for five days, while the *Fly* continued northward following the coastline. The tender *Prince George* was meant to stay at signal distance between the two boats. On this occasion, a hill close to the Gulf of Papua, a few miles up the Kikori River, was baptised Aird Hill, giving a more precise position than can be recognised from the maps produced by the expedition. Having received no news from the other boats for some days, the *Fly* anchored and more boats were sent to find those missing. On 11 May, Blackwood, Jukes, and other members of the expedition explored the shores near Aird Hill in a small boat. Approaching a sandbank, they saw a dozen men armed with bows and arrows: 'We called to them in Erroobian words, which they did not seem to understand, and they shouted words back, which were equally incomprehensible to us.'[11] Apparently frightened at the sight of white men, they fled, but reappeared after some time, keeping themselves at a safe distance. That same day, two other men appeared and one shot an arrow in the direction of the white men who replied with a volley of rifle fire, putting the two to flight.[12]

---

9   Jukes 1847, I: 213.
10 Jukes 1847, I: 215. This is also a rhetorical strategy to morally mask the fear of eventually being killed if a clash occurred; see *infra* fn. 24.
11 Jukes 1847, I: 223.
12 For a discussion of the use of firearms in the 'encounters' in the south-eastern part of New Guinea, see Mosko 2009.

Short of food and concerned about the fate of the missing boats, the party headed back towards the anchored *Fly* and were suddenly confronted by a large fleet of canoes with several armed men. Blackwood gave 'orders, if it were necessary to fire, to aim at first principally at the canoes, so as to give them some notion what our weapons were capable of, and, if possible, frighten them off without bloodshed'.[13] When some arrows were shot, the muskets were fired without inflicting harm but forced the confronting fleet to flee to gain the shore. Here, in the proximity of a village, the warriors rallied and prepared to attack again, jumping into their canoes. Jukes explained that:

> They gradually advanced toward us, and one man seemed inclined to come up alone in a small canoe. We tried him with Erroob words, but he did not seem to understand them, and replied in words unintelligible for us. As we were now so far from the sea, with such a labyrinth of channels to track back, it would evidently never do to proceed with so strong a body of enemies likewise in the rear.[14]

This constituted another failed attempt to use Erubian words to communicate in a potentially dangerous situation.[15]

On 14 May the party rejoined the *Fly* and the following day met the *Prince George*, still with no news of the missing boats. At this point, in considerable apprehension for the fate of their companions, Blackwood sent a boat back to Erub in order to collect information. Four days later, the *Prince George*'s crew reported that there was no news of the missing boats. More days passed searching along the coastline but the bad weather, shortage of provisions, and the threat of attacks forced a decision on Blackwood:

> as a last chance, Captain Blackwood determined to go to Erroob, and endeavour to persuade one or two of its inhabitants to return with us to New Guinea, in order that by their means we might perhaps procure a peaceful interview with some tribe of the New Guinea people, and thus at least learn what had been the fate of our shipmates.[16]

---

13 Jukes 1847, I: 231.
14 Jukes 1847, I: 233.
15 On the importance of local intermediaries in establishing communications with people encountered during the explorations, see Kennedy 2013: 178–181.
16 Jukes 1847, I: 243.

7. MEDIATING THE IMAGINARY AND THE SPACE OF ENCOUNTER IN THE PAPUAN GULF

On 24 May the *Fly*'s crew arrived again in Erub. For three days they tried to persuade Seewai and Mammoos to go with them to New Guinea but the negotiations were complicated by a now open rivalry between the local parties. Analysis of the strategic use of the European presence by the different factions lies outside the scope of this paper, but it is worth noting that the Europeans tried to take advantage of these frictions to serve their goal. Reactions to the request to accompany the Europeans to New Guinea echoed the Torres Strait Islanders' representations of Papuan alterity. Seewai was made aware 'that we wanted him to go with us to talk to the people of Dowdee, that they might inform us where our people were. At this point Seewai shook his head, drew his finger across his throat, and said, "Dowdee no good! arress, aress [war, war]! sarreg [Arrows!]"'.[17] Exploiting Seewai's enmity with Mammoos to exert pressure, the English temporarily convinced the former to join them but women in the village protested energetically. Later, Mammoos showed scars on his body, some of them the result of fights with Papuans. In the end, Blackwood and his crew could not get any Erubian to go on board; it was clear that '[t]hey all seemed to regard Dowdee with considerable horror, and said the people of Dowdee would kill them; making signs, by biting their arms, as if they would also eat them afterward'.[18] Tellingly, this is the first mention in the narrative of cannibalism in relation to the inhabitants of New Guinea.

From this point on, the Europeans' attitude to the deployment of firearms in dealing with the inhabitants of the Gulf of Papua changed significantly: 'We were all well armed and the Prince George's six-pounders were cleaned and got in order', as Jukes wrote.[19] As soon as the expedition approached the Kikori delta, they were confronted by armed men, and 'Captain Blackwood determined to take advantage of the first decided act of hostility on their part, to punish them severely and give them a lesson'.[20] The English also tried to seize prisoners so as to 'acquire some sort of information, or open a communication in a more friendly manner with the rest'.[21] At the first sign of hostility, the cutter crew fired their muskets at a greater rate than expected by Jukes, who justified this course of events by saying, 'The men were just at

---

17 Jukes 1847, I: 247–248.
18 Jukes 1847, I: 261.
19 Jukes 1847, I: 262.
20 Jukes 1847, I: 264.
21 Jukes 1847, I: 265.

this time becoming exasperated, with the loss of their messmates in the boats, and expressed great hatred against the blacks'.[22] According to Jukes, 10 to 12 Indigenous men were killed; an extraordinary number if we consider the casualties that might have gone unrecorded.[23] The next day, the English approached a village and were confronted by a dozen men discharging their arrows at them. Wishing to land, the Europeans decided to clear the zone by firing the six-pounders several times. Here they inspected the long-house, taking some 'ethnological specimens' and killing two pigs.

In sarcastic remorse for this act of theft, Jukes wrote: 'I will so far endeavour to make amends to the inhabitants of Pigville, as we christened this place, as to acknowledge that their pork was excellent.'[24] It is worth noting that the objects 'collected' were compared with the Erubians' material culture, and on a subsequent visit to Erub the Europeans relied on that knowledge to make sense of some objects:

> a cane loop, with a toggle or handle, and a bamboo scoop, with a handle bound round with twine, in which small beads (or seeds) were inserted. I afterwards saw some of these among the natives at Erroob, who said they came from Dowdee ... and said the first was for twisting round people's necks, and the second for cutting their heads off – which merely showed they did not know what their real use was, as they are not at all adapted for those purposes.[25]

---

22   Jukes 1847, I: 265, note. The crew subsequently learned that the missing men had gone in the *Midge* to the English settlement at Port Essington in Arnhem Land. Jukes 1847, I: 302.
23   Bronwen Douglas (pers. comm.) suggests that the number of killings listed in such encounters was often much exaggerated, on the basis of the assumed superiority of European arms. This interpretation is sustained by the convincing argument developed by Dorothy Shineberg (1971) that firearms proved ineffective in the early phase of European exploration of the Pacific, a position that resonates with Kennedy's: 'The technological hubris that inspired many expeditions collided with the constraints of climate, topographies, political economies, and more' (Kennedy 2013: 262). I have argued elsewhere (Di Rosa 2010: 66, chapter 2) that, in the late nineteenth-century exploration of the Gulf of Papua, firearms were often thought of and deployed as a tangible *symbol* of Europeans' supposed superiority. Even if firearms did not prove effective in the humid climate of the Gulf of Papua, it was through these objects that Europeans could hold a sense of confidence to sustain them during the exploration of unknown lands and waters, and the potentially hazardous encounters with the inhabitants of those territories.
24   Jukes 1847, I: 276.
25   Jukes 1847, I: 277–278.

7. MEDIATING THE IMAGINARY AND THE SPACE OF ENCOUNTER IN THE PAPUAN GULF

Michael O'Hanlon has discussed at length the implications of the so-called 'man-catcher' in southern Papua New Guinea, showing the various complex forms of representations that such objects provoked in various sectors of the European colonial community in what was then the Protectorate of British New Guinea.[26]

This is an example of how Erubians associated New Guinea with headhunting practices. Other encounters also took place in New Guinea, mostly marked by tensions, but I want particularly to emphasise the constant English attempt to use Erubian words in order to establish communications there. It is interesting that Jukes thought he could recognise some words from the vocabulary collected in the Torres Strait, segmenting the continuum of the sound-string they were hearing to accord with his expectations. For example, on 29 May, the *Fly*'s crew encountered some men and Jukes described the event:

> When they were within about 100 yards, Captain Blackwood and myself stood up on the taffrail and waved our hats, shouted 'puod, poud,' and told them in Erroob we were friends, and invited them to come to us. They ceased their cries and listened; and *I thought once I heard them say to each other*, 'Errooba.'[27]

On another occasion:

> We again tried them with Erroob words, and, *I think*, they understood 'toorree' (iron), and answered to us, 'nipa' (a knife). We held up hatchets, and again said 'toorree', when they, *I believe*, repeated 'nipa,' and seemed to apply the word to the hatchet, *as if it were a foreign word they had heard, but did not know the exact meaning of*. They certainly never used the word 'sapăra,' which is the Erroobian word for hatchet.[28]

These are further traces of how sustained engagement with some parts of the Torres Strait Islands informed tentative European interactions with people of the Gulf of Papua.

---

26 O'Hanlon 1999.
27 Jukes 1847, I: 265, my emphasis.
28 Jukes 1847, I: 281, my emphasis.

Figure 7.3: H. S. Melville, 'Hut, and Natives of Darnley Id. [Island]', n.d.

Source: *H. S. Melville, Sketches in Australia & the Adjacent Islands*, n.d. [1849?], Plate 18, National Library of Australia.

Although Erubians did not physically accompany Blackwood and his crew to the Papuan coast, they mediated subsequent encounters with Papuans in two ways. They provided a vocabulary that enabled easier engagement in exchanges, thus establishing peaceful encounters. When linguistic communication, no matter how 'raw', failed, the potential for clashes with the Indigenous people encountered became a real threat, as has already been seen. Previous interactions with Indigenous people provided cognitive and behavioural tools to tame the unknown nature of the encounters. When these cognitive resources proved ineffectual, thus failing to 'establish friendly relations', the actions of the Europeans were guided by more familiar stereotypes of 'the Native', which enabled moral justification for the recourse to violence. This brings me to my second point, that sustained engagement with Erubians mediated the European imaginary of the alterity of the inhabitants of the Gulf of Papua. The dialogical construction of Papuan alterity, reified in a gruesome way in the encounters described above, significantly shifted the Europeans' rhetoric and course of actions from 'not shedding unnecessary blood' to 'teaching them a lesson'.[29]

Archaeological, historical and ethnographic evidence shows that Torres Strait Islanders and Papuans of the south coast of New Guinea were entangled in exchange practices, intermarriage, and also raids.[30] Signs of these relationships were in place when Blackwood and his crew arrived in the region. For example, the presence of a New Guinea woman on Darnley Island was recorded by the draughtsman Harden Sidney Melville in one of his sketches entitled 'Hut, and Natives of Darnley Id [Island]': 'Sitting on the left is a New Guinea woman the cause of whose presence on Darnley Island we could not ascertain' (Figure 7.3).[31] Again, Jukes observed that Torres Strait Islanders greatly esteemed the cuscus, which came from the southern New Guinea coast, as did the canoes in use in the Strait. It was from interactions with specific groups on the Papuan coast that Torres Strait Islanders formed images of their alterity, taken by Europeans as applicable to the whole country. Goods generated from the exchanges taking place between

---

29 On the ambiguous relation between violence and ethics during the geographical explorations, see Driver and Jones 2009: 46–47; Kennedy 2013: 204–221. For a discussion of the moral dimension of the deployment of violence in exploring the Kikori area in the Gulf of Papua between the nineteenth and twentieth centuries, see also Di Rosa 2010. For a fruitful analysis of the intersection of morality, violence, and distance see Ginzburg 1994.
30 See, for example, Austen 1948; Allen 1982; McNiven 1998.
31 Melville [1849]: plate 18.

the Torres Strait Islanders and the Papuans of the opposite coast made their way to the Kikori River, and from there were integrated into other exchange routes that stretched as far as the Highlands.[32] These objects, though, travelled by means of personal trading relations, along a sequence of societies with their constellations of enmities and alliances. A long dialect chain of languages is to be found in this part of the Gulf of Papua (Figure 7.4), which rendered unnecessary the development of a common language. Instead, for example, the Motuan language became the *lingua franca* of the *hiri* trade in the eastern part of the Gulf.[33] This enables a more detailed understanding of the complex geopolitics that informed Indigenous constructions of alterity, which in turn impinged on European understandings and engagements with people encountered during the process of exploration. These complex local worlds were often flattened under the category of 'natives'.

As I observed at the beginning of this chapter, Jukes's narrative became a canonical text for later explorations of the Gulf of Papua, becoming itself a mediator of the European imaginary of the Gulf. For example, in 1890 the Lieutenant Governor of the then British New Guinea, William MacGregor, located as Pigville the place where 'during my recent inspection of the western district we were ... completely unsuccessful in our endeavours to establish friendly relations with natives'.[34] But Jukes's legacy runs even further: the anthropologist Alfred Cort Haddon was an eager reader of the *Fly* narrative, and praised the expedition's ethnographic work in Torres Strait in his multi-volume *Report of the Cambridge Anthropological Expedition*.[35] Close reading of this text enabled him, years later while he was working in the Gulf, to locate Pigville as a Kerewo village in the Kikori Delta.[36] It is not of primary importance for me to be able to locate this village exactly, but rather to see how Jukes's narrative, the outcome of the complex kaleidoscopic refractions of representations, operated as a blueprint for understanding encounters in the Gulf of Papua almost 60 years later.

---

32 See Austen 1948: 16–20.
33 The *hiri* trade was an annual voyage undertaken by Motu people, sailing toward the Gulf of Papua in order to exchange mostly clay pots for sago. The so-called Hiri Motu language developed from such interactions; see Dutton 1982.
34 MacGregor 1892: 54.
35 Haddon 1901–35.
36 Haddon 1918: 179.

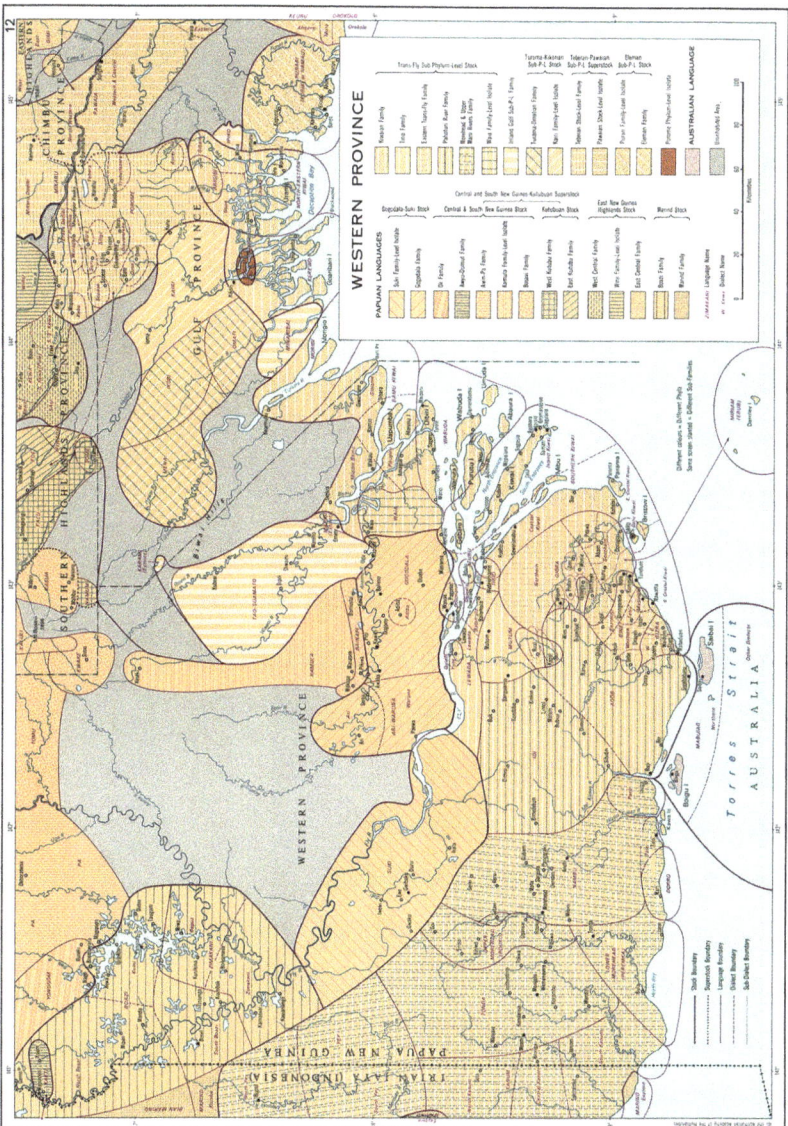

Figure 7.4: Map of languages in Gulf of Papua area, 1981.
Source: C.L. Voorhoeve and Stephen A. Wurm, 'Western Province', in Stephen A. Wurm and Shirô Hattori (eds), *Language Atlas of the Pacific Area*, 1981, Australian Academy of the Humanities; reproduced with permission.

The case analysed in this chapter is not uncommon in Pacific exploration literature and arguably in that of exploration generally. For example, in a narrative of his voyage along the south coast of New Guinea with

Luis Váez de Torres in 1606, Diego de Prado y Tovar recounted that the *indios* ('Indians') of Mailu Island fled at the sight of an African member of the Spanish crew, terrified because he resembled *negros* ('Negroes') who raided them and ate the bodies of their victims. When the Spanish landed on an island in what would become known as Torres Strait and saw skulls in the huts, they assumed that these must be the people the inhabitants of Mailu were frightened of, though they were 'not black', 'but stain themselves to appear more fierce'.[37]

Reading these narratives of encounters with Indigenous people is a reminder of the significance of imagination in shaping the expectations which guided the actions of Europeans toward the people and places they met, readjusting their understanding, and consequently their behaviour, according to whether those *expectations* were met or not. This imaginary was partly formed by interactions with local communities, adhering in the process to 'local' stereotypes which were readily and uncritically naturalised. These revised expectations entered the published accounts consulted by subsequent explorers prior to their own voyages. I am not arguing for a mere analysis of the 'construction of the imaginary' that leads to a mechanistic reading of parties' actions. The imaginary influenced the actions and interactions of Europeans and Indigenous people, whose own imaginary was no less important in their encounters with the white newcomers. For example, in several passages Jukes noted local attitudes toward the white skin and other material signs of European alterity, such as the footprints they left on the ground: 'They seemed to be pointing with great surprise to our foot-marks, wondering no doubt what had become of our toes, and at the extraordinary shaped feet they must have concluded we had from the impressions of our shoes.'[38]

In his unpublished journal of the voyage of HMS *Bramble*,[39] John Sweatman compared the encounters of Blackwood and his crew in the Kikori delta with those they had at Cape Possession, further east

---

37 Prado y Tovar 1930: 160.
38 Jukes 1847, I: 278.
39 John Sweatman was a clerk on HMS *Fly* during the voyage discussed in this chapter and then joined HMS *Bramble*, which conducted explorations in the South Sea after the *Fly* set sail for England. The *Bramble* visited the southern portion of New Guinea in 1846. Sweatman's journal remained unpublished until the 1970s and, as far as is known, only the second volume survives (Sweatman, Journal, n.d., SLNSW MS A1725). We are thus deprived of a different perspective on the *Fly*'s voyage. For a historical contextualisation of this manuscript, see Sweatman 1977.

in the Gulf of Papua. He noted that the people they met were not frightened by their white skin. Sweatman linked this observation to the overall better Indigenous disposition toward the Europeans at Cape Possession, venturing to say that they 'were willing to be as familiar as the Darnley Islanders',[40] who, once again served as the 'yardstick of encounters'. The study of how certain Europeans' imaginaries were formed, both 'at home' and during the temporal frame of the voyages, leads the historian to look at broader questions about the political environment in which Europeans moved. However, this should not diminish the significance of the time-situated actions that these imaginaries reify. Such actions can be partially recovered in the texts, inscribed as Indigenous countersigns.[41]

Stating the relevance of the imagination in shaping knowledge created during the explorations of 'unknown' territories is a scholarly truism. In his work on the British Ornithologists' Union expedition to the interior of what was then Dutch New Guinea, Chris Ballard elegantly reconstructs the history of the 'Pygmy mythology', and the relevance that travel literature pertaining to Central Africa had for understanding the encounters with some human groups in the interior of New Guinea. The nexus between the imagination and its reification during the encounter is well captured by the following quote:

> The discovery of Negritos or Pygmies in the forested highland interior of New Guinea was thus keenly anticipated, and the characteristics of these imagined communities mapped in detail and commonly understood well in advance of the actual encounter.[42]

The case study I examined in this chapter shows that, at least in some cases, Indigenous stereotypes of neighbouring tribes infiltrated into the European's pre-constituted categories of 'the Natives' – something that is often neglected. It would be an exaggeration to attribute the

---

40 Sweatman n.d., NLA Mfm G 27522: 188.
41 For an outline of the fruitful methodology she developed to recover signs and countersigns of Indigenous agency inscribed in written texts, see Douglas 2015; 2014: 18–26.
42 Ballard 2000: 135.

course of events solely to the interactions[43] between the British crew and the Erubians, as the actual physical encounter with people in the Gulf of Papua was no less real and dangerous regardless of the cognitive tools that shaped the *post facto* understanding of it. The magmatic interaction between European and Indigenous imaginations with the uncertainties opened in the space of the encounter, crystallises in texts; in this case Jukes's, which, as I already argued, became a mediator of the imaginary of later explorations of the Gulf of Papua. It was no accident that the naturalist's text became authoritative in a period of transition from fictional accounts to travel literature to scientific reports of geographical explorations. Jukes stated his 'regime of truth' in the Preface to the volume in the following terms:

> in works of this nature, one line of *plain facts* is better than any heightened recollection … For this reason, also, I have avoided all attempts of brilliancy, elegance, or graces of style, and endeavoured to relate with *simplicity and fidelity* whatever I had to tell, either of personal adventure, or of scientific research.[44]

For the subsequent colonial endeavour to understand and tame New Guinea, 'scientific accuracy' was deemed to be absolutely crucial.

Acknowledgements

I thank the organisers and participants of the 'Local Intermediaries in International Exploration' conference at The Australian National University in July 2013 for their fruitful comments. I particularly acknowledge Chris Ballard, Bronwen Douglas and Graeme Whimp for their warm support and thoughtful suggestions.

---

43 Tamisari distinguishes between 'meeting' and 'encounter' on the basis of the intensity and personal involvement of relationship that take place during the ethnographic fieldwork experience, shaping the knowledge produced by the ethnographer. Tamisari's distinction is worth further reflections by historians whose interest revolves around 'intercultural encounters', but this cannot be done in the space of a footnote. What I want to stress here is that the *quality* of relations between the *Fly*'s crew and some Erubian people opened for the permeation of Europeans' imaginary by local stereotypes of inhabitants of 'Dowdee' (Tamisari 2006).
44 Jukes 1847; I: vi; my emphasis. Ballard (2009) convincingly demonstrates that certain literary tropes developed in fictional travel accounts were 'at work' in later texts of a scientific nature. Jukes's regime of truth is echoed by Melville [1849] in his Preface: 'In submitting this little work to the public, I have been actuated by the wish to lay before them facts rather than fancies. As an artist I am well aware of the small merit they posses as *pictures*, and wish to rest their value solely on their being faithful representations of the objects seen.'

References

Allen, Jim 1982, 'Pre-contact trade in Papua New Guinea', in *Melanesia: Beyond Diversity*, Ronald J. May and Hank Nelson (eds), Research School of Pacific Studies, The Australian National University, Canberra, 193–206.

Austen, Leo 1948, 'Notes on the Turamarubi of Western Papua', *Mankind* 4: 14–23.

Ballard, Chris 2000, 'Collecting Pygmies: The "Tapiro" and the British Ornithologists's Union Expedition to Dutch New Guinea, 1910–1911', in *Hunting the Gatherers: Ethnographic Collector, Agents, and Agency in Melanesia, 1870s–1930s*, Michael O'Hanlon and Robert L. Welsch (eds), Berghahn Books, New York and Oxford, 127–154.

—— 2009, 'The art of encounter: Verisimilitude in the imaginary exploration of interior New Guinea, 1725–1876', in *Oceanic Encounters: Exchange, Desire, Violence*, Margaret Jolly, Serge Tcherkézoff and Darrell Tryon (eds), ANU E Press, Canberra, 221–257.

Beer, Gillian 1996, *Open Fields: Science in Cultural Encounters*, Calderon Press, Oxford.

Dening, Greg 1992, *Mr Bligh's Bad Language: Passion, Power, and Theatre on the Bounty*, Cambridge University Press, Cambridge and New York.

Di Rosa, Dario 2010, 'Il caso Goaribari: violenza e saperi nella Papua coloniale', MA thesis, Ca'Foscari University of Venice.

Douglas, Bronwen 2014, *Science, Voyages, and Encounters in Oceania 1511–1850*, Palgrave Macmillan, Basingstoke and New York.

—— 2015, 'Agency, affect, and local knowledge in the exploration of Oceania', *Indigenous Intermediaries: New Perspectives on Exploration Archives*, Shino Konishi, Maria Nugent and Tiffany Shellam (eds), ANU Press, Canberra, 103–130.

Driver, Felix and Lowri Jones 2009, *Hidden Histories of Exploration: Researching the RGS-IBG Collections*, Royal Holloway, University of London, and Royal Geographical Society (with IBG), London.

Dutton, Tom (ed.) 1982, *The Hiri in History: Further Aspects of Long-Distance Motu Trade in Central Papua*, Pacific Research Monograph 8, The Australian National University, Canberra.

Fabian, Johannes 2000, *Out of Our Minds: Reason and Madness in the Exploration of Central Africa*, University of California Press, Berkeley, Los Angeles, London.

Flinders, Matthew 1814, 'General chart of Terra Australis or Australia: Showing the parts explored between 1798 and 1803', engraving, in *A Voyage to Terra Australis: Undertaken for the Purpose of Completing the Discovery of that Vast Country, and Prosecuted in the Years 1801, 1802, and 1803 in His Majesty's Ship the Investigator, and Subsequently in the Armed Vessel Porpoise and Cumberland Schooner ... Atlas*, plate 1, G. and W. Nicol, London.

—— 1822, 'General chart of Terra Australis or Australia: showing the parts explored between 1798 and 1803 by M. Flinders Commr. of H.M.S. Investigator', Admiralty Hydrographical Office, London.

Ginzburg, Carlo 1994, 'Killing a Chinese mandarin: The moral implications of distance', *Critical Inquiry* 21: 46–60.

Haddon, Alfred Cort (ed.) 1901–1935, *Reports of the Cambridge Anthropological Expedition to Torres Straits*, 6 vols, Cambridge University Press, Cambridge.

—— 1918, 'The Agiba cult of the Kerewa culture', *Man* 18: 117–183.

Herzfeld, Michael 2005 [1997], *Cultural Intimacy: Social Poetics in the Nation-State*, second edition, Routledge, London and New York.

Jukes, J. Beete 1847, *Narrative of the Surveying Voyage of H.M.S. Fly, Commanded by Captain Blackwood, in Torres Strait, New Guinea, and Other Islands of the Eastern Archipelago, during the Years 1842–1846: together with an Excursion into the Interior of the Eastern Part of Java*, 2 vols, T. & W. Boone, London.

Kennedy, Dane K. 2013, *The Last Blank Spaces: Exploring Africa and Australia*, Harvard University Press, Cambridge and London.

MacGregor, William 1892, 'Despatch Reporting Further Upon Administrative Visit of Inspection to Western Division', in *Annual Report on British New Guinea 1890–1891*, Appendix M (27 April 1891), Government Printer, Brisbane, Qld, 46–54.

McNiven, Ian J. 1998, 'Enmity and amity: Reconsidering stone-headed club (*gabagaba*) procurement and trade in Torres Strait', *Oceania* 69: 94–115.

Melville, Harden S. [1849], *Sketches in Australia and the Adjacent Islands: Selected from a Number Taken during the Surveying Voyage of HMS "Fly" and "Bramble" under the Command of Capt. FP Blackwood … 1442–1846*, Dickinson & Co., London.

Moore, David R. 1979, *Islanders and Aborigines at Cape York: An Ethnographic Reconstruction Based on the 1848–1850 "Rattlesnake" Journals of O.W. Brierly and Information he Obtained from Barbara Thompson*, Australian Institute of Aboriginal Studies, Canberra.

Mosko, Mark S. 2009 'Black powder, white magic: European armaments and sorcery in early Mekeo and Roro encounters', in *Oceanic Encounters: Exchange, Desire, Violence*, Margaret Jolly, Serge Tcherkézoff and Darrell Tryon (eds), ANU E Press, Canberra, 259–293.

O'Hanlon, Michael 1999, '"Mostly harmless"? Missionaries, administrators and material culture on the coast of British New Guinea', *Journal of the Royal Anthropological Institute* 5: 377–397.

Prado y Tovar, Diego de 1930, 'Relación Sumaria de Don Diego de Prado with an annotated translation', in *New Light on the Discovery of Australia: As Revealed by the Journal of Captain Don Diego de Prado y Tovar*, George F. Barwick (trans.), Henry N. Stevens (ed.), Hakluyt Society, London, 83–205.

Schieffelin, Edward L. and Robert Crittenden (eds) 1991, *Like People You See in a Dream: First Contact in Six Papuan Societies*, Stanford University Press, Stanford.

Shineberg, Dorothy 1971, 'Guns and men in Melanesia', *Journal of Pacific History* 6: 61–82.

Sweatman, John n.d., 'Journal of a surveying voyage in the "Bramble", 1842–1847', State Library of New South Wales, MS A1725; National Library of Australia, microfilm Mfm G 27522.

—— 1977, *The Journal of John Sweatman: A Nineteenth Century Surveying Voyage in North Australia and Torres Strait*, Jim Allen and Peter Corris (eds), University of Queensland Press, St Lucia.

Tamisari, Franca 2006, 'Personal acquaintance: Essential individuality and the possibilities of encounters', in *Moving Anthropology: Critical Indigenous Studies*, Tess Lea, Emma Kowal and Gillian Cowlinshaw (eds), Charles Darwin University Press, Darwin, 17–36.

Thomas, Nicholas 1994, *Colonialism's Culture: Anthropology, Travel and Government*, Princeton University Press, Princeton.

Thomas, Nicolas 2010, *Islanders: The Pacific in the age of empire*, Yale University Press, New Haven.

Wurm, Stephen A. and Shirô Hattori (eds) 1981, *Language Atlas of the Pacific Area. Part 1: New Guinea area, Oceania, Australia*, Pacific Linguistics. Series C, No. 66, Australian Academy of the Humanities [and] the Japan Academy, Canberra.

8

Local agency and William MacGregor's exploration of the Trobriand Islands

Andrew Connelly

At the time of British New Guinea Administrator William MacGregor's first visits to the Trobriand Islands in 1890 and 1891, the islands had been frequented by whalers for over 40 years and by traders for over a decade. However, this long history of European encounter and exchange in the Trobriands failed to result in the construction of a body of knowledge available to MacGregor, since many encounters were not recorded or were buried in ships' logs, published information was widely scattered, and some regular visits were kept secret. Because of this, MacGregor ventured into an informational wilderness to 'discover' the islands for himself. On the other hand, these previous exchanges had produced a local body of shared knowledge that shaped his reception by Trobriand intermediaries, especially local chiefs who attempted to recruit him into exclusive exchange relationships. If not unrecognised by MacGregor, then at least unreported were the surely numerous interactions between Trobrianders and his Polynesian and Melanesian companions, whose presence and conduct would have been as significant for Trobrianders as MacGregor's was.

William MacGregor was born in Scotland and completed medical studies at Edinburgh, gaining his certificate in 1872. He then joined the British colonial service as a medical assistant, working in the Seychelles and Mauritius under Governor Sir Arthur Gordon, who encouraged him to take on administrative tasks as well. It was here that he first developed an interest in 'native' affairs and welfare. MacGregor followed Gordon to Fiji in 1874, where a string of appointments over 14 years amounted to an extended training course in colonial administration.[1]

Figure 8.1: William MacGregor, 1888.
Source: State Library of Queensland.

---

1   Chief Medical and Health Officer, Receiver-General (Treasurer), Colonial Secretary and Acting Governor. Joyce 1971.

8. LOCAL AGENCY & WILLIAM MACGREGOR'S EXPLORATION OF THE TROBRIAND ISLANDS

MacGregor stepped ashore at Port Moresby in September 1888, where he was sworn in as Administrator after proclaiming the former British protectorate's new status as the Crown Possession of British New Guinea. He would lead British New Guinea (long informally and later officially also known as Papua) for a decade, as Administrator until 1894, and as Lieutenant Governor from 1895 to 1898.[2] MacGregor sought to encourage development such as gold mining and copra plantations in British New Guinea but, due to his earlier experiences under Gordon, and perhaps his medical background, he also valued protecting the Indigenous population from exploitation by Europeans.[3] This often brought him into conflict with white elements of settler society. MacGregor viewed exploration as one of the responsibilities of his position and undertook many expeditions large and small to 'discover' and document the Territory's geography, geology, natural history and population. He personally established initial government contact with many Papuan societies, and 'pacification' of hostile or warring groups was a priority. These expeditions were written up in despatches to MacGregor's superior, the Governor of Queensland, and published as appendices in the British New Guinea annual reports. These official despatches, read with interest in colonial offices and drawing rooms across the British Empire, served as a narration of the new government's self-discovery of its own territory and subjects.

When MacGregor first arrived in 1890, Trobrianders had had face-to-face contact with seaborne Europeans for at least half a century, and had been familiar with the sight of European vessels for much longer. A long tradition of regional trade by seagoing canoe meant that Trobrianders were highly mobile, travelling throughout a large area of islands numbering in the hundreds, from Muyuw (Woodlark) in the east and the Louisiades in the south-east, to the D'Entrecasteaux and south-eastern coast of New Guinea to the south. They would have known of and likely interacted with Europeans long before any reached Trobriand shores.

---

2   MacGregor demanded this mainly symbolic promotion after his first five years. Joyce 1971: 118–119; Sinclair 2009: 135.
3   Joyce 1971: 141, 143, 167; see also Sinclair 2009.

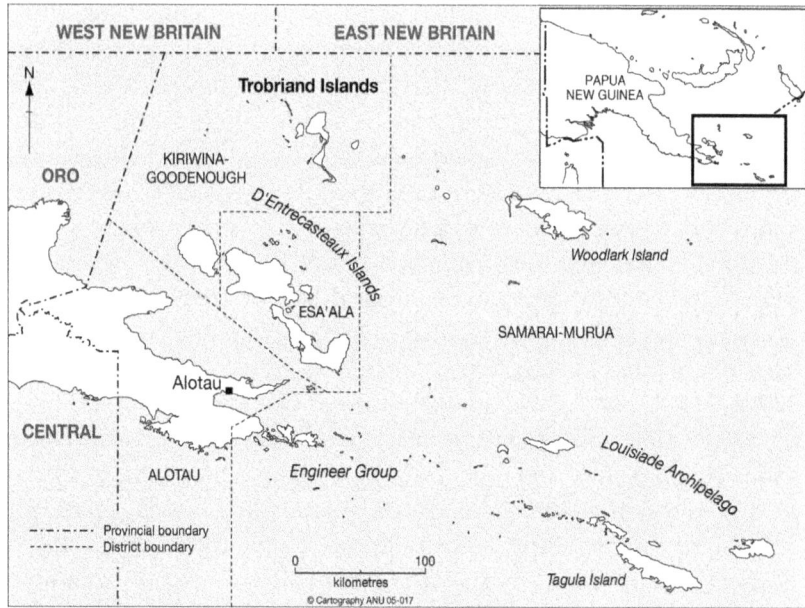

Figure 8.2: Map of Milne Bay Province, south-eastern Papua New Guinea, showing the Trobriands and surrounding islands in the Solomon Sea.
Source: © The Australian National University, CAP Carto GIS.

The first documented sighting of the Trobriands by Europeans was in 1793, when French Rear Admiral Bruni d'Entrecasteaux named the island group after his first lieutenant Denis de Trobriand whilst sailing past, and roughly charted the northern and eastern shores.[4] Thirteen years later, British captain Abraham Bristow was frequenting the area, making contact with nearby Islanders and passing close to islands he logged as being at precisely the latitude of northern Kiriwina.[5] Unrecorded meetings during this time would have been likely between such passers-by and Trobrianders either on the beach or at sea in their large sailing canoes.

---

4   Horner 1995: 183.
5   MacGillivray 1852, I: 175–176.

Figure 8.3: First map of the Trobriands, detail from C. F. Beautemps-Beaupré, 'Carte des Archipels des îles Salomon, de la Louisiade et de la Nouv.^{le} Bretagne; situes a l'est de la Nouvelle Guinee / redigee par C.F. Beautemps-Beaupré, hydrographe sous-chef du depot g.^{al} de la marine en 1806', 1807.

Source: National Library of Australia MAP Ra 82 (Copy 1) Plate 21.

By the early 1830s a more regular form of European contact was taking place, as whalers extended their hunt into the Solomon Sea.[6] The first recorded direct encounter between Europeans and Trobriand Islanders comes through a brief account given by Captain R. L. Hunter of the British whaler *Marshall Bennett*, which dropped anchor off Cape Denis on north-western Kiriwina in October 1836. While Hunter's men remained warily in their whaleboats, the Trobrianders there to receive them showed no hesitation, wading out to the boats with baskets of yams – as Hunter noted, 'in fact, as many as we could find room for, of the finest yams I ever saw', to exchange for hoop iron.[7] Trobriand

---
6 Thomas Beale writes evocatively of being becalmed aboard the British whaler *Kent* north of the Lusancays (just west of the Trobriands) in 1832. Beale 1839: 310.
7 Hunter 1839: 38.

yams were valued by whalers as a staple that was easily stored in barrels and kept well, and Hunter was surely not the first whaler to call into Cape Denis, as the Islanders' readiness to trade indicates a well-worn routine on their part. The Trobriands became known as one of the few places in the region where whalers could safely come ashore to trade for food and gather wood and water without fear of attack, and the islands were regularly visited until the decline of the industry in the 1860s.

By the 1840s, *bêche de mer* collectors and traders had joined the whalers visiting the area. Russian anthropologist Nikolai Miklouho-Maclay briefly visited the Trobriands in late November 1879, aboard the *Sadie F. Caller*, a 'smart three-masted American schooner' engaged in the trade.[8] Five years later, the German ethnologist and naturalist Otto Finsch called in briefly aboard the German steamer *Samoa*. Both men were pressed with carvings for trade. Finsch remarked that he already knew of the Trobriands' 'excellent yams' before visiting, since small trading vessels had been coming down from German New Guinea to barter for them for some years.[9]

While these early visits had been recorded, apparently none of them were known to MacGregor in 1890. Information from these contacts was either buried in whaling logs and thick shipping atlases or published in foreign languages. It may be difficult to imagine today how disconnected various disciplinary, generic, regional and national information flows were at the time.

Furthermore, others had good reason to keep their 'discoveries' in the islands a secret, so much so that facts surrounding this early contact period remain murky. Englishman William Whitten was one of the earliest 'settlers' in the islands of eastern British New Guinea, having arrived in the territory in 1874. Often humbly described as 'a storekeeper at Samarai' (a European settlement in China Strait off the eastern tip of New Guinea), he was a keen and opportunistic entrepreneur, soon making a good business outfitting the many miners that flocked to each new gold strike in the area.[10] According to Leo Austen, an Australian resident magistrate in the Trobriands in the 1930s, Whitten and a Norwegian named Oscar Solberg had

---

8   Webster 1984: 223.
9   Finsch 1888: 204–210. Trobriand passage translated for the author by Hilary Howes.
10 Nelson 1976.

established a 'fishing station' (actually a site for smoking and storing *bêche-de-mer* for occasional collection) on north-west Kiriwina in the 1880s.[11] C. A. W. Monckton wrote that while trading in *bêche de mer*, Whitten became the first European to discover 'that pearls of a fair quality existed in a small oyster forming one of the staple foods of the natives', managing to keep this a secret and to 'purchase large quantities of the pearls from the natives for almost nothing' until the sale of his haul in Australia let the secret out, which 'brought down upon him a host of other competitors'. While denied a possible fortune by the competition, Whitten had 'made enough to bring a younger brother from England, purchase a bigger and better vessel, also a large amount of merchandise', thereby laying the foundation for the formidable Whitten Bros holdings of the next several decades.[12] Austen noted that Whitten's friendships with Trobrianders were memorable enough that 'the people have gone so far as to name a special dance after him. This is known as the *Bwiteni*'.[13] Whitten called at the islands regularly during the period of MacGregor's initial tours (see below).

MacGregor's brief first visit to the Trobriands in July 1890 aboard the government steamer *Merrie England* came on the way back to the mainland after an inaugural trip to Woodlark Island to the east, in company with Reverend George Brown, head of the Australasian Wesleyan Methodist Missionary Society and a veteran of mission work in Oceania, first in Samoa then more recently in the New Britain group north of the Trobriands in German New Guinea.[14] While MacGregor went to Woodlark to investigate the murder of two white traders, he and Brown were also surveying the area for promising locations for new mission stations, as MacGregor felt that missionaries were indispensable to the work of 'civilising' the Papuans. Their first Trobriand stop was the eastern island of Kitava, where they camped on Nurata, a small islet just off the southern coast. MacGregor reported that:

> In the morning at least 200 people came round the coast to the nearest point of Kitava extremely anxious to trade with us. They were very friendly and do not carry arms ... It is clear that they and all the other

---

11   Austen 1936: 10.
12   Monckton 1921: 4–5. While Monckton has garnered a reputation for inaccuracy, in a close study Nancy Lutton concluded that while exaggerating his own adventures, the first two of his three memoirs on British New Guinea are reasonably accurate. Lutton 1972.
13   Austen 1936: 10.
14   Gardner 2006.

natives of the Trobriands have a great aptitude for carving in wood ... We were surprised at the number of people that appeared on Kitava, which was so deeply wooded that it might at a little distance have been thought to be uninhabited.[15]

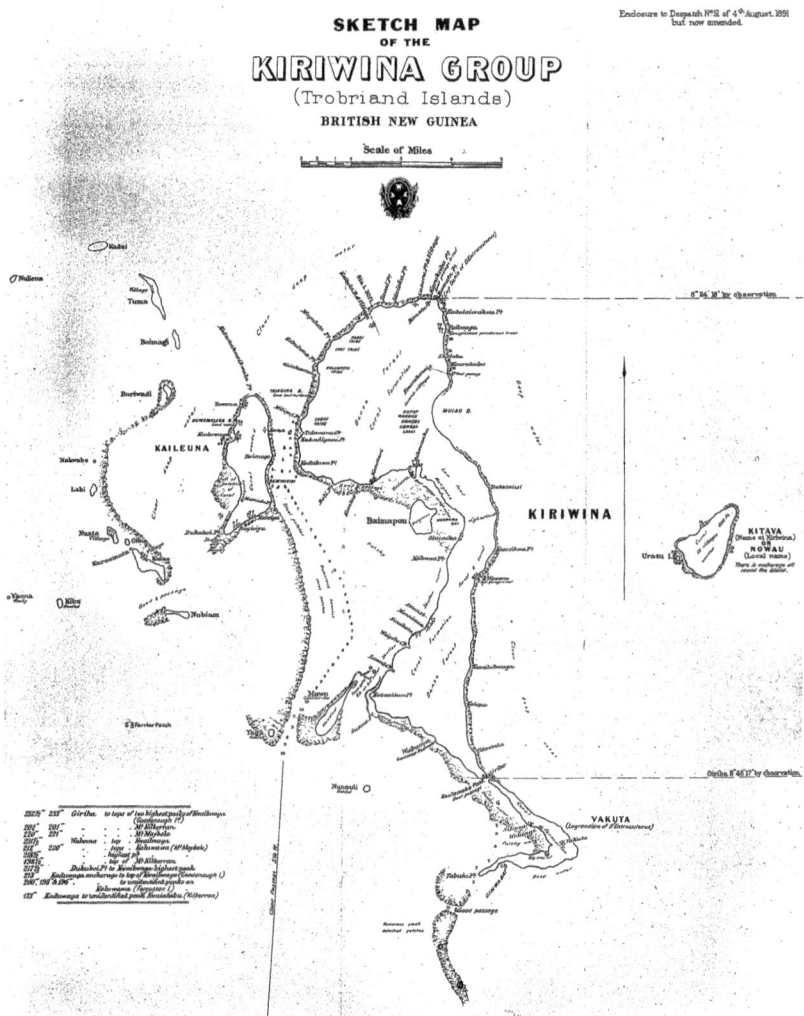

Figure 8.4: William MacGregor, 'Sketch Map of the Kiriwina Group', 1893.
Source: National Archives of Papua New Guinea.

---

15   MacGregor 1892: 7.

The view of Kitava from offshore, with large inland villages lying hidden beyond tall, thickly wooded cliffs, would fool anyone unfamiliar with the island. The spot where the steamer dropped anchor had in fact been one of the preferred stopping places for whalers, so it was no surprise that Kitavans en masse made for the *Merrie England* to trade at first light.

From Kitava the steamer proceeded around Kiriwina's northern end and directly to the large coastal village of Kaduwaga on the western island of Kaileuna, indicating that MacGregor had at least some information about points of interest in the islands, yet not enough to correctly record their names, relying on poor communication with Kitavans to derive 'Waiyova' for Boyowa (a local name for Kiriwina), and 'Avatana' for Kaileuna. As they passed Tauwema village on the north coast of Kaileuna 'some of the natives came out to meet us on canoes, and were very desirous that we should stop there', apparently to trade.

The Trobriand passion for encounter and exchange, as well as MacGregor's growing realisation of the group's popularity amongst traders, was further demonstrated upon arrival at Kaduwaga:

> Before the anchor was down the steamer was surrounded by a crowd of canoes, the occupants of which wished to sell yams. It appears that German traders come to the Trobriands to purchase yams for Matupi [Rabaul in German New Guinea]. A schooner named the 'Hans' is engaged in this trade. We were very kindly received by the people and presented to the chiefs.[16]

MacGregor found that while no English was spoken, a few words of German were known. MacGregor and Brown were 'almost able to hold a sort of broken conversation by means of the languages of Fiji, Murua [Woodlark] and Matupi'. The fecundity of the place was striking to MacGregor, who had seen more of Papua than any other European before him:

> The fertility of the soil was evident from the immense stores of excellent yams stacked up in specially constructed log houses. Nowhere else in the possession have I seen so much food in stock. Besides yams, they brought two pigs to the steamer for sale and a great quantity of newly caught fish.[17]

---

16   MacGregor 1892: 7.
17   MacGregor 1892: 7.

Figure 8.5: Trobriand yam houses, 1897. Photograph by George Brown.
Source: Australian Museum.

The village chiefs paddled out to the steamer the next morning with presents of cooked food.[18] Impressed by what little he saw of the Trobriands on this first visit and charmed by the people, MacGregor hinted at feeling misinformed about the islands:

> The whole [of the Trobriand group] are greatly more important than I had been led to believe, as regards extent, productiveness and population. It will, however, take two or three weeks to inspect the whole, a task I fear must be deferred for some time.

MacGregor's sources for information on the islands would have been the itinerant traders based at Samarai. Many of these were loners and malcontents who would not have been friendly toward the nascent government, and even the more gentlemanly adventurers such as Whitten and Solberg would have at first been ambivalent and rather close-lipped.[19]

---

18   Trobriand society is one of few in Melanesia to possess an hereditary system of ranked chieftainship, but one that includes much room for competition between the various chiefs, or *guyau*. See Malinowski 1922: 62–70; also Mosko 1995.
19   Back in Samarai six months after MacGregor's first visit, when it was clear that he would be paying closer attention to the islands, Whitten offered more detailed geographical and ethnographic information, plus the news that 'they stole several things from [MacGregor's party] at Kaduwaga when we were there'. MacGregor, Diary, 1 January 1891, NLA MS 38.

8. LOCAL AGENCY & WILLIAM MACGREGOR'S EXPLORATION OF THE TROBRIAND ISLANDS

Judging from MacGregor's 'first contacts', by 1890 Trobrianders saw the arrival of a European vessel as an opportunity to trade yams and carvings for valuable iron, and were highly competitive amongst themselves for access to the foreigners. The chiefs' visit on board with gifts of food was part and parcel of this competition, as they attempted to secure the newcomers as exclusive trade partners by opening an exchange relationship and by 'softening' their minds, to use a *kula* term, with gifts.[20]

Trobriand receptions of Europeans were modelled upon long engagement in regional networks such as the *kula*, wherein visiting exchange partners are competitively hosted in order to romance from them objects of desire. *Kula* strategy centres upon impressing counterparts with one's power, attractiveness, influence and generosity, and it is interesting to note that *kula* magic (*mwasila*) is closely linked to the magic of beauty and attraction.[21] Having long experience with visiting Europeans, of different sorts but all intent upon trade, Trobriand chiefs immediately placed MacGregor as another potential trade partner, and each did all in his power to impress and ingratiate this newcomer. MacGregor's Oceanian crew would likely also have been regarded as potential exchange partners, and fêted as well.

MacGregor returned a year later, in July 1891, for a longer tour of introduction and inspection. He was dropped at Kaduwaga with a whaleboat and 'a boat's crew of Papuans and South Sea Islanders', instructing the *Merrie England* to collect the party a week later.[22] MacGregor makes little further mention of this boatload of Oceanians, and so a prominent element of the visit, that of their own encounters with Trobrianders, remains a largely hidden history. MacGregor took a few of his crew along when walking inland from the beaches, but most would have remained with the boat and interacted with locals on their own terms. These kinds of local interactions between Papuans and other Pacific Islanders, unmediated and often unnoticed by Europeans, formed the backbone of the colonial encounter in the Trobriands, as elsewhere in the region.[23]

---

20   Malinowski 1922: 360–361; 1929: 330; Campbell 2002: 43.
21   Malinowski 1929: 186 fn.
22   MacGregor 1893a: 3.
23   See Thomas 2010: 16–17 and *passim*. See also Gammage (1998), offering a detailed account of how a later government expedition in New Guinea was in large part conducted by Indigenous participants, with three European 'leaders' serving as figureheads.

MacGregor's aim on this second visit was to get as comprehensive a view of the islands as possible given his limited amount of time. The visit generated a lengthy despatch, in which a straightforward description of the topography of the group and its people is joined by close observation of those facts and conditions that informed upon future prospects for governance, trade, industry and missionisation, all folded into a narrative of the events of his tour. Great detail is also given to descriptions of the surrounding waters and the suitability of anchorages for ships of various sizes.

Following a short inspection of the outer islet of Buriwadi to the west, the party returned to Kaileuna, from where 'the principal chief of Kaddawaga [sic], Tosieru, and a young man named Puluaiwa, who knew about a dozen words of English slang, accompanied me all over the group up to the moment I left in the steamer'; hence, although barely mentioning them again, MacGregor was never without these elite local intermediaries throughout his tour.[24] With 14 years' experience dealing with the stratified societies of Fiji, he was gratified to find in Papua a similar system of Trobriand chieftainship. MacGregor showed great interest in meeting the chiefs around the islands, and was careful to note the names of all those he met along with village and district names. For his part, Tosieru would have aimed to demonstrate to other chiefs his influence over this distinguished friend and guest by staying at his side throughout his visit. The party spent the night at Tauwema under the care of another solicitous chief:

> The chief of Tawema is Katuwauta, a lame and very amiable man, who was very desirous of making us comfortable. We were very liberally supplied with cooked yams of different kinds, cocoanuts, &c … I there received a visit from Tudava, chief of the neighbouring village of Waigiri. These two chiefs assured me that their people never fight with any other tribes. We saw nothing reprehensible in their conduct, save perhaps that their women are allowed too much freedom with strangers.[25]

---

24   MacGregor's original spelling of place names (which varies at times) is retained in all quotes, while I use more standard spellings employed by Trobrianders and researchers over time. MacGregor learned the next year that Puluaiwa was in fact Paramount Chief Numakala's son. MacGregor 1893b: 28.
25   MacGregor 1893a: 3.

8. LOCAL AGENCY & WILLIAM MACGREGOR'S EXPLORATION OF THE TROBRIAND ISLANDS

From Tauwema the party rowed over to Kaibola on the north coast of Kiriwina. MacGregor initially saw no one, just a few canoes drawn up on the beach where the party made camp, 'but there were 500 or 600 round us before sunset'. Upon hearing the news of the arrival of strangers, everyone within walking or paddling distance who could come to the beach apparently did so, and hence MacGregor got his first taste of an enduring Kiriwinan welcome, the curious throng.

After exploring the rugged east coast of Kiriwina by boat the next day, MacGregor returned to find Tawaguguna, the chief of Kaibola, waiting for him on the beach, 'physically a very fine specimen of the Papuan race, and a very kind and hospitable person, manifesting not the least distrust or suspicion'. On previous explorations elsewhere in the Territory, MacGregor had grown used to encountering people who were shy, afraid or downright hostile to his advances. This enthusiastic welcome by Trobriand crowds, and the easy-going hospitality of the chiefs, were both unexpected and appreciated.

The party passed an uneasy night, not from fear of attack by warriors lurking in the bush, but from the unceasing chatter of what turned into a gigantic slumber party: 'Some 200 or 300 natives camped all night near us; and as at least half of the whole number were ever talking at once, there was not much sleep to be had in our camp.' MacGregor's visit coincided with the harvest celebrations of *Milamala*, so beyond a large contingent from Kaibola, other people would have been socialising away from their villages and staying out through the night.[26]

The next morning MacGregor was welcomed into Kaibola village half a mile from the beach, where he was visited by 'three chiefs ... from other tribes'. He did not realise – nor was he told – that he was being sized up by some of the most important men on the island, the highest ranking members of the senior branch of the chiefly *Tabalu* matriline of northern Kiriwina: 'Each with a number of men came to see me. They were Toula, of Omerakana; Numakala, of Utabala; and Utabalu of Kaisanai; all large men, and two of them with a decided tendency to obesity – a great rarity among Papuan men. They were all very friendly.' MacGregor's 'Toula' was To'uluwa, brother of Paramount Chief Numakala, both of whom would have been residing

---

26 See Malinowski 1929: 212–213.

at Omarakana, so MacGregor's attribution of villages was partly mistaken. To'uluwa succeeded his brother as Paramount Chief in 1899 and held the position until his death in 1933, famously hosting the young anthropologist Bronislaw Malinowski at Omarakana during World War I.[27] Unsure of MacGregor's intentions, Trobrianders withheld Numakala's true status, and the identity of Omarakana as the seat of the Paramount Chief, until his third visit the next year.[28]

MacGregor impressed upon the chiefs the advent of the *Pax Britannica*, and was met with convincing expressions of wholehearted approval:

> When it was pointed out to them that the Government would interfere in future and punish any tribe that molested its neighbors, they protested that they would not fight; that they had no desire to fight, and that they were prepared at once to sell me all their spears … They said that they understood the position of the government. It was quite plain that social matters are in Kiriwina on a footing quite different from that of any other part of British New Guinea.[29]

This turned out to be polite lip service to their guest. Formalised warfare was not suppressed for nearly a decade, fighting waxed and waned throughout the colonial era and through Papua New Guinea's independence in 1975, and loosely organised inter-village fights flare up sporadically to this day.

In the afternoon MacGregor's party rowed down the west coast of Kiriwina, from Kaibola to Boli Point at the north-western edge of the great Kiriwinan lagoon, pitching camp on a secluded beach, '[b]ut our presence soon became known to the people of Kavatari, and by dusk there were probably nearly 200 of them in our camp'. In the morning even more people appeared, and MacGregor walked the two miles to the large lagoon village of Kavataria accompanied by chief Pulitala of Mlosaida (adjacent to Kavataria) and followed by this 'great crowd', while the whaleboat followed along the shore, escorted by a fleet of 53 canoes.[30]

---

27 While clearly another high-ranking kinsman, it is unclear exactly who the third man, 'Utabalu of Kaisanai' [adjacent to Omarakana], was, but he may have been Tagilai, a third brother named by MacGregor in a later despatch (MacGregor 1898: 38). It seems that 'Utabala' (the village) and 'Utabalu' (the man) were misrecognitions of the term 'Tabalu'.

28 MacGregor 1893b: 28.

29 MacGregor 1893a: 3–4.

30 MacGregor 1893a: 4.

Figure 8.6: Paramount Chief Numakala and son
(possibly Puluaiwa), 1897. Photograph by George Brown.
Source: Australian Museum.

MacGregor was keen to note the particulars of Trobriand chieftainship, to him a rare example of hereditary rank in the Territory: 'It was very seldom that a woman or a boy approached a chief except in a crouching attitude; and the chief, called in their language Guiao, is listened to and treated with respect.' MacGregor at once put into play the strategy towards chiefs that would become long-term policy: 'Of course the chief in every instance received special consideration at my hands, but there was no difficulty in putting them in the position of inferior chief towards the administrator. Good opportunities occurred several times for doing this publicly.'[31] An example of this public display of the new order came at Kavataria, in view of a crowd of 1,200 to 1,500 onlookers:

> When we arrived there a small number of leading men were seated in front of the village on a small platform, apparently erected there for that purpose. On landing, I took possession of this, turning them all off, and allowing no one there save the two principal chiefs. This was not regarded at all with ill-humour, as would be the case in many parts of the possession, but was amongst this people at once recognised as the proper course for me to take.[32]

While MacGregor viewed this as a display of his authority, the two chiefs that remained on the platform would have been delighted at this distinguished outsider's public recognition of their locally contested status.[33]

MacGregor continued his tour for another six days, walking inland to visit villages and rowing south along the lagoon to the southern island of Vakuta before returning to Kaduwaga to be picked up by the steamer.

MacGregor's first-person narrative reads like an explorer's account, as he writes of his personal discoveries, and adds them to the fledgling government's knowledge of its territory. But he does not hide the fact that he was a latecomer. Everywhere MacGregor went along the coast he saw people curing *bêche-de-mer* 'for the trader'. At Sinaketa the business was substantial ('They secure a considerable quantity of trepang for trade') but generally it was on a small scale, such as at Labai ('They were also curing a few bêche-de-mer, with which to

---

31 MacGregor 1893a: 4.
32 MacGregor 1893a: 4.
33 One of these two 'principal chiefs' would have been Pulitala, of a junior branch of the chiefly Tabalu, the highest ranking chief on the lagoon and arguably the second most powerful chief in the islands at the time. The other man was most likely either the non-chiefly headman of Kavataria, one of Pulitala's kinsmen, or the Tabalu chief of Gumilababa, a mile inland to the north.

purchase tobacco from the trader') and at Kavataria ('they obtain a few trepang for the trader'). But also at Kavataria MacGregor noted that '[t]his tribe is very keen on trading and are regularly visited by traders', so at least there, more may have been on offer beyond the odd basket of sea slugs. We have seen that German traders had long been coming down from Matupit to Kaduwaga for yams, and it is likely that Kavataria and adjacent villages were also selling them. Carvings and other local wares are also likely to have been offered.[34] While traders apparently had not yet taken up residence around the lagoon (but would by the time the first resident missionary arrived three years later), the trade in pearls, which would form the foundation for Trobriand economic activity for the next 20 years, may already have begun, unbeknownst to MacGregor. Trobrianders would probably not have volunteered such information to MacGregor unless asked directly, and his despatch seems to indicate that lacking a fluent interpreter, the bulk of his information came from direct observation, not questioning. Whitten was likely collecting pearls by this time and, if his secret had already gotten out, other traders would also have had an interest in continuing to keep it under wraps to avoid taxes, duties and other regulation.

What is clear is that by this time Trobrianders had had enough contact with 'the trader' to become inveterate smokers: 'They are all passionately fond of tobacco, and their use of it is more thorough than I have ever observed elsewhere. They seem to swallow the smoke, and learn to retain it for a considerable time, and then emit it through the nostrils.'[35] This passion seems to have taken hold rapidly, since Finsch had reported in 1888 that Trobrianders had no knowledge nor interest in tobacco.[36] Just three years later, the lust for nicotine had eclipsed even the desire for iron tools, and was the key motivation for Trobriand–European interaction for decades, colouring relations with government, traders and missionaries alike. One of the many chiefs to assure MacGregor that fighting was a thing of the past reportedly remarked, 'If I were to fight, where should I get my tobacco from?'[37]

---

34 The Kuboma district near Kavataria had long been home to a local industry turning out wooden bowls and other utensils for inter-island trade. Upon the offer of 'all their spears' for sale at Kaibola, MacGregor, always the astute collector, wrote 'As they were, in most instances, made of ebony, I should gladly have accepted the challenge had it been possible for me to carry them, which was not the case in only a whaleboat with all our stores and baggage'. MacGregor 1893a: 4.
35 MacGregor 1893a: 4.
36 Finsch 1888: 208.
37 MacGregor 1893a: 4.

MacGregor was a keen observer and natural writer, and in 8,000 words left an insightful depiction of the Trobriand Islands in the late 1800s, with descriptions of landscape, culture, subsistence, language, dress, villages, housing and health conditions, all couched in a narrative that includes telling accounts of his interactions with Trobrianders. General appraisals expected from his administrative viewpoint are joined with an ethnographer's eye for small details of observation. Some comments seem to serve only to relate a bit of colour, such as at Obweria, an inland village where a visit from a European was entirely novel: 'The women, especially the old women, were very curious to see a white man, and delighted in peering into my eyes.'[38] There is room for humorous anecdote that lends a sense of humanity to Trobrianders, all too often missing from colonial writing. Upon leaving Obweria:

> Our guide was unable to separate himself from his pig – a fine half-grown animal. This creature would insist on following him like a dog, of which the poor man was greatly ashamed, and he several times in ill-temper severely punished the pig in trying to send it home. But the Papuan pig is certainly the most affectionate, the most active, and the most intelligent of swine; and this devoted adherent, if driven off at one point, soon appeared on the path ahead waiting for its owner.[39]

Throughout his one-week tour MacGregor was greeted, guided and fêted by various chiefs, who appear to artfully manage his visit in order to impress and gratify him, but also to display an easy association with this exotic visitor for their own local benefit. They used him in many ways as a curiosity, just as European nobility had long patronised exotic human beings from faraway lands for their own aggrandisement. On Vakuta, MacGregor observed that, '[t]hey said they had heard all about the government from Murua, and had long been expecting me ... We had the same kind, hospitable and unsuspicious reception here as we had received elsewhere in Kiriwina'.[40] MacGregor was so enamoured with the chiefs that upon finding one away from Vakuta 'on a voyage to the island of Kitava', he pressed on to the next village to enjoy the hospitality of one at home.[41] While the *guyau* of various villages would have conferred about MacGregor's visit, most would have been acting independently

---

38   MacGregor 1893a: 5.
39   MacGregor 1893a: 5.
40   MacGregor 1893a: 6.
41   MacGregor 1893a: 6.

of each other, yet all offered surprisingly similar welcomes, making the party comfortable, offering food in excess, and treating MacGregor as a visiting chief. All were quick to proclaim their friendliness, not only towards the new government but also towards their neighbours.

MacGregor saw the Trobriands as unique from elsewhere in British New Guinea on many levels and, like observers before and after,[42] was quick to note a seemingly Polynesian flavour: '[The Trobriand group] is the point of contact between Papua and the Pacific, tinctured of both.' The chiefs' hospitality had the desired effect on MacGregor, as he summed up his sanguine opinion of the islands:

> Altogether the impression produced on my mind by the people and country is a very favourable one ... In many ways they are a long step in advance of the natives on the north-east coast [of mainland New Guinea] ... the position of the chief is recognised and understood. They are industrious and well fed, and physically they are of superior build.[43]

Not fully aware of the regularity and variety of trade already established, MacGregor opined that '[i]f some new industry could be introduced which would create something for export, there can be no doubt that Kiriwina would become an important trading centre'. As for missionary prospects, 'it is not unlikely that these tribes may possess some trace of that religious sentiment which is so conspicuously absent in the Papuan generally. As a mission field it could be hardly surpassed.'[44]

While an insightful observer in many respects, MacGregor failed to recognise the relatively high status and independence given to women. His earlier remark that they were perhaps 'allowed too much freedom with strangers' might indicate offers of sexual hospitality – he noted in his diary that the missionaries Bromilow and Abel were offered such upon arriving with him on his third visit six months later,[45] or it may simply reflect more generally the social status and

---

42 For instance, Finsch (1888) speculated that Trobrianders were 'a mixed race', a blending of 'Oceanic' and 'Melanesian' blood, and the fact that they were 'noserubbers' (as a greeting) was 'again indicative of Polynesia'. Hagelberg et al. (1999) claim that genetic evidence of 'the remarkable affinity' between Trobrianders and Polynesians 'argues for a recent migration of people east from Polynesia into island Melanesia'.
43 MacGregor 1893a: 6.
44 MacGregor 1893a: 7.
45 MacGregor, Diary, 8 January 1892, NLA MS 38.

freedoms enjoyed by Trobriand women.[46] Regardless, MacGregor's impression of the standing of women, as stated in his conclusion, was mistaken; he concluded they had 'less influence and have much less to say than is the case in many of the ruder tribes on the mainland … this is apparently a consequence of the superior position of the chief in the Kiriwina social system'.[47] It was certainly true that his misconstruction of women's roles had everything to do with the chiefs, but only in that MacGregor's nearly exclusive interactions with chiefs presented him with a limited view of Trobriand society.

MacGregor's experience in the Trobriands was not completely positive. Beyond the women's 'freedom with strangers', he had to deal with a theft whilst receiving Pulitala amongst 'a great crowd' on the beach west of Kavataria: 'A young man stole a looking glass from the travelling bag of one of my boatmen, and the latter promptly seized an ebony bowl belonging to the father of the thief.' A tug-of-war over the bowl ensued that threatened to ignite a 'disturbance' between locals and his crew, but MacGregor took possession of the bowl until, after some misunderstanding, the mirror was returned. He felt this episode worked to his favour: 'this incident established my position as superior chief, and it put a stop to all attempts at pilfering on the part of the natives'.[48] MacGregor literally flexed his muscles upon arriving at the large southern lagoon village of Sinaketa, where he found the people:

> inclined to be somewhat more unruly than they had been elsewhere. One young man asked one of my party for some tobacco, and on being refused struck him on the back with his hand, more in playful impudence than in malice. I saw this, and went up to him and gave his head a wrench, which nearly threw him on his back. When he recovered his balance he fled out of the crowd … after this I was treated with profound respect, and there was no further display of rowdyism.[49]

---

46 See Malinowski 1929; Weiner 1976, 1988; Lepani 2012.
47 MacGregor 1893a: 7.
48 MacGregor 1893a: 4.
49 MacGregor 1893a: 5–6.

This aggressive reaction to a minor display of 'rowdyism' reflects MacGregor's anxiety towards being surrounded by large crowds, which could quickly turn from friendly to violent. His strategy was to tolerate no such displays, even of the most minor sort.

But even at their most friendly, the pressing, noisy crowds that gathered around his camps and attempted to accompany him wherever he went proved tiresome. At Kaibola, '[t]he noise of babbling voices was so great … that it was a great relief to be able to resume our journey down the west side of the island', and upon leaving Teavi to walk inland, '[s]ome 200 or 300 natives wished to accompany me as guides, and it was with the very greatest difficulty that I could reduce my escort to half a score, with two or three of my boat boys'. Later the same day, '[a]s usual, the whole village of Obweba [Obweria] would have gone on to guide me to the next tribe; only one man was constituted official conductor, but a large number followed behind'. Upon anchoring again at Kaduwaga on his third visit, 'a great crowd came out making a frightful row, selling food etc'.[50]

But these irritations were minor compared to the positive image of the Trobriands MacGregor came away with. The artfully managed reception of MacGregor by the chiefs had a long-term effect that is as yet largely unexplored. MacGregor's dispatches, published over 20 years before Malinowski set foot in the islands, were in large part the beginning of a European construction of the Trobriands as a special place in Melanesia, with political and social institutions perceived as akin to an idealised Polynesia. This conception would mark the islands for special treatment for the next 80 years of Anglo-Australian administration and missionisation, and may be one explanation for the oft-noted resiliency of traditional Trobriand culture in the face of those 80 years of colonial and Christian contact.

---

50   MacGregor, Diary, 8 January 1892, NLA MS 38.

Acknowledgements

The research for this chapter was conducted with the support of the School of Culture, History and Language, College of Asia and the Pacific, The Australian National University. The author thanks Chris Ballard, Valerie Bichard, Jay Crain, Allan Darrah, Bronwen Douglas, Dario Di Rosa, Joseph Foukona, Elena Govor, Nicholas Halter, Anna Kwai, Latu Latai, Antje Lubcke, Gonzaga Puas, Cesar Suva, Graeme Whimp and Michael Young for helpful feedback on various drafts.

References

Austen, Leo 1936, 'The Trobriand Islands of Papua', *Australian Geographer* 111(2): 10–22.

Beale, Thomas 1839, *The Natural History of the Sperm Whale… /, to which is added a sketch of a South-Sea whaling voyage… / in which the author was personally engaged*, second edition, John Van Voorst, London.

Beautemps-Beaupré, Charles Francois 1807, *Carte des Archipels des iles Salomon, de la Louisiade et de la Nouv.le Bretagne; situes a l'est de la Nouvelle Guinee / redigee par C.F. Beautemps-Beaupré, hydrographe sous-chef du depot gal. de la marine en 1806*, Depot general des cartes et plans de la marine et des colonies, Paris, Plate 21.

Campbell, Shirley 2002, *The Art of Kula*, Berg, Oxford.

Finsch, Otto 1888, *Samoafahrten: Reisen in Kaiser Wilhelms-Land und Englisch-Neu-Guinea in den Jahren 1884 und 1885 an Bord des deutschen Dampfers "Samoa."* [Second Samoa Cruise: Travel in Kaiser Wilhelm's Land and English-New-Guinea in 1884 and 1885 on board the German steamer "Samoa."], Ferdinand Hirt & Sohn, Leipzig.

Gammage, Bill 1998, *The Sky Travellers: Journeys in New Guinea 1938–1939*, Melbourne University Press, Melbourne.

Gardner, Helen 2006, *Gathering for God: George Brown in Oceania*, Otago University Press, Dunedin.

Hagelberg, Erika, M. Kayser, Marion Nagy, Lutz Roewer, Heike Zimdahl, M. Krawczak, Pietro Lio and W. Schiefenhövel 1999, 'Molecular genetic evidence for the human settlement of the Pacific: Analysis of mitochondrial DNA, Y chromosome and HLA markers', *Philosophical Transactions of the Royal Society of London B: Biological Sciences* 354(1379): 141–152.

Horner, Frank 1995, *Looking for La Perouse: d'Entrecasteaux in Australia and the South Pacific 1792–1793*, Melbourne University Press, Melbourne.

Hunter, R. L. 1839, 'Gower's Harbour, New Ireland', *Nautical Magazine and Naval Chronicle* 8: 37–39.

Joyce, Roger B. 1971, *Sir William MacGregor*, Oxford University Press, Melbourne.

Lepani, Katherine 2012, *Islands of Love, Islands of Risk: Culture and HIV in the Trobriands*, Vanderbilt University Press, Nashville, TN.

Lutton, Nancy 1972, 'C.A.W. Monckton's Trilogy of his Adventures in New Guinea: Fact or Fiction?', Hons thesis, University of Papua New Guinea.

MacGillivray, John 1852, *Narrative of the Voyage of H.M.S. Rattlesnake*, vol. 1, T. & W. Boone, London.

MacGregor, William 1890–1892, Diaries [Manuscript], National Library of Australia, NLA MS 38.

—— 1892, 'Despatch Reporting Expedition to Effect Capture of Murderers of Two Traders at Murua (Woodlark Island)', in *Annual Report on British New Guinea 1890–1891*, Appendix B (16 September 1890), Government Printer, Brisbane, Qld, 4–8.

—— 1893a, 'Despatch Reporting Visits to the D'Entrecasteaux and Trobriand Groups', in *Annual Report on British New Guinea 1891–1892*, Appendix A (4 August 1891), Government Printer, Brisbane, Qld, 2–7.

—— 1893b, 'Despatch Continuing the Report of his Visit of Inspection to the Eastern portion of the Possession', in *Annual Report on British New Guinea 1891–1892*, Appendix G (9 February 1892), Government Printer, Brisbane, Qld, 27–31.

—— 1898, 'Despatch reporting visit to Kiriwina', in *Annual Report on British New Guinea 1897–1898*, Appendix I (8 July 1897), Government Printer, Brisbane, Qld, 37–39.

Malinowski, Bronislaw K. 1922, *Argonauts of the Western Pacific: An account of native enterprise and adventure in the archipelagoes of Melanesian New Guinea*, G. Routledge, London.

—— 1929, *The Sexual Life of Savages in North-Western Melanesia: An ethnographic account of courtship, marriage and family life among the natives of the Trobriand Islands, British New Guinea*, Routledge and Kegan Paul, London.

Monckton, Charles Arthur Whitmore 1921, *Some Experiences of a New Guinea Resident Magistrate*, John Lane, London.

Mosko, Mark 1995, 'Rethinking Trobriand chieftainship', *The Journal of the Royal Anthropological Institute* 1(4): 763–785.

Nelson, Hank 1976, *Black, White and Gold: Goldmining in Papua New Guinea 1878–1930*, Australian National University Press, Canberra.

Powell, Henry A. 1956, 'An Analysis of Present Day Social Structure in the Trobriand Islands', PhD thesis, University of London.

Sinclair, James 2009, *Gavamani: The Magisterial Service of British New Guinea*, Crawford House Publishing Australia, Adelaide.

Thomas, Nicolas 2010, *Islanders: The Pacific in the Age of the Empire*, Yale University Press, New Haven.

Webster, Elsie May 1984, *The Moon Man: A Biography of Nikolai Miklouho-Maclay*, Melbourne University Press, Carlton, Vic.

Weiner, Annette 1976, *Women of Value, Men of Renown: New Perspectives in Trobriand Exchange*, University of Texas Press, Austin.

—— 1988, *The Trobrianders of Papua New Guinea*, Holt, Rhinehart and Winston, New York.

9

Explorers & co. in interior New Guinea, 1872–1928

Chris Ballard

Lagging behind interest in the exploration of central Africa and Australia, the interior of New Guinea scarcely featured in the imaginary of colonial exploration until the 1840s. Joseph Beete Jukes, naturalist and geologist on the surveying expeditions to New Guinea of HMS *Fly* under Captain Blackwood between 1842 and 1846, famously exclaimed that:

> I know of no part of the world, the exploration of which is so flattering to the imagination, so likely to be fruitful in interesting results, whether to the naturalist, the ethnologist, or the geographer, and altogether so well calculated to gratify the enlightened curiosity of an adventurous explorer, as the interior of New Guinea. New Guinea! The very mention of being taken into the interior of New Guinea sounds like being allowed to visit some of the enchanted regions of the Arabian Nights, so dim an atmosphere of obscurity rests at present on the wonders it probably contains.[1]

If the exploration of coastlines was founded on the ability to chart their material presence, interiors invited acts of imagination, projective leaps beyond the visible.[2] Johannes Fabian has identified the quality

---
1 Jukes 1847, I: 291.
2 Glen 2000.

of the anticipated interior as that of 'a political vacuum, nothing but "geography"';[3] but the unfolding history of interior exploration witnesses an inexorable shift from geography to ethnography and then politics, from a concern for surveying the landscape accurately, to engaging its inhabitants and plotting their distribution and disposition, and then seeking to control them.

In the broadest of terms, the early exploration of interior New Guinea moved through a series of stages, with transitions from one to the next accompanied by transformations in the nature of the relationship with its inhabitants. Between 1825 and 1850, the Morse code of New Guinea's coastline was gradually replaced by a more bounded form, fixed in place by the method propagated by d'Entrecasteaux's surveyor, Charles-François Beautemps-Beaupré, which consisted of triangulating the heights of prominent landmarks from a distance of about 40 miles off the coast.[4] Curiously, much of the earliest detailed cartographic knowledge of New Guinea was thus produced largely by standing off its shores, rather than landing, and the scope for engagement with local communities and consequent dependence on intermediaries were thus correspondingly limited. The chagrin of the naturalists on board HMS *Fly* and, later, HMS *Rattlesnake* under Captain Owen Stanley, who were frequently denied opportunities to land and collect, was almost palpable, evident in the youthful Thomas Huxley's declaration: 'If this is surveying, if this is the process of English discovery, God defend me from any such elaborate waste of time and opportunity.'[5]

When the time came (and it came relatively late in New Guinea), the earliest strategies for terrestrial exploration beyond the beach generally took two forms: either navigation by boat up and then back down the largest rivers; or walking to visible features, such as distant peaks, and returning. Few had struck out from the security of rivers or away from direct line of sight to a mountain peak. The earliest European attempts to move beyond the safety of rivers were cautious affairs by comparison with contemporary interior exploration in Africa and

---

3   Fabian 2000: 34.
4   Kingston 2007: 146.
5   Huxley 1936: 130.

Australia.⁶ As late as 1877, Andrew Goldie could make the proud boast that 'I have the honour to be the first European … to penetrate by land for a considerable distance into the interior of New Guinea' – 'considerable distance' at this time being reckoned at about 40 miles.⁷ Over the next 30 years, others would go further: the indefatigable Lieutenant Governor William MacGregor ascended every major river in Papua to its navigable limit, crossed twice from Port Moresby to the Mambare River on the north coast of British New Guinea, and in 1889 climbed Mt Victoria, at that time the highest point reached by a European in New Guinea.⁸ Only later did explorers seek to strike out from one river catchment across the watershed to another catchment, placing themselves increasingly (if reluctantly) in the hands of local communities; it is the changes in relations with local intermediaries contingent on this transition that are the subject of this paper.

Following Driver and Jones, I adopt a generous notion of the intermediary in exploration, which encompasses the roles of locals and non-locals, guides, native police, carriers, paramours and other expedition members, amongst others, and introduces the possibility of more elaborate categories or hierarchies of intermediary than the simple opposition between explorer and auxiliary.⁹ This chapter addresses the ways in which intermediaries are produced or acknowledged at the intersection of narrative templates for exploration and the material circumstances (objectives, topography, distance, funding, and so on) that prescribe some of the terms for an expedition's progress.

Unlike Africa or Australia, there was no ready supply on or near the coast of professional native guides for the interior of New Guinea. New Guinea's celebrated linguistic and cultural diversity, and ubiquitous raiding and feuding, ensured that few assistants acquired on arrival were familiar with either the physical or social topography more than a few miles from the coast.¹⁰ Thus early expeditions leaving Port Moresby by foot were accompanied by relays of different guides

---

6   See Kennedy 2013 on Australia and Africa. Despite sporadic attempts at the establishment of government, trading and mission stations since the 1790s, sustained European settlement on the main island of New Guinea began only in the 1870s. Souter 1963.
7   Goldie 1877–78: 219.
8   Souter 1963.
9   Driver and Jones 2009.
10 Simpson 1975; Kennedy 2013.

and relied for their local information on double interpretation.[11] To an unusual degree, the early European exploration of interior New Guinea was undertaken with assistants from the broad region (carriers and police from elsewhere in British New Guinea or Papua, for example) but with few or no local guides for periods longer than a few days. The process of learning to travel in interior New Guinea required a degree of trust between explorers and local communities that was seldom achievable at the speed with which most exploring parties travelled.

Rather than attempt a comprehensive history of the European exploration of New Guinea's interior, I want to consider the contrasting experiences of a handful of different expeditions, spanning the period from the 1870s to the 1920s, but focused on just two of the largest Papuan rivers: the Fly and the Kikori (Figure 9.1). The series of ascents of the Fly River by the Italian naturalist D'Albertis, between 1875 and 1877, nicely illustrate the nature and the limitations of riverine exploration; administrator Staniforth Smith's disastrous attempt to cross the watershed between the Kikori and Strickland rivers from 1910 to 1911 is perhaps the textbook case of 'misguided' interior exploration; while the North-West Patrol from the headwaters of the Fly to the Sepik, led by patrol officers Karius and Champion between 1926 and 1928, follows the conventional narrative of perseverance and breakthrough. In each of these vignettes, the roles of intermediaries are critical and, in each case, these roles are brought into sharpest relief at moments of crisis, in which the entire enterprise of the expedition is at risk of foundering. Local knowledge remained critical to every expedition to interior New Guinea, but it was not just that this knowledge was effaced in European accounts; rather it was often actively disregarded and undervalued in the very act of exploration.[12]

---

11   See, for example, Forbes 1888: 407.
12   Burnett 2002.

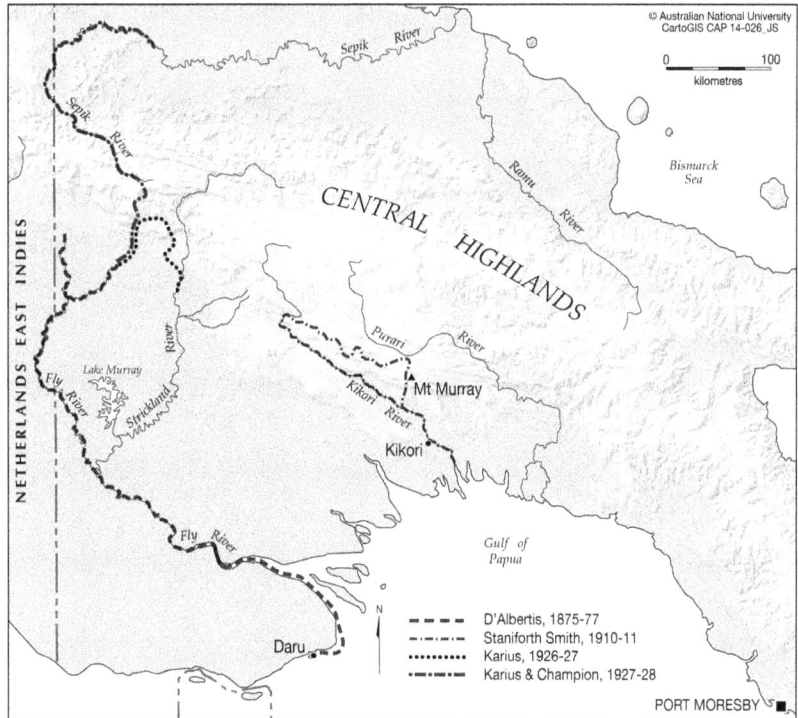

Figure 9.1: Interior New Guinea, showing explorers' routes.
Source: © The Australian National University CartoGIS.

If the shifting relationship between explorers and intermediaries is brought on or even forced in part by the changing nature of exploration, the second part of my argument is that the crises which illuminate these shifts are also an essential feature of the exploration narrative. Changes in the nature and structure of explorer narratives thus play an equally critical part in the transformation of the relationship between explorers and intermediaries. Fabian notes that the literary genre of travelogue reinforces the stereotype of the solitary hero, but it does so because the moral narratives of either transformation or unflinching maintenance of the self operate through the individual – other Europeans, as well as local actors, take a back seat.[13] The first of my vignettes is a compact illustration of the role of these narrative conventions in the description, the deployment and the fate of local intermediaries.

---

13 Fabian 2000: 24.

Captain John A. Lawson, 1872–1873?

In June 1872, shortly before Captain John Moresby set out on HMS *Basilisk* to complete the coastal surveys initiated by d'Entrecasteaux, Blackwood and Stanley, Captain John Lawson landed on the south coast of New Guinea.[14] Accompanied by a Lascar, Toolo, and two Australian Aboriginal 'bearers of baggage', Joe and Billy, he engaged the services of two Papuan assistants, Aboo and Danang, from the coastal village of Houtree. Together, they struck out on foot for the interior of New Guinea, crossing vast plains and wide rivers, and ascending a snow-peaked mountain, Mt Hercules. Disaster struck when they were attacked at an unnamed village just 30 to 40 miles from the north coast, and the expedition returned to Houtree, having walked for almost eight months. Of Lawson's five companions, only two survived: Toolo succumbed to madness and committed suicide, and Danang and Joe were killed in the skirmish near the north coast.

Lawson's companions featured prominently, if not always creditably, as porters, servants and dependents in his account of the expedition. Following Toolo's death, Lawson reflected on their three years together, during which Lawson 'had grown to look upon and treat him more like a companion and friend than a servant', reflecting Toolo's faithfulness and 'that remarkable attachment to my person which is so often found in natives of the East towards those who have treated them with kindness'.[15] The deaths of Danang and Joe were lesser events; Lawson mourned the loss during their flight from the attack of most of his 'goods and chattels', listing the items of clothing and weapons, 'to say nothing of the loss of two faithful servants'.[16] The two survivors, the Australian Billy and the Papuan Aboo, were studies in contrast: fearful, lazy, rebellious and prone to drunkenness, Billy was thrashed by Lawson on at least two occasions; Aboo, on the other hand, was both a reliable source of local information and interpretation, and a stalwart but submissive companion – still a dependent, but dependable; an 'ideal intermediary'.[17]

---

14 Lawson 1875a.
15 Lawson 1875a: 184–185.
16 Lawson 1875a: 215.
17 Kennedy 2013: 162.

Lawson's book, published in London in 1875, was roundly condemned by the majority of reviewers, who regarded it as a work of fiction and 'not even', sniffed Alfred Russel Wallace, the celebrated naturalist and early visitor to New Guinea, 'a clever fiction'.[18] Moresby's return to London from his New Guinea surveys led to open warfare in the pages of the *Athenæum* between Lawson and his critics. When Moresby himself challenged Lawson's claims, point after point, Lawson retorted that, unlike Moresby, he had actually set foot in the interior, and was not to be contradicted on the truth of his experience.[19]

Unconstrained by the exigencies of reporting facts, Lawson's account of his companions served to elicit and illustrate different facets of his own character, as an idealised explorer, including his mastery of native truculence, his personal fortitude at the head of the expedition, and his capacity for benevolence towards servants. In terms of the structure of Lawson's narrative, the loss of his companions was both a necessary sacrifice and a measure of his own endurance and good fortune. Much like the disposable sidekicks of cinema and television, expendable companions emerge as an early staple of expedition accounts.

Luigi Maria D'Albertis, 1875–1877

The Italian naturalist Luigi Maria D'Albertis may have 'thrown aside with contempt the book relating Captain Lawson's travels across New Guinea', but his own adventures offer a number of close parallels.[20] By 1875, when he joined London Missionary Society (LMS) missionary Samuel Macfarlane's *Ellangowan* expedition up the Fly River, D'Albertis had been collecting intensively in north-west and south-east New Guinea for almost three years. For the next four years, he was consumed by the desire to penetrate further and collect deeper into New Guinea's interior than any before him, and in the course of two further expeditions up the Fly River, in 1876 and again in 1877, he largely succeeded in his aims. On both occasions, the expedition ascended the Fly on the shallow-draught steam-powered vessel *Neva*, with only occasional forays to the river's banks for wood, collection and

---

18   Wallace 1875.
19   *Athenæum* 1875; Lawson 1875b; Moresby 1875; Ballard 2009.
20   D'Albertis 1880, II: 2.

hunting, to the farthest point deemed either navigable or wise, before returning. If sufficient funds had been available through his sponsor, the Sydney-based physician and naturalist George Bennett, D'Albertis had also planned to walk from the Upper Fly to Port Moresby or Yule Island over six to eight months, a venture of Lawsonesque ambition.[21]

The map that accompanies his book carries annotations that are revealing of D'Albertis's optimism and ambition, and indicative of the harsh reality of early interior exploration, including 'Highest point[s] reached' by the *Ellangowan* in 1875 and the *Neva* in 1876; 'Gold probably to be found'; 'Attacked by Natives 1876'; and 'Natives hostile, several fights with them'. All three expeditions were marred by violence, both against local communities along the river and within the expedition parties, and D'Albertis played a central role in this violence. Attacks on his boats were common, but initial restraint quickly gave way to pre-emptive strikes. D'Albertis delighted in the use of dynamite charges timed to explode beneath pursuing canoes, or signal rockets loaded with dynamite fired into settlements or massed warriors. Heads from some of the victims of this slaughter were collected and pickled, joining mummified corpses and body parts stacked against the gunwales of the *Neva* in a macabre mobile tableau.

In his choice of companions, D'Albertis outdid Lawson. He arrived in south-east Papua with three servants: Tomaselli from Genoa, who quickly left his service, and two 'Cingalese', Tom and Arnold, recruited en route in Colombo. A large retinue of 'South Sea Islanders', drawn from New Britain and the New Hebrides, and acquired through exchange with Captain Redlich, also decamped from his earlier collecting station on Yule Island. Considering himself 'alone' after the departure of Tomaselli, D'Albertis joined Macfarlane, and Henry Chester, the police magistrate at Somerset, on the *Ellangowan*'s Fly River expedition, along with six Queensland Native Police, four Loyalty Islanders and Maino of Mowatta village on the New Guinea mainland, as a local guide.[22]

Assuming the leadership of the two subsequent expeditions, D'Albertis recruited men who he felt were capable of defending themselves, but who were also cheap to hire and susceptible to

---

21   Goode 1977: 156.
22   Macfarlane 1876.

his control. Three Europeans accompanied him on the second expedition: the engineer and naturalist Lawrence Hargrave, a seaman John Moreman, and a very youthful collecting assistant, Clarence Wilcox; but only one European, the engineer Clement Preston, could be induced to join the third expedition. At various times, D'Albertis had under his employ two Jamaican Africans (Palmer, a former naval hand, and the well-educated Jackson), Fiji Bob, John from Hawaii, Filipino Tommy Xavier, Johnny Caledonia, Samoan Jack, and a Chinese cook, Tiensin. Maino of Mowatta, who had made clear his reluctance to travel beyond the mouth of the Fly River on the first expedition, was pressed into service again, and induced through the judicious display of trade goods to persist. The most tragic figures amongst his recruits were the four Chinese men who joined D'Albertis's third expedition on the vague promise of a goldfield at the head of the Fly.

None of his companions survived unscathed. D'Albertis's volcanic temper and Kurtzian paranoia grew with each mile that the two expeditions progressed upriver, rising to a climax on both occasions when the decision had to be taken to turn back. Hargrave was hounded throughout the second expedition and blamed for every mishap before being discharged; Moreman was chained to the mast and whipped; and the Chinese were repeatedly flogged if they failed to collect specimens in sufficient quantity. Only the two youths, Clarence Wilcox and Tommy Xavier, were spared his public displays of temper, possibly because they served D'Albertis in other ways. On the third expedition, all four of the Chinese crew members (fully half his crew) died: one presumed executed, another beaten to death by D'Albertis, and the last two killed by local warriors when they deserted. Those that survived were broken: D'Albertis had Bob and Jack gaoled for theft, mutiny and rebellion on their return to Somerset; Preston developed epilepsy; and Hargrave nursed to his grave a grudge against D'Albertis.[23]

Not surprisingly, D'Albertis was never content with his human colleagues, reserving his affection for pets, including his Newfoundland dog, Dash, whose death he mourned in terms of friendship; a pet snake he described as 'a true friend and companion' and – with another snake – as 'my friends, for I loved them and they loved me'.[24]

---

23 Goode 1977: 205–6, 223–4.
24 D'Albertis 1880, I: 315, 376; II: 194.

For D'Albertis only pets and objects – a flag or a treasured ring – were singled out and named individually as 'companions' in what he evidently regarded as a rather solitary adventure. Distant friends in Italy or Australia could be recalled with fondness, and natives could be friendly and hailed as friends if they remained that way, but few of his companions on expedition were ever identified as such. Although D'Albertis employed it most frequently to describe the close confidants of others, 'companion' was a privileged term in his writing. He might on occasion refer to the other members of his expeditions collectively as 'companions', but only Tomaselli, perhaps as a fellow Italian, attained the status of an individualised companion. Instead, the other members of his expeditions were identified in terms of their functional roles, as appendages to his enterprise: thus Hargrave was always 'the engineer', Tiensin 'the cook', and most others were simply 'servants'. Without companions, or those with whom he felt some sort of social parity, D'Albertis could thus describe himself as 'almost alone in New Guinea, in the midst of savages'.[25]

The security of riverine expedition – the protection of the water, the bounds of the expeditionary vessel, and the Ariadne's thread of an obviously reversible direction – also produced constraints. The feverish intensity of relations on board a small vessel, matched with D'Albertis's capacity for violence, strained bonds beyond breaking point. Contacts with local communities were fleeting and often violent, and once beyond the mouth of the Fly River, there were no attempts to seek local guidance. Each account of D'Albertis's Fly River expeditions rose with mounting excitement as he ascended the river, culminating in the crisis of the decision to return, forced upon him in every instance by the shortcomings of his assistants or equipment. D'Albertis is also exemplary in the way in which his narrative comes to efface all traces of effective metropolitan support, companionship or local assistance in focusing on his own agency.

---

25   D'Albertis 1880, II: 184.

Miles Staniforth Cater Smith, 1910–1911

The Staniforth Smith expedition of 1910–1911, which sought to cross from the Purari River to the Kikori and then to the Strickland River, is perhaps the classic example of misguided interior exploration.[26] In 1910, Miles Staniforth Cater Smith was the Commissioner for Lands in the Territory of Papua. Taking advantage of his position as Administrator in the absence of the Lieutenant Governor, Hubert Murray, whose post he coveted and whose authority he was actively seeking to undermine, Smith launched an ambitious expedition. His ostensible purpose was to confirm earlier reports by the Mackay–Little expedition of coal seams in the area of Mt Murray, on the watershed between the Purari and Kikori rivers.[27] Daunted by the flow of the Purari, Smith instead established a base camp at the highest navigable point of the Kikori, and then advanced north towards Mt Murray with a small overland party. Though inexperienced himself in New Guinea conditions, Smith was accompanied by a large party, including a number of officers more familiar with the Papuan bush.

The base of Mt Murray was reached after just two weeks on foot, but food supplies were already low. At this point, ambition got the better of Smith, and he decided to make a push for glory by traversing from the Kikori to the Strickland River, which he planned to descend by raft to the Fly River. He sent back the larger part of his team, including the most experienced of his officers, retaining just Resident Magistrate Leslie Bell and surveyor A. E. Pratt, who had been a member of the Mackay–Little expedition up the Purari, along with 11 native police and 17 carriers. In the well-populated Samberigi Valley, the expedition was able to acquire food supplies, and negotiated its contacts with the local community without reported loss of life. Thereafter, they struggled through limestone country in which rivers, which plunged underground or over waterfalls, proved impossible to follow or raft. When they met a river large enough to be the Strickland, it lay at the bottom of a 1,200-foot gorge, down which they scrambled to build rafts. Tragically, within 200 yards, all four rafts were overturned on

---
26 Smith 1911a, 1912; Schieffelin and Crittenden 1991: 33–40.
27 Mackay 1912.

the first rapid: seven carriers drowned, almost all of the equipment was lost, and the survivors found themselves washed up on opposing banks of the river.

Walking downriver, they encountered some 'wild savages, who had never seen a white man before', but who nevertheless held up baked sago and enticed Smith's small group across the river to eat their fill. Joined by the others, the expedition (if that is what it could still be called) was taken to a nearby village, where they were fed more sago and understood that the 'natives had evidently heard about us'.[28] After another month of walking with little to eat along the river, which was still too dangerous to raft, they were welcomed hospitably at a second village, and ventured onto canoes again, only to be overturned the following day. Reduced again to walking beside the river, they stumbled on the next day into a campsite of tents which they recognised, to their astonishment, as their original base camp on the Kikori. They had travelled an estimated 374 miles by foot and 150 miles by canoe or raft, in a circle.

For this feat of endurance, Smith was lionised in England on his return in 1912, addressing the Royal Geographical Society and receiving awards including the Society's Founder's Medal, and the British Empire medal from the King.[29] Back in Papua, Murray took particular delight in declaring the expedition 'disastrous': 'The loss of a third of the party is something quite unprecedented in Papuan exploration.'[30] Smith was much more generous than D'Albertis in his estimation of his companions, or at least of the European officials and native police; the carriers he tended to despise as insufficient to the task, though he made a show of endowing the orphans of the lost carriers with 10 pounds 'to pay the cost of their maintenance as long as I was in the Territory'.[31] The hospitality of the local communities along the banks of the Kikori he ascribed to their knowledge of the 'great care we had

---

28   Smith's bluff and understated account of his travails contrasts strongly with that of his companion Bell, who described finding 'our leader sitting disconsolately on a heap of stones … Mr Smith had aged considerably in the short time, and bore all the evidence of having endured great privations. His cheeks were sunken, and he was much thinner. He was clad only in a light singlet and a pair of trousers cut off at the knees. On his feet were sandshoes, with the soles nearly worn out. His legs were one mass of festering New Guinea sores, and he was in agony from the bites of sandflies.' Bell 1911: 60–61.
29   Bayliss-Smith 1992.
30   Murray 1911: 6.
31   Smith to Murray, 29 June 1911, NLA/MS1709, Folder 15.

exercised in seeing that those we had previously met had been justly treated'; hinting, in a rather backhanded manner, at the presence of webs of local connection.[32] As W. N. Beaver, one of the officers charged with tracing the fate of the Staniforth Smith expedition by following their route, observed, 'communication and intercourse are maintained right from our starting point to our limit. The natives right along the course of the Kikori are in touch with one another.'[33] Long-distance trading routes and kinship ties connected communities at the mouth of the Kikori with all of the areas through which the expedition had travelled, and news of its passage had passed in advance and then back to the coast long before Smith's men emerged from their ordeal.[34]

Beyond the corporal punishment inflicted on members of his own party either directly by Smith or on his orders, for which he was later chastised, neither the various written accounts of the expedition nor the local memories of its passage describe any of the conflict, either internally or with local communities, that shadowed the movements of D'Albertis;[35] but there was also remarkably limited consultation about direction, or guidance offered. In part, this reflected the confidence that Europeans of this period in New Guinea expressed repeatedly about their ability to overcome the challenges of the landscape, and about their sense of purpose and hence direction. Cutting across or against the social grain of the landscape, 'blindly … like moles burrowing underground', as Smith later ruefully acknowledged, the expedition confounded local understandings of purpose and direction, and offers of guidance were frequently regarded by the expedition, in turn, as attempts at deception or obstruction.[36] Pratt's map, based on his salvaged survey notes, was later proved to be surprisingly accurate in its depiction of latitude but well wide of the mark on longitude, which accounts for the expedition's belief that it had reached the

---

32 Smith 1912: 319.
33 Beaver 1911: 185.
34 Schieffelin and Kurita 1988.
35 Little to Mahon, 8 February 1912, NLA MS 1709, Folder 11; Schieffelin and Kurita 1988.
36 Smith 1912: 313.

Strickland River.[37] The three relief parties sent out to find Smith's expedition covered much more ground and ultimately contributed more substantially to the exploration of the Territory.[38]

Charles Karius and Ivan Champion, 1926–1928

The subsequent exploration of interior New Guinea was a task shared fairly equally between miners, missionaries and government officers, each with their own local staff and methods;[39] but it was the government patrol officer who became the crystallising figure, and frequently the author, of the New Guinea exploration narrative. If there was little by way of a scramble for territory in interior New Guinea, there was certainly a scramble to publish, and expeditionary tales by government officers became a small but significant literary genre in their own right. Perhaps the jewel in the exploratory crown in New Guinea was the first crossing of the island at its widest point, and Lieutenant Governor Murray was keen that this be first achieved by the staff of his Papuan administration. Appointing two officers with considerable experience in the bush for their age, Charles Karius and Ivan Champion, he directed them to cross from the headwaters of the Fly River to the Sepik River. Between December 1926 and June 1928, the North-West Patrol, as it became known, launched two attempts at this crossing.[40] The first was turned back by a seemingly impenetrable mountain wall, but the second succeeded in threading a path over the central range and down into the Sepik basin. The key to this success lay in the convergence of explorer and local interests.

Karius, as the senior officer, took it upon himself to lead the first attempt, delegating Champion to a support role at a base camp established on the Luap River, in the foothills around the head of the Fly River. Over 36 days, Karius and a small team worked their way

---

37 Bayliss-Smith 1992: 323.
38 The extended absence of the Smith expedition led to a major and wide-ranging relief effort coordinated by Judge Herbert, who sent several patrols up the Strickland River, the Kikori River and along the actual route taken by Smith; Murray happily published their lengthier reports along with that of Smith in the Territory's annual report. Herbert 1911; Beaver 1911; Massey-Baker 1911.
39 Nelson 1976; Radford 1987; Schieffelin and Crittenden 1991.
40 Champion 1932, 1966.

north, before being pushed eastwards by a massive wall of mountains; coming across a large river which they took to be the Strickland River, they followed it down to a point where they were able to purchase canoes at a village and proceed down to the Fly River.[41] As Barry Craig has demonstrated, in a forensic analysis of the expedition diary, Karius – like most explorers in New Guinea without the requisite navigational equipment or experience – was wildly optimistic in his estimation of distance. In fact, he had neither reached a pass marking the watershed with the Sepik, nor joined the Strickland River until it had already debouched from the mountains.[42]

Champion, who would later recall that 'Karius didn't have much of a sense of direction', had been born and raised in Papua, and made more constructive use of his time at the base camp, establishing contact and talking with mountain people living nearby, gathering word lists and local names for the features already named by Karius for fellow patrol officers.[43] Ignoring his instructions to return to the Palmer River, Champion took it upon himself to explore the headwaters of the Luap. He came upon a series of hamlets where he recognised some of the young men who had been visiting the base camp, and they guided him over a pass into the Bol River valley. One of the carriers, Simodi, a prisoner from Goaribari Island, had inadvertently continued when the patrol made camp, and when they found him the following day, he was surrounded by a group of men and youths, whom one of the constables reported as describing a large river with sago (a lowland staple) to their north. Together they walked down to the more substantial village of Bolivip, and into what was perhaps the most significant encounter in the history of New Guinea's exploration.

> Out of the crowd stepped a short stocky man with Jewish features, huge chest and shoulders, wearing the customary cassowary plumes and Job's tears. He embraced me, saying, 'Num seno, seno, sene'. He then banged his chest with his open palm, and made a sweeping flourish with his arm, which included the people, the village, and the surrounding country; then stooped, and with his closed fist struck the ground, at the same time exclaiming loudly, and in a high-pitched voice, 'Bolivip! Bolivip! Bolivip!' He rose and patting my chest, pointed to my carriers, and then patting his chest pointed to his

---

41   Karius and Champion 1928.
42   Craig 2014.
43   Sinclair 1988: 55.

people talking the while, meaning that as I was the chief of my people he was chief of Bolivip. I looked at my subjects and then at his, and I must admit that I envied him.⁴⁴

There is no photograph of this moment, but an imaginative woodcut or linocut illustration published in a 1955 school primer edition of Champion's narrative meets all the requirements of convention, with Champion centrally positioned and a suitably noble chief in greeting (Figure 9.2). Over the course of a few further days of conversation and forays out from Bolivip, Champion established that two communities – the Feramin and the Kelefomin (Telefomin) – occupied large valleys to the north of Bolivip, in which the rivers flowed to the north and west, presumably as tributaries of the Sepik. People at Bolivip could also describe the sequence of river junctions to their south for 100 miles, indicating the regional extent of their knowledge and relationships.

Once Champion and Karius were reunited, much of their time between the two attempts was taken up by the onerous but vital task of relaying and staging rice and other supplies along their route in preparation for a final push. By April of 1927, the North-West Patrol was in position to make its next attempt, and this time Champion's route was followed, bringing the patrol back to an enthusiastic welcome at Bolivip. From Bolivip, the 'Chief' led them along a slender track up the precipitous mountain wall and over a high, waterless plateau to a grassy ridge above Feramin in the Sepik catchment. The panorama viewed from a small rock at the base of this ridge was breathtaking: 'Never before have I seen anything so wonderful', exulted Karius.⁴⁵

As soon as they had descended to Feramin, the 'Chief', now identified as Tamsimara (or Tamsimal), took complete control of the encounter, as he had at Bolivip, giving speeches both to the patrol officers and to the assembled Feramin. After one final word of advice to the Feramin, 'Suddenly, and seemingly in the middle of a sentence, he snatched his sling bag from behind him on the floor of the tent, rushed outside, called out for his Bolivip followers, and disappeared down the track at a trot. That was the last we saw of Tamsimara and the Bolivip.'⁴⁶

---

44   Champion 1928: 108.
45   Karius 1929a: 98.
46   Karius 1929a: 99.

Figure 9.2: Patrol Officer Ivan Champion meets the 'Chief' of Bolivip Village. Untitled illustration by Pamela Lindsay.
Source: Ivan Champion, *Across New Guinea*, Bonito Edition, Longmans Green and Co., p. 10.

Tamsimal of Bolivip

The success of the North-West Patrol turned upon a number of factors. The experience of the patrol officers and in particular Champion's willingness to engage with the region's inhabitants and anchor the patrol's route in local knowledge and toponymy were obviously critical, but the encounters and breakthroughs in understanding were substantially negotiated by a range of intermediaries including the carrier, Simodi; the policemen making enquiries of their own; the villagers who trekked down to visit the base camp and led Champion towards Bolivip; and of course Tamsimal. The question this now poses is whether any of these individuals regarded themselves as 'intermediaries'. To an important extent, Champion and Karius had been recruited as auxiliaries – companions even – in Tamsimal's rise to regional prominence, and the Bolivip community is dominated today by his descendants, as testimony to his prowess as a leader and his success in attracting wives.[47]

In a misguided moment of my own, I joined some friends, led by Michael Bird, in a 70th anniversary re-walk of the 1926 North-West Patrol. Our goal, which was to follow as closely as possible the original route of the patrol (without Karius's detour) proved difficult, as the walking tracks and connections between communities had been radically realigned by the development of the large gold mine at Ok Tedi, to the west of our route. At every opportunity, we sought to confirm the authenticity of our own trip by taking photographs that matched exactly those taken 70 years earlier by Karius and Champion, whose negatives we had been able to copy. Less authentic was our reliance on a helicopter to relay our supplies, though we still depended heavily on local guides and carriers.

When we duly arrived at Bolivip, our presence was brokered in part by a resident anthropologist from Cambridge, Tony Crook. On the evening before we left Bolivip, Michael was ceremonially presented with a taro, much as Karius had been in 1927; and we were then treated to a series of three historical dramas or skits, performed in the church. During the day, various pieces of our equipment – a hat, a camera, some bags of rice – had been borrowed, and these

---

47   Crook 2007: 15–16.

resurfaced in the first skit, which re-enacted the meeting between Tamsimal and Champion. One Bolivip villager, dressed as Champion, led the patrol, taking photographs as he came (a wincingly accurate depiction of our own arrival). The Bolivip warriors approached these strangers, threatening them with drawn bows and whoops, only for Tamsimal to appear between the two parties, reassuring Champion on one side while trying to dampen the ardour of his men on the other. Finally, both sides acknowledged his authority, he shook hands with Champion, and peaceful contact was effected. The other skits dealt with subsequent events in the life of Tamsimal and the community, including Tamsimal's defence of one of his wives from a marauding policeman or carrier (possibly in 1942), and the community's acquisition of its first shotgun; situating the encounter with the North-West Patrol within a longer run of encounters, in each of which the central roles were played by Bolivip villagers.[48]

Something of the contrast between Karius and Champion is conveyed in images taken at the Brumtigin rock overlooking the Sepik catchment. In the first image, of which there was more than one variant, Karius stands upright on the rock, pointing dramatically towards the Sepik, carriers and police posed before him and a crouching Bolivip man behind him (Figure 9.3). The second image, taken by Karius, shows Champion and Tamsimal in seemingly natural conversation, seated together on the rock (Figure 9.4). When we chanced upon the same rock in 1997, we could not resist the opportunity to recreate and rework these images, and shot off rolls of film with different members of our group posed more or less dramatically: Figure 9.5 shows geology student Philip Pousai as Champion, and one of Tamsimal's many grandchildren, Ray Kisol, as the great man himself.

---

48 The very lateness of European exploration of interior New Guinea has provided a wealth of Indigenous perspective and response that is perhaps exceptional globally. Connolly and Anderson 1987; Schieffelin and Crittenden 1991; Kituai 1998; Gammage 1998.

Figure 9.3: Charles Karius and company at Brumtigin rock, 1927. Photograph by Ivan Champion.
Source: By permission of the Champion family.

Figure 9.4: Ivan Champion and Tamsimal at Brumtigin rock, 1927. Photograph by Charles Karius.
Source: By permission of the Champion family.

Figure 9.5: Philip Pousai (left) and Ray Kisol (right) at Brumtigin rock, 1997. Photograph by Chris Ballard.
Source: Author's collection.

9. EXPLORERS & CO. IN INTERIOR NEW GUINEA, 1872–1928

The intermediary position

I want to make just three brief points in conclusion, teasing out both the common elements and the transitions evident in this series of vignettes. The first point, returning to Fabian's observations on the conception of exploration as a matter of geography rather than politics, is that the early history of European exploration of interior New Guinea, from the 1870s to the 1920s, illustrates a shift from exploring the country to finding, and being found by, people – a slow and often painful process of discovering that ethnography, or a grasp of social relationships, and not geography was what mattered. Once the initial objectives of exploration had been achieved – mapping shorelines, ascending large rivers, and climbing mountain peaks close to the coast – explorers of this period found themselves almost entirely dependent on local knowledge, goodwill and food.

The second addresses the ascription of agency in narratives and the irresistible emergence in explorer narratives of the local intermediary. In each of the published accounts discussed here, a politics of accreditation – of the granting of credit or recognition – is at work. Lawson provides the literary templates: the faithful and truculent servants, the expendable companions, and the unreachable and savage locals. D'Albertis, for whom intermediaries are a practical and narrative hindrance, labours to deny companionship and effective agency to all around him. Staniforth Smith is more generous in his recognition of the roles of both his companions and local people – or perhaps has that generosity thrust upon him in the extremity of his situation on the banks of the Kikori. While Karius and Champion effectively submit to the authority of Tamsimal, placing their trust in him, and their narrative within his.

Finally, through the example of Tamsimal at Bolivip, the situated understandings of the role of 'guides' and other intermediaries invite us to reflect on the intermediary position. Narrative conventions play a central part in defining the intermediary, whether these conventions are those of the skits at Bolivip or the published accounts of gentlemanly exploration. Indeed, my selection of vignettes extends the enduring tradition of organising exploration history around its notional leaders. But the broader contexts for each of these expeditions reminds us that even the narrators, as the central figures in their own accounts of exploration, are positioned as intermediaries in other narratives, whether D'Albertis in the context of his Sydney sponsor, George Bennett, or Staniforth Smith, Karius and Champion in Lieutenant Governor Murray's authoritative accounts of colonial exploration in Papua. Which of these figures – and indeed who amongst us – is not an intermediary in someone else's narrative?

Acknowledgments

I continue to be grateful to Michael Bird and the other members of the North-West Patrol re-walk of 1996–1997, as well as the communities and other institutions that supported and sustained us, including The Australian National University and other generous sponsors. Thanks also to Barry Craig for discussions about Karius's missteps, Dario Di Rosa for sharing his findings on Staniforth Smith, and colleagues of ANU's Pacific History reading group for their close criticism of a draft of this paper.

References

Athenæum 1875, 'The interior of New Guinea', *The Athenæum*, 17 April, 2477: 518–519; 1 May, 2479: 585–586; 8 May, 2480: 622; 26 June, 2487: 858.

Ballard, Chris 2009, 'The art of encounter: Verisimilitude in the imaginary exploration of interior New Guinea, 1725–1876', in *Oceanic Encounters: Exchange, Desire, Violence*, Margaret Jolly, Serge Tcherkézoff and Darrell Tryon (eds), ANU E Press, Canberra, 221–258.

Bayliss-Smith, Tim 1992, 'Papuan exploration, colonial expansion and the Royal Geographical Society: Questions of power/knowledge relations', *Journal of Historical Geography* 18(3): 319–329.

Beaver, W. N. 1911, 'Report by W.N. Beaver, Esq., on the search party led by him in connexion with the Kikori Expedition', Appendix A(2) to Smith 1911, 178–187.

Bell, Leslie Livingstone 1911, 'Exploring in Papua', *Victorian Geographical Journal* 28: 31–63.

Burnett, D. Graham 2002, '"It is impossible to make a step without the Indians": Nineteenth-century geographical exploration and the Amerindians of British Guiana', *Ethnohistory* 49(1): 3–40.

Champion, Ivan 1928, 'North-West Patrol, Report of sub-patrol, Made by Ivan Champion, P.O., 1st May to 14th July 1927', Appendix B in *Annual Report for the Territory of Papua 1926–27*, 102–117.

——— 1932, *Across New Guinea from the Fly to the Sepik*, Constable, London.

——— 1955, *Across New Guinea*, Bonito Edition, Longmans Green and Co., London.

——— 1966, *Across New Guinea from the Fly to the Sepik*, Lansdowne Press, Melbourne.

Connolly, Bob and Robin Anderson 1987, *First Contact*, Viking Penguin, New York.

Craig, Barry 2014, '"How Karius found a river to the north": The first 1927 attempt to cross New Guinea from the Fly to the Sepik', Upper Sepik-Central New Guinea Project, uscngp.com/papers/37, accessed 14 February 2014.

Crook, Tony 2007, *Exchanging Skin: Anthropological Knowledge, Secrecy and Bolivip, Papua New Guinea*, Oxford University Press for The British Academy, Oxford.

D'Albertis, Luigi Maria 1880, *New Guinea: What I Did and What I Saw*, 2 vols, Sampson Low, Marston, Searle & Rivington, London.

Driver, Felix and Lowri Jones 2009, *Hidden Histories of Exploration: Researching the RGS-IBG Collections*, Royal Holloway, University of London, and Royal Geographical Society (with IBG), London.

Fabian, Johannes 2000, *Out of Our Minds: Reason and Madness in the Exploration of Central Africa*, University of California Press, Berkeley.

Forbes, Henry O. 1888, 'On attempts to reach the Owen Stanley Peak', *The Scottish Geographical Magazine* 4: 401–415.

Gammage, Bill 1998, *The Sky Travellers: Journeys in New Guinea*, Miegunyah Press, Melbourne.

Glen, David 2000, 'The Last Elusive Object', MA thesis, The Australian National University, Canberra.

Goldie, Andrew 1877–78, 'A journey in the interior of New Guinea from Port Moresby', *Proceedings of the Royal Geographical Society* 22(3): 219–223.

Goode, John 1977, *Rape of the Fly: Explorations in New Guinea*, Thomas Nelson (Australia), Melbourne.

Herbert, Justice 1911, 'Report by Mr. Justice Herbert on the search for the Kikori Expedition', Appendix A(1) to Smith 1911, 171–177.

Huxley, Thomas H. 1936, *T.H. Huxley's Diary of the Voyage of HMS Rattlesnake*, Huxley, Julian (ed.), Doubleday, Doran & Co., Garden City, NY.

Jukes, Joseph Beete 1847, *Narrative of the Surveying Voyage of HMS Fly, Commanded by Captain FP Blackwood, RN in Torres Strait, New Guinea, and Other Islands of the Eastern Archipelago, During the Years 1842–1846*, 2 vols, T. & W. Boone, London.

Karius, Charles 1929a, 'Expedition across the island of New Guinea, 17th September, 1927, to 30th January, 1928', Appendix D in *Annual Report for the Territory of Papua 1927–28*, 87–108.

—— 1929b, 'Exploration in the interior of Papua and north-east New Guinea: The sources of the Fly, Palmer, Strickland, and Sepik rivers', *The Geographical Journal* 74(4): 305–322.

Karius, Charles and Ivan Champion 1928, 'Report of North-West Patrol, 3rd December, 1926, to 10th June, 1927', Appendix A in *Annual Report for the Territory of Papua 1926–27*, 91–101.

Kennedy, Dane 2013, *The Last Blank Spaces: Exploring Africa and Australia*, Harvard University Press, Cambridge, MA.

Kingston, Ralph 2007, 'A not so Pacific voyage: The "floating laboratory" of Nicolas Baudin', *Endeavour* 31(4): 145–151.

Kituai, August Ibrum K. 1998. *My Gun, My Brother: The World of the Papua New Guinea Colonial Police, 1920–1960*, University of Hawai'i Press, Honolulu.

Lawson, John A. 1875a, *Wanderings in the Interior of New Guinea*, Chapman & Hall, London.

—— 1875b, 'The interior of New Guinea', *The Athenæum*, 1 May, 2479: 585; 8 May, 2480: 622; 12 June, 2485: 786–787.

Little, J. to Hugh Mahon, MHR re Staniforth Smith expedition, 8 February 1912, Staniforth Smith Papers, NLA MS 1709, Folder 11.

Macfarlane, Samuel 1876, 'Ascent of the Fly River, New Guinea', *Proceedings of the Royal Geographical Society* 20(4): 253–266.

MacKay, Donald 1912, 'An exploration in New Guinea', *Report of the Thirteenth Meeting of the Australasian Association for the Advancement of Science* 13: 385–389.

Massey-Baker 1911, 'Report by Mr. Massey-Baker on his trip up the Fly and Strickland rivers in search of the Kikori Expedition', Appendix A(3) to Smith 1911, 187–194.

Moresby, John 1875, 'The interior of New Guinea', *The Athenæum*, 29 May, 2483: 718–720; 26 June, 2487: 855.

Murray, J. H. P. 1911, 'Lieutenant-Governor's report', *Annual Report for the Territory of Papua 1911*, Government of the Commonwealth of Australia, Melbourne, 5–6.

Nelson, Hank 1976, *Black, White and Gold: Goldmining in Papua New Guinea, 1878–1930*, Australian National University Press, Canberra.

Radford, Robin 1987, *Highlanders and Foreigners in the Upper Ramu: The Kainantu Area, 1919–1942*, Melbourne University Press, Melbourne.

Schieffelin, Edward L. and Robert Crittenden 1991, *Like People You See in a Dream: First Contact in Six Papuan Societies*, Stanford University Press, Stanford.

Schieffelin, Edward L. and Hiroyuki Kurita 1988, 'The phantom patrol: Reconciling native narratives and colonial documents in reconstructing the history of explorations in Papua New Guinea', *The Journal of Pacific History* 23(1): 52–69.

Simpson, Donald 1975, *Dark Companions: The African Contribution to the European Exploration of East Africa*, Paul Elek, London.

Sinclair, James 1988, *Last Frontiers: The Explorations of Ivan Champion of Papua*, Pacific Press, Gold Coast, Qld.

Smith, Miles Staniforth 1911, 'Kikori Expedition', *Annual Report for the Territory of Papua 1911*, Government of the Commonwealth of Australia, Melbourne, 165–171.

—— 1912, 'Exploration in Papua', *The Geographical Journal* 39(4): 313–331.

Smith, Miles Staniforth to Murray, 29 June 1911, Staniforth Smith Papers, NLA/MS1709, Folder 15.

Souter, Gavin 1963, *New Guinea: The Last Unknown*, Angus & Robertson, Sydney.

Wallace, Alfred Russel 1875, 'Lawson's "New Guinea"', *Nature* 12(292): 83–84.

www.ingramcontent.com/pod-product-compliance
Lightning Source LLC
Chambersburg PA
CBHW040319170426
43197CB00022B/2967